iWork®

PORTABLE GENIUS
2nd Edition

iWork®

PORTABLE GENIUS
2nd Edition

Guy Hart-Davis

WILEY

iWork® PORTABLE GENIUS, 2nd Edition

Published by
John Wiley & Sons, Inc.
10475 Crosspoint Blvd.
Indianapolis, IN 46256
www.wiley.com

Credits

Acquisitions Editor
Aaron Black

Project Editor
Amanda Gambill

Technical Editor
Paul Sihvonen-Binder

Senior Copy Editor
Kim Heusel

Director, Content Development & Assembly
Robyn Siesky

Vice President and Group Executive Publisher
Richard Swadley

About the Author

Guy Hart-Davis writes about computers, phones, tablets, and technologies. His other books include *iMac Portable Genius, Teach Yourself VISUALLY iPhone 5s and iPhone 5c, Teach Yourself VISUALLY iPad*, and *Teach Yourself VISUALLY MacBook Air.*

This book is dedicated to Teddy.

Acknowledgments

I'd like to thank the following people for making this book happen:

- Stephanie McComb for getting the book approved and signing me up to write it.

- Aaron Black for supervising the revision and focusing the coverage.

- Amanda Gambill for running the editorial side of the project.

- Paul Sihvonen-Binder for reviewing the book for technical accuracy and making many helpful suggestions.

- Kim Heusel for copyediting the book with a light touch.

Contents
at a Glance

Contents

chapter 1

How Do I Get Started with iWork?   2

chapter 2

How Do I Work with Documents in iWork Apps? 40

chapter 3

How Do I Work with Text in iWork Apps? 66

How Do I Use Common Features in iWork Apps? 102

chapter 5

How Do I Create Attractive Documents in Pages? 158

chapter 6

What Extra Features Do I Get
Using Pages on OS X?   194

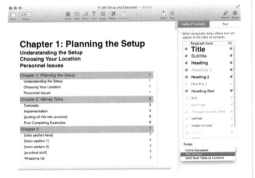

chapter 7

How Do I Design and Lay Out
Spreadsheets in Numbers?   210

chapter 8

How Do I Perform Calculations in Numbers Spreadsheets? 238

chapter 9

How Can I Create Dynamic
Spreadsheets? 264

chapter 10

How Do I Use the Extra Features
in Numbers for OS X? 296

chapter 11

How Can I Create Compelling Presentations with Keynote? 316

chapter 12

How Do I Give Presentations Using Keynote? 342

How Can I Use the Extra Features for Keynote in OS X?

Connected to Keynote on Den
Mac mini.

Play Slideshow

Introduction

To complement its market-leading Macs and iOS devices, Apple builds some terrific software. For several years now, the iWork suite of apps has enabled Mac users to create slick and professional documents quickly and with minimal effort, and share them easily in person, on paper, or via the Internet. But now Apple has taken iWork to the next level by making the apps run not only on Macs and iOS devices but also on the iCloud website. Today you can create and edit your documents no matter where you are and no matter which computer or device — Mac, PC, iPhone, iPad, or iPod touch — you are using.

iWork Portable Genius shows you how to get the most out of the iWork applications. Here's a taste of what you can do with this book:

- **Get up and running with iWork.** Get started with iWork in mere minutes by downloading the apps if you don't have them and setting up iCloud on your computer or iOS device. Navigate the iWork interface, create new documents, and upload your existing documents to iCloud.

- **Bring yourself up to speed on core skills.** Make sure you know all the essential maneuvers you can use in any of the iWork apps — everything from inputting text quickly and efficiently and formatting it consistently, to adding pictures, shapes, charts, and tables to your documents. Become expert in sharing and printing your documents, and choose preferences and settings to suit your needs.

- **Create professional-quality documents in Pages.** Build your word-processing documents and page-layout documents fast and smoothly whether you work from scratch or harness the power of templates. Control the page layout, track changes, and bring in text from outside sources when you need it. Learn how to deal with problems when exchanging documents with Microsoft Word.

- **Build spreadsheets and crunch data in Numbers.** Pick the best template as a starting point, and then organize your data logically into sheets and tables. Use cell formatting to make Numbers format values exactly the way you want them. Make the most of the built-in functions in Numbers, and create powerful formulas that perform exactly the calculations you need.

- **Create persuasive presentations in Keynote.** Choose an effective look for your presentation by selecting the right theme. Develop the presentation's outline quickly by using the Outline pane, or simply open a PowerPoint presentation so that you can create a Keynote version of it. Use the Light Table view to arrange your slides in the right order, set extra slides to be skipped, and add presenter notes that will help you hit every key point in order.

- **Deliver your presentation powerfully and convincingly.** You can deliver a presentation from an iPad or other iOS device, but for ultimate power, you probably want to use a Mac. Set up your presentation display to show precisely the information you need, then rehearse the presentation and make sure your timings work. Connect your Mac to an external projector or display and give the presentation, controlling it with the keyboard, the mouse, or an iPhone or iPod touch. When you can't give a presentation in person, create a presentation that runs itself — great for a kiosk or trade show — or share the presentation online.

How Do I Get Started with iWork?

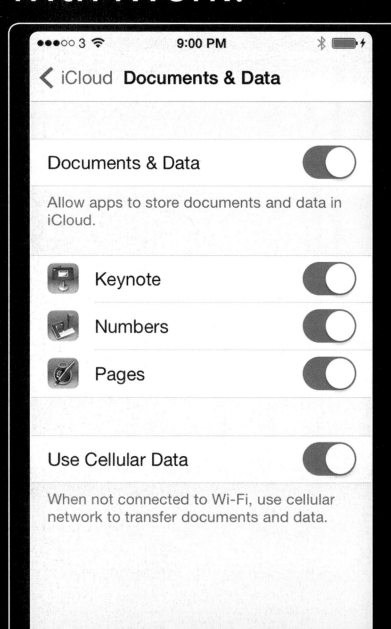

The iWork suite from Apple consists of three apps — Pages, Numbers, and Keynote — that enable you to create beautiful documents, powerful spread-sheets, and convincing presentations. The iWork apps run on OS X on Macs; on iOS on the iPhone, iPad, and iPod touch; and on the iCloud online service that Apple offers. You can create documents on any of the platforms, store them on iCloud, and then work with them on other platforms. This chapter shows you how to get iWork on the platforms you're using. It also covers how to navigate the iWork user interface smoothly and effectively.

Understanding iWork for OS X, iOS, and iCloud

iWork is a suite of three apps produced by Apple:

- **Pages.** An app for word processing and document layout. Pages includes templates that enable you to create many document types quickly, ranging from letters, resumes, and reports to posters, project proposals, and flyers. Pages can import and export documents in the Microsoft Word formats.

- **Numbers.** An app for creating spreadsheets, tables, and charts. Numbers comes with templates that make it easy to create anything from a basic spreadsheet containing data of your choice to business spreadsheets, such as employee schedules and expense reports, or personal spreadsheets, such as a savings tracker or a mortgage calculator. Numbers can import and export spreadsheet files in the Microsoft Excel formats.

- **Keynote.** An app for creating and delivering presentations. Keynote includes a set of visual themes for creating visually striking presentations containing whatever material you need to show to your audience, be it in a business setting or a personal setting. Keynote can import and export presentation files in the Microsoft PowerPoint formats.

Understanding the three platforms iWork supports

The iWork apps run on the three main platforms Apple supports:

- **OS X.** The operating system for Macs, previously known as Mac OS X. Macs range from the diminutive MacBook Air, the smallest of which has an 11-inch screen, to the high-powered Mac Pro, which can drive several massive monitors at the same time, and give you a huge amount of space. OS X, which, at this writing, is in its tenth major version (numbered OS X 10.9 and codenamed Mavericks) is the longest standing of the three platforms, has the greatest maturity, and offers the most power and features. To run the iWork apps on OS X, you download the apps from the Mac App Store, install them, and run them like any other app. Figure 1.1 shows Pages running on OS X. You can expand the Pages window to full screen, and give commands using the menu bar, toolbars, and the panel on the right.

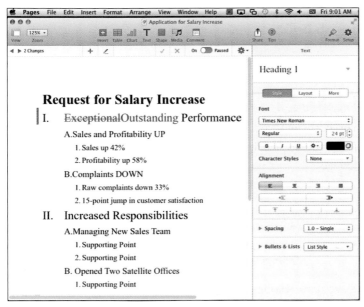

1.1 On OS X, Pages appears in a window that you can expand to full screen.

iOS. The operating system for the iPad, iPhone, and iPod touch. Both of the latest iPhone models, the 5s and 5c, have a four-inch screen, as does the iPod touch, providing only limited space for apps to display content to the controls for manipulating it. The iPad comes in two models, the iPad Air with a 9.7-inch screen and the iPad mini with a 7.9-inch screen, which give enough space for the apps to display larger amounts of content and to keep some essential controls displayed all (or most) of the time. To run the iWork apps on iOS, you download the apps from the App Store, install them, and run them like other apps. Figure 1.2 shows Pages running on iOS on the iPad. You give commands by tapping buttons on the toolbar, and then using the pop-up palettes.

Note   Apple released the first version of iOS with the first iPhone in 2007. At that point, Apple didn't give the operating system a name, describing the iPhone as running OS X. In 2008, Apple released a beta version of the iPhone's operating system to developers, calling it iPhone OS. In 2010, after releasing the iPad, Apple rebranded the operating system to iOS.

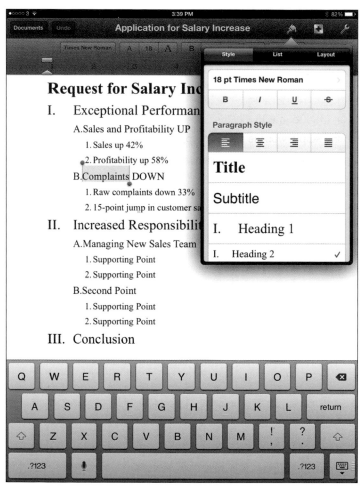

1.2 On iOS, Pages appears full screen, like all iOS apps.

- **iCloud.** The Apple web service for creating, storing, and sharing data and documents online. Apple launched iCloud in October 2011, and has been adding capabilities to it since then, including the iWork apps in the autumn of 2013. To use the iWork apps on iCloud, open a web browser and go to the iCloud website at www.icloud.com. Figure 1.3 shows Pages running on iCloud in a browser on a Mac. You give commands by tapping the buttons on the toolbar, and then using the pop-up palettes.

Web Browsers Compatible with iCloud

To use the iCloud versions of the iWork apps, you need a browser that iCloud supports. As of January 2014, iCloud supports the following browsers:

- **Safari.** A web browser developed by Apple, Safari is available for OS X, iOS, and Windows. OS X and iOS include Safari. You can download Safari for Windows from the Apple website (http://support.apple.com/kb/DL1531).

- **Firefox.** Developed by the Mozilla Foundation, Firefox is a widely used and powerful web browser that is available for OS X, Windows, Linux, Android, and other platforms. You can download Firefox from the Mozilla website (www.mozilla.org).

- **Internet Explorer.** A web browser developed by Microsoft, Internet Explorer is available only for Windows. Most versions of Windows include Internet Explorer; if not, you can download Internet Explorer from the Microsoft website (http://windows.microsoft.com/en-us/internet-explorer/download-ie).

Safari, Firefox, and Internet Explorer are three of the big four browsers; the fourth is Google Chrome, which iCloud doesn't support. iCloud also doesn't support less widely used browsers, such as Opera, OmniWeb, SeaMonkey, IceDragon, or Camino.

If you try to use an unsupported browser, iCloud either warns you it is unsupported and prevents you from logging in or displays the login screen but with its login controls disabled. Either way, you cannot use iCloud.

How the iWork apps work on the different platforms

Given that the three platforms on which the iWork apps run are very different from each other, it's no surprise that the apps themselves look different on each platform to make the most of the space and features available. Figures 1.1, 1.2, and 1.3 give you an idea of how different Pages looks on OS X, iOS on the iPad, and iCloud.

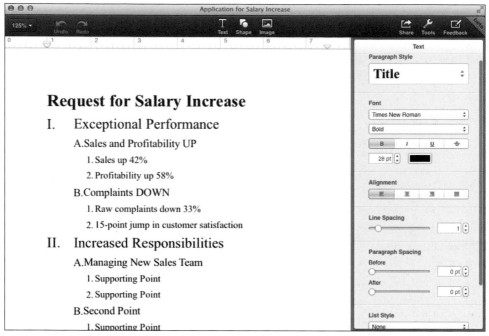

1.3 On iCloud, Pages appears in the browser window.

The iWork apps also work differently on the three platforms, as you probably expect if you know how iOS devices differ from Macs. These details are covered in the chapters about each app — but for now, here are the two main differences:

- **How you navigate and give commands.** The interfaces of the OS X apps are designed to be easy to navigate using the keyboard and mouse (or equivalent pointing device, such as a trackpad), whereas the interfaces of the iOS apps are designed to be controlled by fingers on the touchscreen. Fingers are much less precise than the mouse pointer, so the controls on the iOS apps are necessarily larger and more widely spread than the controls on the OS X apps. You can see this in Figure 1.4, which shows the Text pane of the Format inspector from the OS X version of Pages, and Figure 1.5, which shows the Text panel in the iPad version of Pages. The sets of commands in the Text pane and the Text panel have some overlap, but aren't identical; the next section explores such differences further.

- **The actions the platform allows for apps and files.** On a Mac, OS X allows you to take a wide range of actions with apps and files. For example, you can launch apps in a wide variety of ways, from using the Dock and Launchpad to launch an app by opening a file associated with it; and you can manage your files and folders directly by using the Finder, placing them, more or less, wherever you want in the Mac's file system. None of this is remarkable in the context of computer operating systems — but iOS restricts apps and files far more tightly. So, on iOS devices you typically launch an app only from the Home screen or by using the Open In command for a file you have received via an app such as Mail. Each app stores its files in its own area of the file system that other apps cannot access. iOS offers no equivalent of Finder for managing your files directly, so you either manage the files through the app itself (for example, using Numbers to delete one of its own spreadsheet files) or use iTunes to transfer files to and from your computer. Similarly, on iCloud, you use the apps themselves to manage their files.

Understanding how iWork features work on each platform

To enable the iWork apps to work with the same file format on all three platforms, Apple has removed various advanced features that used to be in the OS X versions of Pages, Numbers, and Keynote. Even so, at this writing, the OS X apps still have features that the

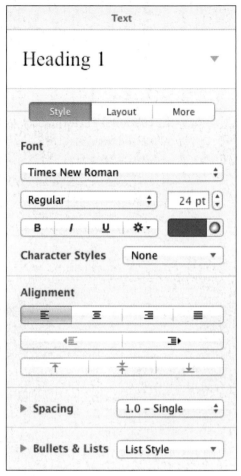

1.4 The interfaces of OS X apps are designed for precise control using the mouse or an equivalent pointing device.

iOS and iCloud versions do not yet have. However, Apple has been adding features gradually to the iOS and iCloud versions, and it seems likely to continue to do so.

These core features work on all platforms:

- **Creating documents based on templates.** On each platform, each app enables you to create new Pages documents, Numbers spreadsheets, and Keynote presentations based on a variety of attractive or functional templates. The selection of templates varies depending on the app and platform, but there are plenty of templates to get you started.

You can also create a blank document and build it out with the content and formatting you need. Another option is to use third-party templates to give your documents a kick-start. You can do this on OS X or iOS, but at this writing, not on iCloud.

- **Opening, editing, and saving documents.** On each platform, you can open, edit, and save documents you have created in the iWork apps, on either that platform or another. If the document was created in an older version of iWork, the app warns you that you will need to use the new version of the app from now on (see Figure 1.6). Click Open to proceed; click Don't Open if you prefer not to open the document.

- **Working with text, media, tables, charts, and shapes.** On each platform, you can create, edit, and format essential content. Pages even supports Track Changes, which enables you to track inserted and deleted text, and view the document with or without the changes highlighted.

1.5 The interfaces of iOS apps, designed for touch, have larger controls with more space between them. You may need to scroll to reach some of the controls.

Open in Pages

Your document will open in the new Pages for iOS. To open it on a Mac, you'll need to install the latest Pages on OS X Mavericks.

Open

Learn More

Don't Open

1.6 An iWork app warns you if the document was created in an older version of iWork.

Understanding the Numbering of the iWork Apps

When you need to troubleshoot an iWork app or look up information about it, it's helpful to know the app's version number. Apple has changed its version numbering, so the numbers aren't in sync. Here are the current OS X version numbers:

- **Pages.** The current version is Pages 5. Earlier versions included Pages '08, which had an internal version number of Pages 3, and Pages '09 (Pages 4).

- **Numbers.** The current version is Numbers 3. Earlier versions were Numbers '08 (Numbers 1) and Numbers '09 (Numbers 2).

- **Keynote.** The current version is Keynote 6. Earlier versions included Keynote '08 (Keynote 4) and Keynote '09 (Keynote 5).

Updates to the apps use point numbering, such as Numbers 3.0.1. To find out the exact version numbers for the apps on OS X, click the application menu, and then click About (for example, choose Pages ⇨ About or Numbers ⇨ About).

Here's how to find out the version numbers for the apps on iOS:

1. **Press the Home button to display the Home screen.**
2. **Tap the Settings icon to display the Settings app.**
3. **Tap Keynote, Numbers, or Pages to display the app's settings.**
4. **Look at the Version readout.**

The iCloud versions of the apps do not show a version number.

Note

At this writing, the iWork for iCloud apps do not let you edit inline objects such as tables, but Apple says this capability is coming soon.

- **Formatting document elements.** On each platform, you can apply mainstream formatting such as paragraph styles, font formatting (including bold, italic, and underline), alignment, line spacing, paragraph spacing, list styles, and indents.

- **Laying out document elements.** On each platform, you can lay out document elements on the document canvas that forms the background of each iWork document. You can resize objects, adjust masks and wrapping, flip objects horizontally or vertically, and move objects forward or back in the stack of objects to control which parts of which are visible. You can also lock objects in place to prevent yourself from moving them accidentally.

- **Find and Replace.** Each platform lets you search documents for specific text and replace it with other text. You can choose whether to limit the search to matching case or to whole words only.

- **Printing and sharing your documents.** Each platform enables you to share your documents via e-mail, either keeping the document in its native format (for example, as a Pages document), exporting it to the equivalent Microsoft Office format (for example, exporting a Pages document to a Microsoft Word document), or converting it to a Portable Document Format (PDF) file. The OS X apps and iOS apps also enable you to print your documents.

Note

At this writing, you can print only to a PDF file from the iWork for iCloud apps. You can then download this file to a computer and print it.

- **Formulas and functions in Numbers.** On each platform, you can create formulas freely to perform calculations. You can also use the scores of functions built in to Numbers.

The key elements that are available on OS X but not on iOS or iCloud are mostly advanced features. Here are some examples:

- **All apps.** Reverting to earlier versions of the document. Saving a document as a template for other documents. Advanced layout features, such as aligning objects or distributing them horizontally or vertically.

- **Pages.** Document navigation features, such as bookmarks and page thumbnails. View options, such as the option to display invisible characters (tabs, line breaks, and so on). Proofreading tools, including grammar checking.

- **Numbers.** Advanced options, such as filtering tables. Creating styles for objects, such as charts and tables.

- **Keynote.** Advanced animations. Defining chart masters, text placeholders, and media placeholders. Rehearsing and recording slide shows.

Getting iWork

Before you can start using the iWork apps on OS X or iOS, you must download and install the apps. With iCloud, you must sign up for an account, and then sign in to it.

Which Version of iWork Should You Get?

As discussed in the previous section, the iWork apps have the same core functionality on each platform but, beyond that, have different capabilities on OS X, iOS, and iCloud. So, you may be wondering which version of iWork you should get.

To some extent, this depends on what exactly you will be doing with iWork. However, generally speaking, you can get the most out of iWork by using it on each platform available to you. So, if you have an iOS device, buy the iOS versions of the iWork apps — or download them free if your device qualifies for free downloads — so that you can create and edit documents wherever you go. In addition, if you have a Mac, buy the OS X versions of the iWork apps you will use on it so that you have access to the most advanced features when you need them.

Whichever versions you buy, you will most likely want to use the iCloud versions of the apps as well, so you can work on your documents from any Mac or PC. Even if you take your iOS device everywhere you go, you will most likely find it helpful to work on a larger screen sometimes, especially with long or complex documents.

Getting and installing iWork for OS X

To get and install the iWork apps for OS X, you use the App Store app to buy the app or apps from the Mac App Store. You can then launch the apps in any of the standard ways for OS X.

Here's how to buy and download iWork for OS X:

1. **Click the App Store icon on the Dock.** If the App Store icon doesn't appear on the Dock, click Launchpad on the Dock or press F4 to display the Launchpad screen, and then click the App Store icon.

2. **Click in the Search box in the upper-right corner of the window, type *iWork*, and then press Return.** A list of search results appears (see Figure 1.7).

3. **Click the price button for the app you want to buy.**

4. **Click Buy App.**

5. **Provide your payment information when App Store prompts you to do so.** App Store then downloads the app and installs it automatically.

After installing some or all of the iWork apps on your Mac, you can launch them in any of the following ways:

- **Launchpad.** Click the Launchpad icon on the Dock or press F4 to open the Launchpad screen, and then click the app's icon.

1.7 You can quickly locate the iWork apps in the Mac App Store by opening the App Store app and searching for iWork.

Note

To locate an app's icon quickly on the Launchpad screen, type the first few letters of the app's name — for example, type *pa* to locate the Pages icon. As you type, Launchpad narrows down the list of apps to those that have words starting with those letters.

● **Dock.** If you've added the app to the Dock, click the app's Dock icon to launch it. If you haven't yet added the app to the Dock, click the Launchpad icon on the Dock to display

the Launchpad screen, and then drag the app to where you want it on the Dock. If you've launched the app already, Control-click its Dock icon, highlight Options on the context menu, and then click Keep in Dock (see Figure 1.8).

● **Finder.** Click the Desktop to activate the Finder, then choose Go ➪ Applications or press ⌘+Shift+A to open a window showing the Applications folder. You can launch any app from here by double-clicking it, but that's more effort than using Launchpad or the Dock. What you may want to do instead is add apps to the Finder sidebar by selecting

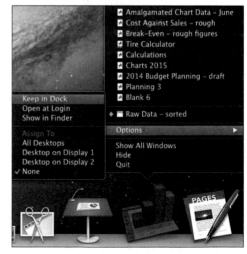

1.8 You can choose Options ➪ Keep in Dock to add a running app's icon to the Dock quickly.

the app, and then choosing File ⇨ Add to Sidebar. Once you've done this, you can drag a document to the app's icon on the sidebar to open the document in that app. This is especially useful when you want to open a document in an app other than the default app, where double-clicking the document in a Finder window would open it in the default app.

 Launch on login. If you need one of the iWork apps each time you use your Mac, set the app to launch when you log in. The easiest way to do this is to Control-click the app's Dock icon, click Options, and then click Open at Login. You can also choose Apple ⇨ System Preferences to open the System Preferences app, click Users & Groups, click the Login Items tab to display the Login Items pane, and then click the Add (+) button to add each app to the list of items that open automatically when you log in.

Getting and installing iWork for iOS

You can get started quickly with the iWork for iOS apps by buying the apps from the App Store, and then downloading them to your iPhone, iPad, or iPod touch.

Note

If you have bought a new iPhone, iPad, or iPod touch, you can download the iWork apps for free from the App Store.

Here's how to buy and download Pages, Numbers, or Keynote for iOS:

1. **Press the Home button to display the Home screen.**
2. **Tap the App Store icon to open the App Store app.**
3. **Tap the Search button to display the Search screen.**
4. **Type *iWork,* and then tap the Search button.**
5. **Scroll through the search results, and then tap the price button for the app you want to buy.**
6. **Tap the Buy button that replaces the price button.** iOS downloads the app and installs It. You can then launch the app from the Home screen.

Genius

If you have Keynote, you probably want to download the free Apple Keynote Remote app. It enables you to use an iOS device as a remote to control a Keynote presentation running on a Mac or other iOS device. For example, you can use your iPhone to control a presentation you're giving with your iPad.

Here's how to launch an app on your iPhone, iPad, or iPod touch:

1. **Press the Home button to display the Home screen.**

2. **Locate the icon for the app.** You can swipe either left or right until you reach the Home screen that contains the icon, or pull down on the Home screen to display the Search box, and then start typing the app's name.

3. **Tap the icon.**

Genius

You can also launch an app from a document you have received in Mail or another app that receives files. Touch and hold the app's icon to display the Share sheet, and then tap the Open In button for the app you want to use. For example, tap Open in Numbers to open the file in the Numbers app.

Getting and Launching iWork for iCloud

To get started with iWork for iCloud, you must get an Apple ID if you don't already have one. You can then sign in to iCloud and use the iWork apps. To sign up for an Apple ID, go to the My Apple ID web page (https://appleid.apple.com), and then click Create an Apple ID. This brings you to a page on which you choose the Apple ID and password, set a security question and answer, and then type your name and address.

Once you have your Apple ID, you can sign in to iCloud like this:

1. **Open your web browser and go to the iCloud website (www.icloud.com).**

2. **Type your Apple ID and password.**

3. **Select the Keep me signed in check box if you want to stay signed in to iCloud.** This is usually a good idea when you're using your own computer, because it saves you having to sign back in repeatedly. Don't select this check box when you're using someone else's computer or a public computer such as one in an Internet café.

4. **Press Return or click the Sign In arrow (see Figure 1.9).**

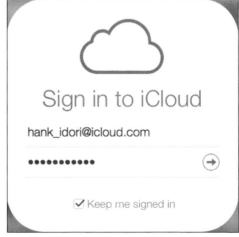

1.9 Select the Keep me signed in check box if you want your computer to store your Apple ID and password. Click the arrow button to sign in.

Do You Already Have an Apple ID?

If you've set up an iCloud account on a Mac or on an iOS device, you already have an Apple ID you can use for the iWork apps on iCloud. Both OS X and iOS press you to create an Apple ID, so if you're using either of these devices, chances are you already have an Apple ID.

If you have an Apple ID but have forgotten the password, go to the My Apple ID web page (https://appleid.apple.com), and then click the Reset Your Password link. You then type your Apple ID, choose between authentication via e-mail or by answering your security questions, and then reset your password.

If you're not sure whether you have an Apple ID, go to the My Apple ID web page (https://appleid.apple.com), and then click the Find Your Apple ID link. This takes you to a page on which you can fill in your name and your current and prior e-mail addresses and then click Next to search for your Apple ID.

Setting Up iCloud on Your Computer or iOS Device

At this point, you need to set up iCloud on your computer or iOS device unless you've already done so. This section explains how to set up iCloud and choose suitable settings. OS X and iOS offer the same configuration options for iCloud, so I deal with them together. Windows needs you to install iCloud Control Panel and gives you fewer options, so Windows is covered separately.

Opening the iCloud pane on a Mac

Here's how to open the iCloud pane in System Preferences on the Mac:

1. **Choose Apple ⇨ System Preferences from the menu bar to open the System Preferences window.**

2. **Click the iCloud icon to display the iCloud pane.**

Genius

An even quicker way to open the iCloud pane in System Preferences is to Control-click the System Preferences icon on the Dock and then click iCloud on the context menu.

3. **If the Sign in with your Apple ID prompt appears, type your Apple ID and password, and then click Sign In (see Figure 1.10).** System Preferences signs you in to iCloud and then displays the next iCloud screen.

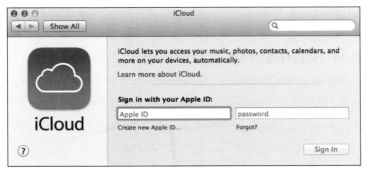

1.10 If you have not yet signed in to iCloud, type your Apple ID and password, and then click Sign In.

4. **Select the Use iCloud for mail, contacts, calendars, reminders, notes, and Safari check box (see Figure 1.11) if you want to use iCloud for some (or all) of these items.** You can easily change your settings afterward if necessary.

1.11 Choose which iCloud features to use, and then click Next.

5. **Select the Use Find My Mac check box if you want to use the Find My Mac feature, which enables you to locate your Mac if it goes missing.** This feature is usually helpful for Macs, especially for MacBook models.

6. **Click Next.** The iCloud controls appear, and you can configure iCloud, which is described later in this chapter.

Genius

Find My Mac can only be active for one user of any Mac. If another user has already turned on Find My Mac and you try to turn it on, System Preferences warns you that enabling Find My Mac for you will disable it for the other user. Click Continue to proceed or Cancel to stop.

Displaying the iCloud screen on iOS

Here's how to display the iCloud screen on iOS:

1. **Press the Home button to display the Home screen.**

2. **Tap Settings to display the Settings screen.**

3. **Tap iCloud to display the iCloud screen.**

4. **If the Apple ID and password fields appear, type your Apple ID and password, and then tap Sign In (see Figure 1.12).** The Settings app signs you in to iCloud, and then displays the Allow iCloud to use the Location of Your iPad? dialog.

Genius

To input a domain quickly (such as .com or .org), touch and hold the period (.) key until a pop-up menu of domains appears, and then tap the appropriate one.

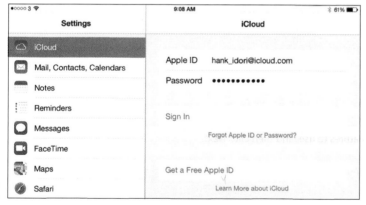

1.12 To set up iCloud on your iOS device, type your Apple ID and password on the iCloud screen in the Settings app, and then tap Sign In.

5. **Tap OK (see Figure 1.13) if you want to turn on the Find My iPad feature (which is called Find My iPhone for the iPhone or Find My iPod for the iPod touch).** Turning this feature on is normally a good idea, because it enables you to locate your iOS device if you mislay it or someone takes it.

6. **If the Merge with iCloud? dialog opens (see Figure 1.14) offering to merge your existing data with your iCloud account, tap Merge or Don't Merge, as appropriate.**

Choosing settings for iCloud

After displaying the iCloud pane on the Mac or the iCloud screen on iOS, you can choose settings for iCloud. These settings fall into five categories:

Allow iCloud to Use the Location of Your iPad?

This enables Find My iPad features, including the ability to show the location of this iPad on a map.

| Don't Allow | OK |

1.13 Choose whether to allow iCloud to use the location of your iOS device.

Merge with iCloud?

Your Safari data, reminders, calendars and contacts on this iPad will be uploaded and merged with iCloud.

| Don't Merge | Merge |

1.14 In the Merge with iCloud? dialog, tap Merge if you want to merge your existing data on the iOS device with the data in your iCloud account.

- **Application data.** You can choose which of Mail, Contacts, Calendars, Reminders, Notes, and Safari to sync.

- **iCloud Keychain.** You can set up iCloud Keychain to secure your private data.

- **Photos.** You can turn on photo streams and photo sharing.

- **Documents & Data.** You can choose which apps can store documents and data in iCloud.

- **Find My iPhone.** You can turn on or off this feature for finding your iOS device or Mac if it goes missing.

Genius

If you choose not to turn on the Find My iPhone, Find My iPad, or Find My iPod touch feature at this point, you can turn it on at any time by setting the Find My iPhone switch (or the Find My iPad switch or the Find My iPod switch) on the iCloud screen in the Settings app to On. In the On position, the switch has a green background; in the Off position, the background is white.

At the top of the iCloud pane or screen, you can turn on or off synchronization for Mail, Contacts, Calendars, Reminders, Notes, and Safari. On iOS, set each switch to On or Off, as needed. On the Mac, select or deselect each check box.

Note Safari can sync your bookmarks, open tabs, and Reading List. Syncing the open tabs enables you to pick up your browsing on one device right where you left off browsing on another. Syncing the Reading List enables you to carry with you the pages you have saved to read later.

Setting up iCloud Keychain on iOS

To secure your data online, you can set up iCloud Keychain. This section shows screens from an iPad. To set up iCloud Keychain on iOS, follow these steps:

1. **Give the command for turning on iCloud Keychain in one of the following ways:**

   - **OS X.** Select the Keychain check box in the iCloud pane in System Preferences.

   - **iOS.** Tap the Keychain button on the iCloud screen in Settings to display the Keychain screen, and then move the iCloud Keychain switch to On (see Figure 1.15). In the On position, the switch has a green background; in the Off position, the background is white.

2. **If the Sign In to iCloud dialog appears, type the password for your Apple ID, and then tap OK.** Your Mac or iOS device signs in to iCloud.

1.15 On the Keychain screen, set the iCloud Keychain switch to On to use iCloud Keychain.

3. **In the Keychain Setup dialog or screen (see Figure 1.16), type the security code you want to use, and then retype it when prompted.** You can mix lowercase letters, capital letters, numbers, and symbols to create a code that's harder to guess or crack. If you want to use a complex security code or have iCloud create a random code for you, tap Advanced Options to display the Advanced Security Code Options screen (see Figure 1.17) or Advanced Security dialog.

1.16 In the Keychain Setup screen or dialog, you can either type four digits to create your iCloud Security Code or tap Advanced Options for alternatives.

Then, perform the appropriate substep in the following list:

- **Complex security code.** Tap Use a Complex Security Code, which places a check mark next to it, and then tap Next. On the next screen, type the security code you want to use, and then tap Next. iOS prompts you to retype your security code. Do so, and then tap Next to reach the screen for typing your phone number.

 1.17 On the Advanced Security Code Options screen, tap Use a Complex Security Code or Get a Random Security Code.

Genius A complex security code must be a minimum of four characters, but it's better to use a much longer code. If your code is seven characters or fewer, iOS warns you that it can be guessed easily, and prompts you to change it. Tap Change to change the code; tap Use Code to proceed with it.

- **Random security code.** Tap Get a Random Security Code, which places a check mark on it, and then tap Next. The Keychain Setup screen displays a random complex security code. Write it down carefully, store it somewhere safe, and then tap Next.

Genius On the Advanced Security Code Options screen, you can tap Don't Create Security Code if you want to set up your iCloud Keychain without creating a security code. This is seldom a good idea because it compromises the security of iCloud Keychain. If you don't create a security code, the procedure for setting up iCloud Keychain on a Mac or another device is more complex.

4. **After you choose your security code, pick your country, and then type your phone number on the next Keychain Setup screen (see Figure 1.18).** The phone number must be able to receive SMS (text) messages, so don't input a landline number.

5. **Touch Next.** iOS sets up your iCloud Keychain and then displays the Keychain screen again.

1.18 On this Keychain Setup screen, choose your country, and then type a phone number that can receive text messages.

6. **Touch iCloud at the top of the screen to return to the iCloud screen.**

Setting up iCloud Keychain on a Mac

Here's how to set up iCloud Keychain on a Mac:

1. **Click the Keychain check box in the iCloud pane in System Preferences.**

2. **If the Sign In to iCloud dialog appears, type the password for your Apple ID, and then click OK.** The Settings app signs you in to iCloud.

3. **In the Create an iCloud Security Code dialog, choose which of the following types of security codes to create:**

   - **Regular security code.** Type a four-digit numeric code (see Figure 1.19). The Enter a phone number that can receive SMS messages dialog then appears.

   - **Complex security code.** Click Advanced in the first Create an iCloud Security Code dialog to display the second Create an iCloud Security Code dialog (see Figure 1.20). Select the Use a complex security code radio button, and then click Next. In the third Create an iCloud Security code dialog (see Figure 1.21), type the code you want, and then click Next. Retype the code in the next Create an iCloud Security code dialog, and then click Next again. The Enter a phone number that can receive SMS messages dialog appears.

   - **Random security code.** Click Advanced in the first Create an iCloud Security Code dialog to display the second Create an iCloud Security Code dialog. Select the Get a random security code radio button, and then click Next.

1.19 To create a regular security code of four digits, type them in the first Create an iCloud Security Code dialog.

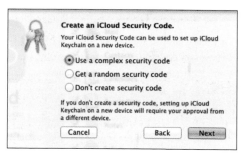

1.20 To create a complex security code containing as many characters as you like, select the Use a complex security code radio button, and then click Next.

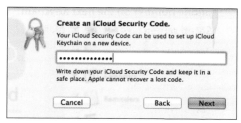

1.21 Type the characters for your complex security code in the third Create an iCloud Security Code dialog, and then click Next.

Write down the security code that the next Create an iCloud Security Code dialog displays, and then click Next. The Enter a phone number that can receive SMS messages dialog then appears.

Genius

An easy way to record your iCloud security code is to capture a screenshot of it. Press @cmd+Shift+4 to activate the ScreenCapture app and set it to capture a selection, press Spacebar to specify you want to capture a window, and then click the iCloud window. By default, the ScreenCapture app places the image file on your desktop.

- **No security code.** Click Advanced in the first Create an iCloud Security Code dialog to display the second Create an iCloud Security Code dialog. Select the Don't create security code radio button, and then click Next. The Enter a phone number that can receive SMS messages dialog then appears.

Caution

If you don't create an iCloud security code, when you set up iCloud Keychain on a new iOS device or Mac, you must request approval from one of your devices that already uses iCloud Keychain. Normally, it is best to create an iCloud security code and use it to secure your iCloud Keychain.

4. **In the Enter a phone number that can receive SMS messages dialog (see Figure 1.22), choose your country.**

5. **Type or paste a phone number that can receive SMS messages.**

6. **Click Done.** The Settings app sets up your iCloud Keychain and selects the Keychain check box in the iCloud pane.

1.22 Choose your country, and then type a phone number that can receive SMS messages.

Setting up Photo Streams and Photo Sharing on your iOS device or Mac

Here's how to set up Photo Streams and Photo Sharing on your iPhone, iPad, or iPod touch:

1. **Tap Photos on the iCloud screen to display the Photos screen.**

2. **Set the My Photo Stream switch to On (see Figure 1.23) to use the My Photo Stream feature.** My Photo Stream automatically uploads the pictures you take with the Camera app to iCloud and downloads the new photos you have taken with your other iOS devices or added to iPhoto (on the Mac) or your designated Photos folder (on Windows).

3. **Set the Photo Sharing switch to On to use the Photo Sharing feature.** Photo Sharing enables you to create shared photo streams on iCloud, invite other people to join them, and even let those people add photos to the streams.

4. **Tap iCloud at the top of the screen to return to the iCloud screen.**

Here's how to set up Photo Streams and Photo Sharing on your Mac:

1. **Select the Photos check box in the iCloud pane in System Preferences.**

2. **Click Options to display the iCloud Photo Options dialog.**

3. **Select the My Photo Stream check box (see Figure 1.24) if you want to use the My Photo Stream feature.** This feature automatically uploads the pictures you take with the Camera app to iCloud and downloads the new photos you have taken with your other iOS devices or added to iPhoto (on the Mac) or your des- ignated Photos folder (on Windows).

4. **Select the Photo Sharing check box to use the Photo Sharing feature.** Photo Sharing enables you to create shared photo streams on iCloud, invite other people to join them, and even let those people add photos to the streams.

5. **Click OK to close the iCloud Photo Options dialog and return to the iCloud pane in System Preferences.**

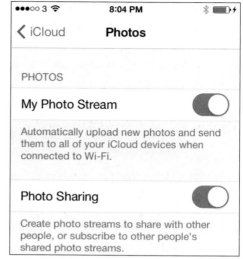

1.23 On the Photos screen, choose whether to use the My Photo Stream and Photo Sharing features.

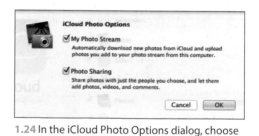

1.24 In the iCloud Photo Options dialog, choose whether to use the My Photo Stream or Photo Sharing features.

Genius

If you turn on the My Photo Stream feature, your photo stream also includes photos you save from e-mail messages, instant messages, web pages, and similar sources. Your iOS device adds these pictures to the Camera Roll album in the Photos app, which adds them to your photo stream.

Setting up Documents and Data on your iOS device or Mac

Here's how to set up the Documents & Data feature on your iOS device:

1. **Tap Documents & Data on the iCloud screen to display the Documents & Data screen.**

2. **Set the Documents & Data switch to On (see Figure 1.25) if you want to store documents and data in iCloud.** You need to store documents and data in iCloud to get the most out of iWork.

3. **In the Allow apps to store documents and data in iCloud area, set the switch for each app to On or Off, as needed.** Normally, you want to set the switches for Keynote, Numbers, and Pages to On. If you have only a few other iCloud-enabled apps, you may want to allow each of them to store documents and data in iCloud. If you have many apps, you may want to permit only some; or you may want to disallow apps that you find use too much data for your cellular plan.

4. **On an iPhone or a cellular iPad, set the Use Cellular Data switch to On or Off, as needed.** Syncing your documents and data via the cellular network is great for keeping up to date and maximizing your productivity, but large documents can quickly run through your data allowance. This switch does not appear on the iPod touch and Wi-Fi–only iPads.

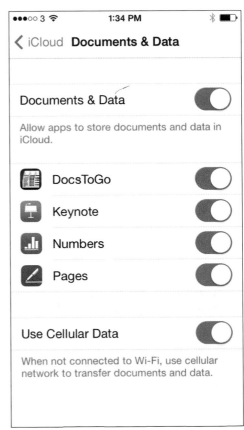

1.25 On the Documents & Data screen, set the Documents & Data switch to On, and then choose which apps you will allow to store documents and data in iCloud.

5. **Tap iCloud at the top of the screen to return to the iCloud screen.**

Here's how to set up the Documents & Data feature on your Mac:

1. **Select the Documents & Data check box in the iCloud pane in System Preferences.**

2. **Click Options to display the Documents & Data Options dialog.**

3. **Select the check box for each app you want to be able to store documents and data in iCloud (see Figure 1.26).** Normally, you want to select the check boxes for Keynote, Numbers, and Pages if you're using iWork in iCloud.

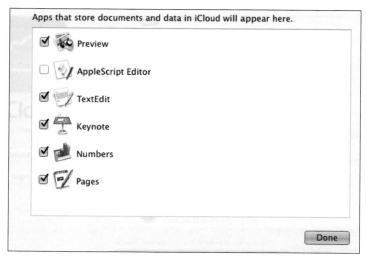

1.26 In the Documents & Data Options dialog, choose which apps may store documents and data in iCloud.

4. **Click Done to close the Documents & Data dialog and return to the iCloud pane in System Preferences.**

Setting your iOS device to back up your data to iCloud

As well as using iCloud to sync your app data, documents and data, and photos, you can also use it to back up your iOS device. Backing up to iCloud gives you an iOS backup you can access from anywhere when your iOS device suffers a failure or goes missing.

Note

On the Storage & Backup screen, tap Manage Storage to view the list of backups, documents and data, and mail stored on your iCloud account. You can delete back-ups and documents you no longer need. From the Storage & Backup screen, tap Change Storage Plan to display the Buy More Storage screen, from which you can buy more iCloud space.

Here's how to back up your iOS device to iCloud:

1. **On the iCloud screen, tap Storage & Backup to display the Storage & Backup screen.** Figure 1.27 shows the Storage & Backup screen on an iPhone.

2. **Set the iCloud Backup switch to On if you want to back up your iOS device to iCloud.** This feature backs up the pictures in the Camera Roll album, your account details, your documents, and your settings.

3. **Tap Back Up Now if you want to create a backup now.** Otherwise, iOS automatically backs up your iOS device when it is plugged in to power, connected to a Wi-Fi network, and locked (so you are not using it).

4. **Tap iCloud at the top of the screen to return to the iCloud screen.**

Setting up iCloud on Windows

Before you can set up iCloud on your Windows computer, you need to add iCloud Control Panel to Windows. You can then open iCloud Control Panel and choose settings for iCloud.

Adding the iCloud Control Panel to Windows

Here's how to add iCloud Control Panel to Windows:

1.27 On the Storage & Backup screen, you can set your iOS device to back up critical data (including photos and documents) to iCloud.

1. **Open your web browser and go to** http://support.apple.com/kb/DL1455.

2. **Click the Download button for iCloud Control Panel.**

3. **If your browser gives you the choice between running the iCloudSetup.exe file or saving it, click Run.** Otherwise, download the file and then double-click it in a Windows Explorer window to launch the iCloud installer. Either way, the first screen of the iCloud installer appears (see Figure 1.28).

4. **Click Next to start the installation.**

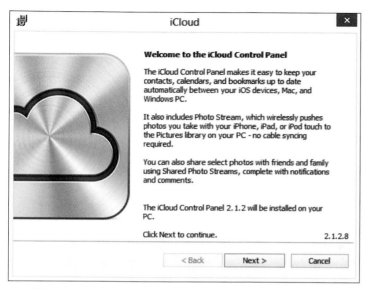

1.28 Click Next on the first screen of the iCloud installer to install iCloud Control Panel on Windows.

5. **Follow through the installation screens.** After you accept the license agreement (which you must do to complete the installation), your only choice is on the Installation Options screen, where you can click Change to select a different destination folder for the files you're installing. Normally, the default folder (the \Common Files\Apple\Internet Services\ folder In your Program Files folder) is the best choice.

6. **On the final screen of the iCloud installer (see Figure 1.29), select the Open the iCloud Control Panel check box if you want to open iCloud Control Panel automatically.** Click Finish.

Opening the iCloud Control Panel and choosing settings

Now that you've added iCloud Control Panel to Windows, open it so you can choose settings for iCloud. Here's how to open iCloud Control Panel on Windows 8:

1. **Move the mouse pointer to the upper-right corner of the screen to display the Charms bar.**

1.29 If you want to open iCloud Control Panel immediately, select the Open the iCloud Control Panel check box.

2. **Click Start to display the Start screen.**

3. **Click iCloud.** iCloud Control Panel opens.

Here's how to open iCloud Control Panel on Windows 7, Windows Vista, or Windows XP:

1. **Choose Start ⇨ Control Panel to open a Control Panel window.**

2. **If Control Panel opens in category view (that is, showing categories instead of icons for the different control panels), click View By, and then click Large Icons or Small Icons, whichever you prefer.**

3. **Click iCloud.**

After opening iCloud Control Panel, you can sign in to your iCloud account and choose settings for iCloud. Follow these steps to choose iCloud settings:

1. **Type your Apple ID in the left field of the iCloud Control Panel window (see Figure 1.30).**

2. **Type your password in the right field.**

3. **Click Sign In.** iCloud Control Panel signs you in to iCloud, and then displays the iCloud controls (see Figure 1.31).

1.30 On the iCloud Control Panel sign-in screen, type your Apple ID and password, and then click Sign In.

1.31 Use the iCloud Control Panel for Windows to choose which iCloud features to use.

4. **Select the Mail, Contacts, Calendars, & Tasks with Outlook check box if you want to use Outlook for your iCloud e-mail, contacts, calendars, and reminders.** This works only if you have Outlook installed on your PC. If not, iCloud Control Panel allows you to select this check box but returns an error when you click Apply.

Note If you need to make changes to your Apple ID, such as changing your password or contact information, click Account options in iCloud Control Panel, and then click Manage Apple ID in the Account Options dialog. To buy more storage, click Manage, and then use the controls in the dialog that opens.

5. **Select the Bookmarks check box if you want to sync your bookmarks from Internet Explorer or Safari.** The readout after the button shows which browser is selected — for example, *Bookmarks with Internet Explorer*. To change browsers, click Options on the

Bookmarks line to display the Bookmarks Options dialog (see Figure 1.32), click Internet Explorer or Safari as needed, and then click OK.

6. **Select the Show iCloud status in Notification Area check box if you want the iCloud icon to appear in the notification area toward the right end of the status bar.** This icon gives you an easy way to open iCloud Control Panel and go to the iCloud website, so it is usually helpful.

7. **Click Apply to close iCloud Control Panel.**

Bookmarks Options

Use iCloud Bookmarks with:

Internet Explorer

Safari ✓

OK   Cancel

1.32 In the Bookmark Options dialog, click Internet Explorer or Safari to set the browser with the bookmarks you want to sync with iCloud, and then click OK.

Genius

If you choose to display the iCloud icon in the notification area, make it appear permanently, not just when it has notifications. Right-click the iCloud icon, and then click Customize notification icons on the context menu to open the Notification Area Icons dialog. Click the drop-down list for iCloud item, click Show icon, click notifications, and then click OK.

Navigating the iWork Interface

Now that you have iWork installed and working, it's a good idea to make sure you know the best ways to navigate the iCloud apps. The apps on each platform work in the same way, so this section covers one app on each platform: Pages on OS X, Numbers on the iPad, Keynote on the iPhone, and Keynote in iCloud.

Opening Pages on OS X and navigating its interface

To meet the Pages interface, open Pages by clicking the Launchpad icon on the Dock and then clicking Pages on the Launchpad screen. If you have put Pages on the Dock, simply click the Pages icon there.

Note If Pages displays the Pages – Documents dialog, click the document, and then click Open. If you want to create a new document, click New Document to display the Template Chooser dialog. You can then click the appropriate document type and click Create.

With Pages open, you should see something like Figure 1.33. As covered later in this book, Pages and the other OS X apps are highly customizable, so some of the elements of the user interface may not appear.

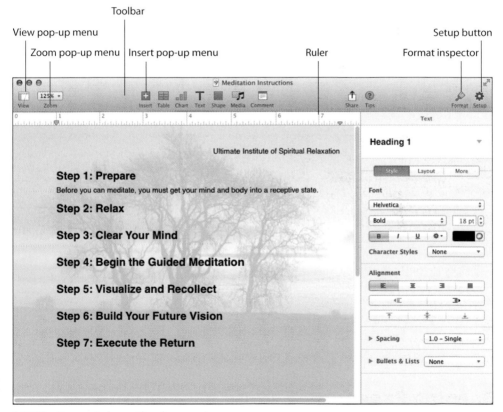

1.33 The Pages window with a document open.

Here's what these elements do:

- **View pop-up menu.** This enables you to change the view and the Pages elements displayed. For example, you can display or hide the ruler.
- **Zoom pop-up menu.** Enables you to zoom in and out of the document.

33

- **Toolbar.** Provides buttons and pop-up menus for common actions and displaying other tools (such as the Format inspector). You can customize the toolbar to contain the tools you need.

- **Insert pop-up menu.** Enables you to insert frequently used items, such as page breaks, page numbers, and footnotes.

- **Editing status.** Shows whether the document has been edited since it was last saved ("Edited" appears after the document's name).

- **Ruler.** Enables you to control the horizontal placement of text, tabs, and other elements.

- **Format inspector.** This panel displays controls for formatting the current selection. The Format inspector displays different panes depending on the object you select. For example, the Text pane appears when the selection is text.

- **Format button.** Displays or hides the Format inspector.

- **Setup button.** Displays or hides the Document Setup inspector, a panel that contains controls for configuring the document's setup.

Opening Numbers on the iPad and navigating its interface

To meet the Numbers interface, open Numbers on your iPad or other iOS device. Follow these steps:

1. **Press the Home button to display the Home screen.**

2. **Navigate to the Home screen that contains the Numbers icon.** You can swipe left or right to move from one Home screen to another.

Genius

If the Home screen on your iOS device contains so many icons that you have trouble locating the app you need, search for it. Touch and pull down a little way on the Home screen to display the Search box and the on-screen keyboard, and then start typing the app's name. When you see the app's icon, tap it to launch the app.

3. **Tap the Numbers icon to launch Numbers.**

Figure 1.34 shows Numbers on the iPad with a spreadsheet open.

These are the main components of the Numbers interface on iOS:

- **Toolbar.** The toolbar contains buttons that give you access to the tools that Numbers provides.

- **Spreadsheets button.** Tap this button to return to the Spreadsheets screen, on which you navigate among your existing spreadsheets or create new spreadsheets.

● **Tabs.** Each sheet or form appears as a tab you can tap to display its contents.

● **Format button.** Tap this button to display the pop-up panel that provides commands for formatting or manipulating the object you have selected.

● **Add button.** Tap this button to display the pop-up panel for adding media, tables, charts, or shapes to the active sheet.

● **Tools button.** Tap this button to display the Tools pop-up panel, which gives you access to tools such as Share and Print, Find, and Settings.

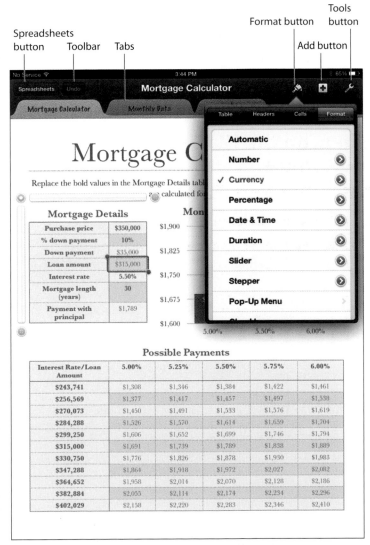

1.34 Numbers in iOS represents each sheet or form as a tab, and provides pop-up panels for formatting, adding objects, and accessing tools.

Opening Keynote on the iPhone and navigating its interface

To meet the Keynote interface, open Numbers on your iPhone or iPod touch. Follow these steps:

1. **Press the Home button to display the Home screen.**

2. **Navigate to the Home screen that contains the Keynote icon.** You can swipe left or right to move from one Home screen to another.

3. **Tap the Keynote icon to launch Keynote.**

Note If Keynote displays the iCloud for Keynote screen, prompting you to store your presentations in iCloud so they are available on all your devices, tap Use iCloud. If you don't want to use iCloud at this point, tap Later.

4. **On the Keynote screen, tap the presentation you want to open, or tap the + button, and then tap Create Presentation to create a new presentation.**

Figure 1.35 shows Keynote on the iPhone with a presentation open.

These are the main elements of the Keynote window on the iPhone or iPod touch:

- **Toolbar.** The toolbar at the top of the window contains buttons for accessing Keynote's tools, plus the Play button for setting your presentation playing.

- **Presentations button.** Tap this button to return to the Presentations screen, on which you navigate among your existing presentations or create new presentations.

- **Slides pane.** The Slides pane on the left of the window enables you to navigate among your slides, change their order in the presentation, and promote and demote them.

- **Current slide.** The current slide appears in the main part of the window.

- **New Slide button.** This button enables you to add new slides to your presentation. You can choose between adding a blank slide and adding one with content, layout, or formatting.

- **Format button.** This button displays the Format panel, which you use to apply formatting.

- **Add button.** This button displays the Add panel, which you use to add objects to your slides.

- **Tools button.** This button displays the Tools screen, which you use to access tools.

- **Play button.** This button starts the slide show.

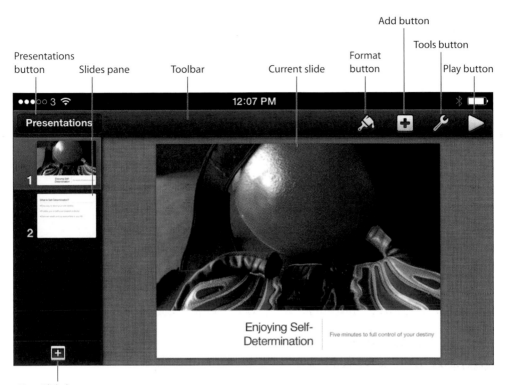

Presentations button · Slides pane · Toolbar · Current slide · Format button · Add button · Tools button · Play button

New Slide button

1.35 Keynote on the iPhone or iPod touch provides the Slides pane for navigating among your slides, and the toolbar for displaying the tools you use to build presentations.

Because the screen of the iPhone and iPod touch is so small, Keynote's main tools necessarily take up much or all of the screen when displayed instead of appearing at the same time as the presentation content. For example, tapping the Tools button on the toolbar displays the Tools screen (see Figure 1.36), which contains commands such as Transitions and Builds, Share and Print, and Find.

Opening Keynote in iCloud and navigating its interface

To meet the Keynote interface in iCloud, follow these steps to open Keynote in your web browser:

1. **Launch your web browser.** For example, on a Mac, click the Safari icon on the Dock.

2. **Go to the iCloud website at www.icloud.com, and then sign in.**

3. **Click the Keynote icon on the main iCloud screen to launch Keynote.**

Figure 1.37 shows Keynote in iCloud with a presentation open.

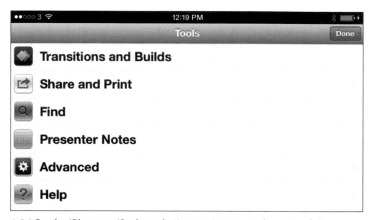

1.36 On the iPhone or iPod touch, Keynote's main tools appear full screen.

Slides pane   Toolbar   Current slide   Format panel

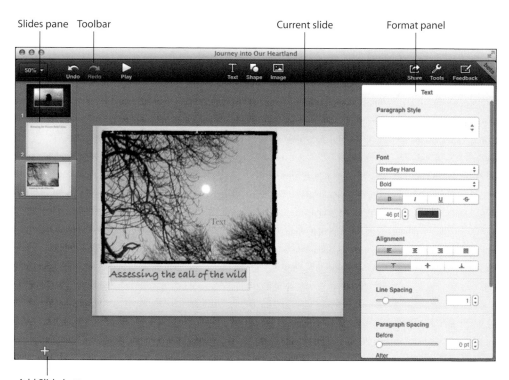

Add Slide button

1.37 Keynote in iCloud features a stripped-down user interface with easy access to the available tools and features.

These are the main elements of the Keynote window in iCloud:

- **Toolbar.** The toolbar at the top of the window contains several widely used tools, such as Zoom and Undo, and provides buttons for accessing the other tools.

- **Slides pane.** The Slides pane on the left side of the window enables you to navigate among your slides, change their order in the presentation, and promote and demote them.

- **Current slide.** The current slide appears in the main part of the window.

- **Add Slide button.** This button enables you to add new slides to your presentation. You can choose between adding a blank slide and adding one with content, layout, or formatting.

- **Format panel.** This panel contains the main tools for formatting text and objects on your slides. You can display the Format panel by clicking the Tools button on the toolbar and then clicking Show Format Panel. The contents of the Format panel automatically change to suit the object you select.

How Do I Work with Documents in iWork Apps?

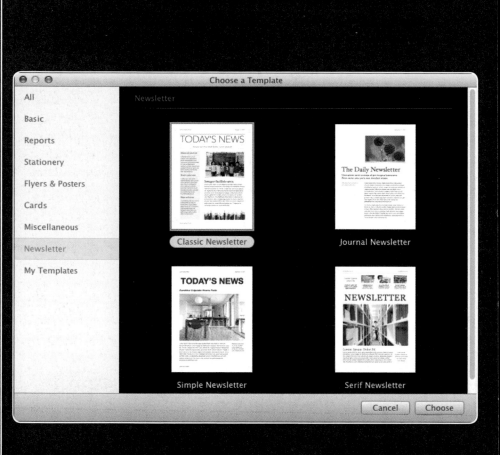

After setting up the iCloud and iWork apps on your computer or iOS device, you're ready to start creating documents. In this chapter, I cover the various formats in which Pages, Numbers, and Keynote can import and export documents. I also go through how to create new documents, as well as how to save, close, or reopen them when needed on any of the iWork platforms. This chapter also covers how to manage your documents and transfer them between your devices and iCloud.

Understanding Which Document Formats Are Supported by iWork Apps

Each iWork app has its own file format for storing documents:

- **Pages.** Pages uses the Pages format with the .pages file extension.

- **Numbers.** Numbers uses the Numbers format with the .numbers file extension.

- **Keynote.** Keynote uses the Keynote format with the .key file extension.

Each app can also open documents in other file formats and export its documents to different file formats.

Document formats supported by Pages

Pages can import documents in the following formats:

- **Plain text files.** These files can contain only text with no formatting and have the file extension .txt.

- **Rich Text Format files.** These files can contain text, formatting, and objects such as graphics. They have the file extension .rtf or .rtfd.

- **Microsoft Word.** These files can contain text, formatting, and a wide variety of objects, such as graphics, tables, and equations. Pages can import both the .doc file format, often described as Word 97–2003 format on Windows or Word 98–2004 format on the Mac, and the .docx format that subsequent versions of Word use by default. Pages can successfully import some but not all objects from Word documents; those objects it cannot import, it removes.

- **AppleWorks 6 word processing.** (Pages for OS X only.) These are files created in the AppleWorks 6 format. Apple stopped supporting AppleWorks in 2007, so relatively few people are using it now. However, if you have old files in the AppleWorks 6 word-processing format, you can import them into Pages. These files have the .cwk extension.

Pages can export documents in the following formats:

- **Pages '09.** (Pages for OS X only.) If you work with people who use this older version of Pages, you can export documents in the Pages '09 format to make sure the people can use the documents.

- **Microsoft Word.** You can export your Pages documents in this widely used format. Pages creates a document in the .doc format rather than the .docx format.

The conversion may remove some complex formatting and layout from the document, but the text, formatting, and most objects will be retained.

- **PDF.** You can export Pages documents as Portable Document Format files, creating files that look just like the Pages documents but are not easily editable. Exporting to PDF is great for sharing a finished document.

- **Rich Text Format.** (Pages for OS X only.) You can export Pages documents in Rich Text Format, but doing so loses some formatting and objects. Normally, you would export a Pages document to Rich Text Format only when you need to share the document with someone who cannot use either a Pages document or a Word document.

- **Plain Text.** (Pages for OS X only.) You can export the text from a Pages document to a plain text file. Doing so retains only the text of the document, removing all formatting and objects.

- **ePub.** (Pages for OS X only.) You can also create an ePub file from a Pages document. ePub is a format widely used for e-books.

Spreadsheet formats supported by Numbers

Numbers can import documents in the following formats:

- **Comma-separated value (CSV).** Files in this format contain text with no formatting or objects. A comma marks the division between each cell.

- **Tab-separated values.** Also known as tab-delimited format, files in this format contain text with no formatting or objects. A tab marks the division between each cell.

- **Microsoft Excel workbook.** Numbers can import both the .xls file format, often described as Excel 97–2003 format on Windows or Excel 98–2004 format on the Mac, and the .xlsx format that subsequent versions of Excel use by default. Numbers can successfully import some objects, such as charts and graphics, in Excel documents. Numbers removes any objects it cannot import.

- **Open Financial Exchange (OFX).** This format, based on the Extensible Markup Language (XML), is used by banks and some financial software. Many U.S.-based banks enable their customers to download bank statements in OFX format.

Numbers can export documents in the following formats:

- **Numbers '09.** (Numbers for OS X only.) If you work with people who use this older version of Numbers, you can export a spreadsheet in the Numbers '09 format to make sure those people can open it.

- **Microsoft Excel workbook.** You can export a Numbers spreadsheet in this widely used format. Numbers creates a file in the .xls format rather than the .xlsx format. The conversion may lose complex formatting and layout.

- **PDF.** You can export Numbers spreadsheets as Portable Document Format files. These files look just like spreadsheets, but are not easily editable. For example, you might create PDFs so that you can share a finished spreadsheet via e-mail.

- **Comma-separated value (CSV).** When you need to retain only the values in a spreadsheet, you can export it to CSV format. Exporting to CSV strips out all the formatting and objects. Normally, you would export a Numbers spreadsheet to CSV only when you need to share it with someone who cannot open either a Numbers spreadsheet or an Excel workbook.

Presentation formats supported by Keynote

Keynote can import presentations only in the Microsoft PowerPoint presentation file format. Keynote can import both the .ppt file format, often described as PowerPoint 97–2003 format on Windows or PowerPoint 98–2004 format on the Mac, and the .pptx format that subsequent versions of PowerPoint use by default. Keynote can import slides, charts, graphics, and other objects from PowerPoint presentations, but may remove complex builds and animations that it doesn't support.

Keynote can export documents in the following formats:

- **Keynote '09.** (Keynote for OS X only.) If you work with people who use this older version of Keynote, you can export a presentation in this format to make sure they can open it.

- **Microsoft PowerPoint presentation.** Keynote can export to the .ppt file format, not to the .pptx file format.

- **PDF.** You can export a presentation as a PDF file, creating a file that shows the slides and their layout but is not easily editable.

- **JPG, PNG, or TIFF image files.** (Keynote for OS X only.) You can export a Keynote presentation as a sequence of image files.

- **HTML.** (Keynote for OS X only.) You can export a Keynote presentation to an HTML file so that people can view it in a web browser.

- **QuickTime movie.** (Keynote for OS X only.) You can export a Keynote presentation to a QuickTime movie that will play on a computer, an iPod, or an iOS device (for example, an iPad).

Dealing with Documents in Unsupported Formats

If you have documents in formats the iWork apps cannot open, try these two moves:

- **Save the document to a common format.** Open the document in an app that supports it, and then save it to a common format, such as RTF for a word-processing document or CSV for a spreadsheet. You can then import that file into the iWork app.

- **Paste the data into the iWork app.** Open the document in an app that supports it, copy the data, and paste it into the iWork app.

Both of these steps are much easier on a Mac or PC than they are on an iOS device or in iCloud.

Creating a New Document

You can either create a blank document or a document based on one of the many templates that iWork includes. Create a blank document when you want to create the entire document or design from scratch. Base a document on a template when you want to create the document more quickly and give it a consistent look. You can create your own templates containing exactly the document elements you need or give yourself a quick boost by adding third-party templates.

Note Pages and Numbers use templates, but Keynote uses themes. So, where Pages and Numbers provide the Template Chooser dialog for choosing the template on which to base a document or spreadsheet, Keynote has the Theme Chooser dialog for choosing the theme to use for a presentation.

Creating a new document on OS X

Here's how to create a new document in an iWork app on OS X:

1. **Open the iWork app if it's not running, or switch to it if it is.** This example uses Pages.

Note If you want to create a blank document instead of a document based on a template, you can simply choose File ➪ New or press ⌘+N.

2. **Choose File ➪ New from the Template Chooser or press Shift+⌘+N to display the Template Chooser dialog.** This dialog shows the templates available for the iWork app you're using.

3. **In the left column, click the category of templates you want to view (see Figure 2.1).**
   For example, click Newsletter to view the templates for creating newsletters.

2.1 In the Template Chooser dialog, click the template category in the left column to browse the templates.

4. **Click the template you want to use.**

5. **Click Choose.** The iWork app creates a new document based on the template and opens it in a window.

Adding Your Own Templates to Template Chooser or Theme Chooser

Pages comes with a selection of templates to create everything from a business letter to an invitation. Numbers provides spreadsheet templates that range from tracking your weight to sending out invoices. Also, Keynote provides an attractive variety of themes for presentations. However, you probably want to use your own custom templates and themes.

To create a template from a document in Pages or Numbers, choose File ⇨ Save as Template. Similarly, you can create a theme from a document in Keynote by choosing File ⇨ Save Theme. The iWork applications store your custom templates and themes in these folders (where the tilde, ~, represents your home folder):

- **Pages templates.** ~/Library/Application Support/iWork/Pages/ Templates/My Templates

- **Numbers templates.** ~/Library/Application Support/iWork/Numbers/ Templates/My Templates

- **Keynote themes.** ~/Library/Application Support/iWork/Keynote/Themes

To save templates or themes from elsewhere, copy them to the appropriate folder using the Finder. To reach the Library folder in your user account, open a Finder window, click the Go menu, hold down Option (the Library command then appears on the Go menu; otherwise, it's hidden), and then select Library.

The built-in templates and themes are stored inside the package files for the applications themselves. So, you can find the Pages templates by opening your Applications folder, Control+clicking the Pages application in the iWork folder, choosing Show Package Contents, and then drilling down to the /Contents/Resources/Templates folder. You can't modify these templates and themes.

Creating a new document on an iOS device

Here's how to create a new document on the iPhone, iPad, or iPod touch:

1. **Open the iWork app or switch to it.**

Genius

Whether the iWork app is running or not, you can open it or switch to it by pressing the Home button and then tapping the app's icon on the Home screen. When the app is running, press the Home button twice in rapid succession to display the app-switching screen, scroll until the app's listing appears, and then tap the app.

2. **If the iWork app displays a document, tap the button in the upper-left corner of the screen to return to the Pages, Numbers, or Keynote screen.**

3. **Tap the + button in the upper-left corner to display the panel for creating and adding documents.**

4. **Tap the Create button.** This button's name is Create Document in Pages, Create Spreadsheet in Numbers (see Figure 2.2), and Create Presentation in Keynote. The Templates screen appears.

5. **Tap the template you want to use (see Figure 2.3).** The app creates a document based on that template and displays it.

2.2 To create a new spreadsheet in Numbers on iOS, tap the + button, and then tap Create Spreadsheet.

2.3 On the Templates screen, tap the template you want to use for the new document.

Creating a new document in iCloud

Here's how to create a new document in iCloud:

1. **Open the appropriate iWork app.** For example, click Pages on the iCloud Home screen. The app's Home screen appears — in this case, the Pages for iCloud screen.

2. **Click the Create button (see Figure 2.4).** This is the button with the large + sign and the text Create Document (in Pages), Create Spreadsheet (in Numbers), or Create Presentation (in Keynote). The Choose a Template dialog appears.

3. **Click the template you want to use (see Figure 2.5).** You may need to scroll up or down the window to see all the templates.

4. **Click Choose.** The app creates the document and displays it in a new window.

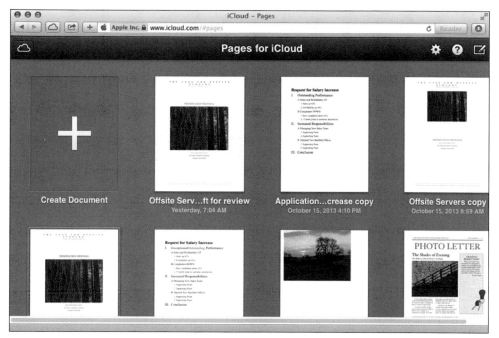

2.4 Click the Create Document button in the Pages for iCloud window to start creating a new Pages document.

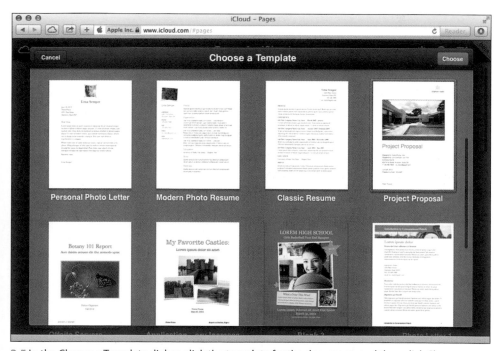

2.5 In the Choose a Template dialog, click the template for the document, and then click Choose.

Saving a New Document

After creating a new document on a computer, you normally save it if you want to keep it. Saving a document is an elementary and straightforward move, but it happens in different ways on the different iWork platforms.

On each of the three platforms, the iWork apps automatically save your documents for you. On OS X, the apps save your documents only after you have named the documents and chosen their location. On iOS and iCloud, the iWork apps automatically save all your documents.

Saving a document on OS X

Here's how to save a document in an iWork app on OS X:

1. **With the document active, choose File ⇨ Save to display the Save As sheet.** The Save As sheet may open at either its smaller size (which shows only the Save As field, the Tags field, and the Where pop-up menu) or its full size (which provides a full file-system browser and extra options).

2. **Type the document name in the Save As box (see Figure 2.6).**

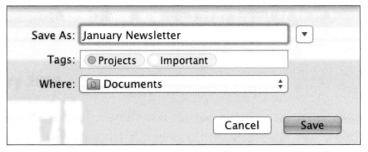

2.6 In the smaller version of the Save As sheet, you can name your document, assign tags, and select the folder.

3. **Add any tags needed to the Tags box.**

4. **Click the Where pop-up menu, and then choose the folder in which to save the document.** Choose iCloud if you want to save the document in your iCloud account.

Note When you select iCloud in the Where pop-up menu, the app disables the down-arrow button to the right of the Save As box in the Save As sheet.

5. **If the Save As sheet is displayed at its smaller size and you want to navigate to areas of your Mac's file system that don't appear on the Where pop-up menu, click the down-arrow button to the right of the Save As box.** The Save As sheet switches to its larger size.

6. **Navigate to the folder in which you want to store the document (see Figure 2.7).**

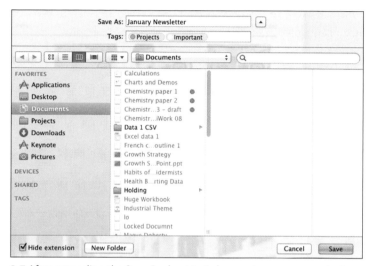

2.7 After expanding the Save As sheet to its larger size, you can navigate your Mac's file system.

7. **Click Save.** The app saves the document.

Saving a document on iOS or iCloud

On iOS and iCloud, the iWork apps automatically save each new document you create and periodi- cally save changes to it. The app gives the new document a name based on its template, such as Recipe or Term Paper (or a name such as Recipe 2 or Term Paper 2 if a document with that name already exists). You can subsequently rename the document manually from the Pages screen, Numbers screen, or Keynote screen.

Here's how to rename a document on iOS:

1. **If the document is currently open, tap the button in the upper-left corner of the screen to return to the document-management screen.** These are the buttons:

   ● **Pages.** Tap the Documents button to return to the Pages screen.

   ● **Numbers.** Tap the Spreadsheets button to return to the Numbers screen.

   ● **Keynote.** Tap the Presentations button to return to the Keynote screen.

2. **Tap the document's name to display the Rename Document screen, Rename Spreadsheet screen, or Rename Presentation screen.**

51

3. **Type the new name for the document (see Figure 2.8).**

4. **Tap Done.** The app applies the name to the document and then displays the Pages screen, Numbers screen, or Keynote screen again.

Here's how to rename a document in iCloud:

1. **In your web browser, display the Pages for iCloud screen, the Numbers for iCloud screen, or the Keynote for iCloud screen, as appropriate.**

2.8 Use the Rename screen to rename a document you've created on iOS.

Note You can rename an iCloud document even when it is open in another window.

2. **Click the document's name to select it.**

3. **Type the new name for the document.**

4. **Press Return or click elsewhere in the window.**

Closing or Opening a Document

When you finish working with a document, you can close it to get it out of the way. On OS X, you can open pretty much as many documents as you want in separate windows; and on iCloud, you can likewise open multiple documents in separate windows. However, on iOS, you can open only a single document at a time in each iWork app. To open another document in that app, you must close the open document.

Genius Technically, it's possible to open enough iWork documents to slow your Mac down or cause the app you're using to crash. In practice, this problem seldom arises unless your Mac is short of memory (RAM) or drive space.

Here is how to close a document on each of the iWork platforms:

- **OS X.** Choose File ➪ Close. Provided you've already named the file and chosen the location in which to save it, the app automatically saves any unsaved changes before closing the document. If the document is a new one that you haven't saved, the iWork app prompts you to save it (see Figure 2.9). Either type a name for the document, apply any tags needed, choose where to save it, and click Save; or click Delete if you want to get rid of the document.

iOS. Tap the button in the upper-left corner of the screen — the Documents button on Pages, the Spreadsheets button on Numbers, or the Presentations button on Keynote. The iOS app automatically saves any unsaved changes in the document and displays the document-management screen. You can then create a new document or open an existing document.

2.9 iWork on OS X prompts you to save an unsaved document you try to close.

iCloud. Click the Close button on the document's tab (if the document is in a tabbed window) or the close button on its window (if it is in its own window). You can also choose File ➪ Close Window (or press Shift+⌘+W in Safari on the Mac) or File ➪ Close Tab (or press ⌘+W on the Mac). The iCloud app automatically saves any changes to the document and closes it.

When you want to resume work with a document you've previously created or closed, you open it again. You can also open documents you have received from other sources — for example, documents you receive via e-mail or that you copy from a WebDAV server. Follow these steps to open a document on OS X:

1. **Open the iWork app associated with the document.**

2. **Choose File ➪ Open to display the Open dialog.** This dialog's title bar shows the app's name — for example, Keynote.

3. **Click iCloud or the title bar in On My Mac (see Figure 2.10) to control which set of documents is displayed.**

4. **Click the document you want to open.**

5. **Click Open.** The document opens in the app.

Note

You can also open documents in OS X in several other ways, such as directly from the Finder or from the Dock. See Chapter 1 for details.

2.10 In the Open dialog, which displays the app's name, you can easily switch between the documents in your iCloud account and those stored in your Mac's file system.

Here's how to open a document on iOS:

1. **Open the appropriate iWork app on your iOS device.**

2. **If the iWork app displays a document, tap the button in the upper-left corner of the screen to return to the Pages, Numbers, or Keynote screen.**

3. **Tap the document you want to open.**

Genius

You can sort the documents either by date or by name. To change the sorting, tap the Pages screen, the Numbers screen, or the Keynote screen and pull down a little way, so that the Date button and Name button appear at the top. Tap the button for the type of sort you want.

To open a document in iCloud, follow these steps:

1. **Open the appropriate iWork app.** For example, click Numbers on the iCloud Home screen. The app's Home screen appears — in this case, the Numbers for iCloud screen.

2. **Locate the document you want to open.** You can sort the documents either by date or by name. To change the sorting, click the Settings button (the cog icon) on the toolbar and then click Sort by Date or Sort by Name, as needed.

3. **Double-click the document.** The iCloud app opens it in a new window, and you can start working with it.

54

Managing Documents

In this section, I explain how to manage your iWork documents. You can quickly add your existing documents to iCloud, transfer documents from iCloud to your Mac or PC, and copy documents between your computer and your iOS device. You can also duplicate documents or delete documents you no longer need.

Adding your existing documents to iCloud

By putting your documents into iCloud, you can make them available to your Macs, your iOS devices, and the iCloud apps in whichever supported browser you use. Here's how to add your existing documents to iCloud:

1. **Open a browser window, go to the iCloud website, and then sign in to your account.**

2. **Click the app that contains the documents you want to transfer.** For example, click Pages. The document-management screen appears.

3. **Click the Action button (the cog icon) on the toolbar, and then click Upload Document to display the Upload dialog.**

4. **Select the documents you want to upload (see Figure 2.11).**

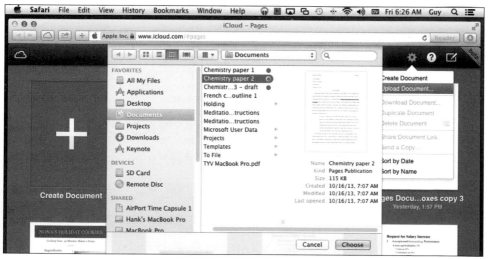

2.11 To upload a document, choose Action⇨Upload Document, select the document in the Upload dialog, and then click Choose.

5. **Click Choose.** Your computer uploads the files to iCloud.

Genius

You can also upload files and folders by dragging them from a Finder window on your Mac or a Windows Explorer window on your PC to the iCloud document-management screen in your web browser.

Transferring iCloud documents to a Mac or PC

Here's how to transfer a document from iCloud to your Mac or PC:

1. **Open a browser window, go to the iCloud website, and then sign in to your account.**

2. **Click the app that contains the documents you want to transfer.** For example, click Pages. The document-management screen appears.

3. **Select the document(s) you want to download to your computer in one of the following ways:**

   - To select a range of contiguous documents, click the first document, and then Shift+click the last.

   - To select noncontiguous documents, click the first document, and then ⌘+click each of the others.

   - You can also select a range of contiguous documents by using the Shift+click technique, and then either add to or remove the selected documents by ⌘+clicking them.

4. **Click the Action button (the cog icon) on the toolbar, and then click Download Document or Download Documents on the menu.** The Choose a download format dialog appears.

5. **Click the format in which you want to download the document (see Figure 2.12).** Your choices are the current iWork format (such as Pages), PDF, or the equivalent Microsoft Office format (such as Word for a Pages document).

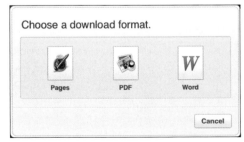

Choose a download format.

Pages   PDF   Word

Cancel

2.12 In the Choose a download format dialog, click the format to use.

6. **Wait while the iWork app processes the documents you've requested, and then downloads them to your default downloads folder (such as the Downloads folder in your user account on a Mac).** If your computer contains an app associated with the documents, they open automatically.

Putting desktop documents on an iOS device

You can put your desktop documents on your iPad, iPhone, or iPod touch in several ways:

- **Use iTunes File Sharing to copy the documents to the iOS device, and then use the Open from iTunes command to open them.**
- **E-mail the documents.**
- **Use a file-transfer service, such as Dropbox.**
- **Open a document from a WebDAV server.**

Transferring documents using iTunes File Sharing

If the document you want to put on your iOS device is on your Mac or PC, you can transfer it easily by using the iTunes File Sharing feature built in to iTunes. You can also use iTunes File Sharing to copy documents from your iOS device to your computer. Here's how to transfer documents using iTunes File Sharing:

1. **Connect your iOS device to your computer.**

Note You can connect your iOS device to your computer either via USB or wirelessly. Before you can connect wirelessly, you must connect the iOS device via USB; click the Summary tab in iTunes; select the Sync with this iPhone over Wi-Fi check box, Sync with this iPad over Wi-Fi check box, or Sync with this iPod over Wi-Fi check box; and then click Sync.

2. **Click the iOS device's button on the navigation bar to display the management screens for the device.** If you've chosen to display the iTunes sidebar, click the iOS device's entry in the sidebar.

Genius iTunes gives you two means of navigation: the navigation bar, which appears across the top of the window below the playback controls, and the sidebar, which appears on the left side of the window. Current versions of iTunes display the navigation bar by default. To display the sidebar, choose View ⇨ Show Sidebar or press Option+⌘+S.

3. **Click the Apps button on the navigation bar to display the Apps screen.**
4. **Scroll down to the bottom of the Apps screen so that you can see the File Sharing section.**
5. **In the Apps box on the left, click the app to which you want to add files or from which you want to copy them (see Figure 2.13).** The list of documents already in the app appears in the Documents box on the right. This box shows the app's name and "Documents" — for example, Pages Documents.

2.13 Use the File Sharing section of the Apps screen in iTunes to quickly copy documents from your computer to your iOS device, or vice versa.

6. **To copy files from your computer to the iOS device, follow these steps:**

    a. **Click the Add button to display the Add dialog.**

    b. **Select the file(s) you want to add to the iOS device.**

    c. **Click the Add button.** iTunes copies the files to your iOS device.

7. **To copy files from the iOS device to your computer, follow these steps:**

    a. **In the Documents box on the right, select the file(s) you want to copy to your computer.**

    b. **Click the Save to button to display the Save to dialog.**

    c. **Navigate to the folder in which you want to put the copies.**

    d. **Click the Save to button.** iTunes copies the files to the folder you chose.

8. **Click Done.** You can then disconnect your iOS device from your computer.

Genius

To update a document on your iOS device, click Add in the File Sharing section of the Apps screen, select the document in the Add dialog, and then click Add. iTunes displays a dialog warning you that an older version of the document already exists on the iOS device. Click Replace to replace the existing version with the new version.

Opening a document from iTunes

After copying a document from your computer to your iOS device using iTunes File Sharing, you use the Copy from iTunes command to open it in the appropriate app. Here's what to do:

1. **Open the appropriate iWork app on your iOS device.**

2. **If the iWork app displays a document, tap the button in the upper-left corner of the screen to return to the Pages, Numbers, or Keynote screen.**

3. **Tap the + button in the upper-left corner to display the panel for creating and adding documents (see Figure 2.14).**

4. **Tap Copy from iTunes to display the Copy from iTunes dialog.**

5. **Tap the document you want to copy (see Figure 2.15).** The app copies the document and then displays the Pages screen, Numbers screen, or Keynote screen, which now lists the copied document.

6. **Tap the document to open it.**

2.14 Tap the + button, and then Copy from iTunes to copy a document you have placed on your iOS device using iTunes File Sharing.

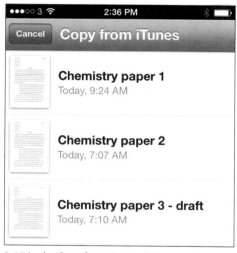

2.15 In the Copy from iTunes dialog, tap the document you want to copy to the iWork app.

Transferring documents via e-mail

Sending files attached to e-mail is a great way to transfer documents quickly and easily either to other people or to your computer or iOS device.

Caution Mail servers may reject attachments larger than 5MB, so it's best to use e-mail only for smaller documents.

Here's how to send an iWork document via e-mail from an iOS device:

1. **Open the app.**

2. **Open the document in the app.**

3. **Tap the Tools icon on the toolbar to display the Tools screen or Tools pane.**

4. **Tap Share and Print to display the Share and Print screen or Share and Print pane.**

5. **Tap the Email button.** This button's name is Email Document in Pages, Email Spreadsheet in Numbers, or Email Presentation in Keynote. The Email Document, Email Spreadsheet, or Email Presentation screen or pane appears.

6. **Tap the button for the file format you want to send.** Your choices are the app's native format (for example, the Pages format for Pages), the equivalent Microsoft Office format (for example, Word for Pages), and PDF. The iWork app causes Mail to create a new message with the document attached.

7. **Address the message, give it a subject and any explanatory body text needed, and then send it.**

Here's how to send an iWork document via e-mail from an iWork app on the Mac:

1. **Open the document in its iWork app.** For example, open a document in Pages.

2. **Click Share on the menu bar to open the Share menu.**

3. **In the Send via Mail category at the top of the menu, click the format you want to use.** Your choices are the app's native format (for example, the Numbers format for Numbers), the equivalent Microsoft Office format (for example, Excel for Numbers), and PDF. The iWork app causes Mail to create a new message with the document attached.

4. **Address the message, give it a subject and any explanation needed, and then send it.**

Genius You can also send files via e-mail by attaching them to messages in either Apple Mail or another e-mail app. In Mail, start a message, click the Attach button (the paperclip icon) on the toolbar, click the file, and then click Choose File. Alternatively, start the message, and then drag in the file from a Finder window or the desktop.

Here's how to send an iWork document from iCloud:

1. Open the document in the iWork app in iCloud.

Genius

You can also send a document from the document-management screen for the iCloud app — for example, the Keynote for iCloud screen. Control+click the document you want to send, and then click Send a Copy on the contextual menu to display the Choose a format to send via iCloud Mail dialog. You can then choose the format as described in step 3.

2. Click Share to display the Choose a format to send via iCloud Mail dialog.

3. Click the format in which you want to send the iCloud Mail (see Figure 2.16). Your choices are the app's native format (for example, the Keynote format for Keynote), the equivalent Microsoft Office format (for example, PowerPoint for Keynote), and PDF. The iWork app creates a copy of the presentation and then displays a dialog telling you it is ready.

2.16 In the Choose a format to send via iCloud Mail dialog, click the format you want to use.

4. Click the Email button. An iCloud Mail window opens, containing a new message with the document attached.

5. Address the message, give it a subject and any explanation needed, and then send it.

Transferring documents via file-transfer services

Another easy way of transferring documents is to use a file-transfer service such as Dropbox (www.dropbox.com). If you want to use the service to get documents to and from your iOS device, make sure the service provides an iOS app.

Once the file-transfer service is set up on your computer and devices, you can easily copy files back and forth. For example, here's how to open a Pages document in Pages from the Dropbox app on iOS:

1. **In the Dropbox app, tap the document's listing (see Figure 2.17).** The document opens in the iOS viewer, a mini-app that displays documents in various formats.

2. **Tap the Action button in the lower-right corner to display the Action dialog.**

3. **Tap Open In to display the dialog of available actions.**

4. **Tap Open in Pages (see Figure 2.18) to open the document in Pages.**

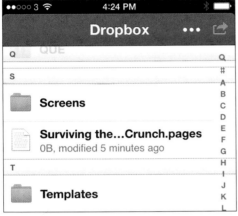

2.17 Tap the document's listing in Dropbox to open it in the iOS viewer.

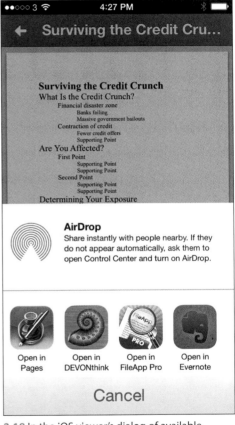

2.18 In the iOS viewer's dialog of available actions, tap Open in Pages to open the document in Pages.

Opening a document from a WebDAV server

The iWork apps can also open documents stored on WebDAV servers. This is handy if your company or organization uses a WebDAV server for sharing documents on the Internet.

Note WebDAV is the acronym for Web Distributed Authoring and Versioning, a protocol for storing files on web servers.

Here's how to open a document from a WebDAV server:

1. **Open the appropriate iWork app on your iOS device.**

2. **If the iWork app displays a document, tap the button in the upper-left corner of the screen to return to the Pages, Numbers, or Keynote screen.**

3. **Tap the + button in the upper-left corner to display the panel for creating and adding documents.**

4. **Tap Copy from WebDAV to display the WebDAV Sign In screen.**

5. **Type the server address (see Figure 2.19).**

6. **Type your user name for the server.**

7. **Type your password for the server.**

8. **Tap Sign In.** The app signs in to the WebDAV server and then displays the listing of files and folders.

9. **Tap the document you want to copy.** The app copies the document to its local storage and then displays the Pages screen, Numbers screen, or Keynote screen, which now lists the copied document.

10. **Tap the document to open it.**

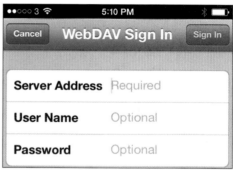

2.19 On the WebDAV Sign In screen, type the server address, your username and password, and then tap Sign In.

Duplicating or deleting a document

If you want to work with a copy of a document, leaving the original untouched, you can quickly duplicate it. Also, when you no longer need a document, you can delete it.

Here's how to duplicate a document in the iWork apps:

- **OS X.** Choose File ⇨ Duplicate, type the new name for the document in the title bar, and then press Return.

- **iOS.** On the document-management screen, tap Edit to start the document icons jiggling; you can also tap and hold a document to start the icons jiggling. Tap the document you want to dupli-cate, and then tap Duplicate (the + icon) on the toolbar (see Figure 2.20). You can then rename the copy by tapping its name and working on the Rename screen that appears.

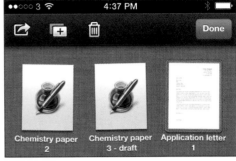

2.20 To duplicate a document in iOS, tap Edit, tap the document, and then tap Duplicate (the plus sign, +) on the toolbar.

- **iCloud.** On the Pages for iCloud screen, Numbers for iCloud screen, or Keynote for iCloud screen, Control+click the document, and then click the Duplicate command on the con-textual menu. (This command is called Duplicate Document in Pages, Duplicate Spreadsheet in Numbers, and Duplicate Presentation in Keynote.) You can then rename the copy by clicking its name, typing the new name, and then clicking elsewhere.

Here's how to delete an iWork document:

- **OS X.** In a Finder window, Control+click the file, and then click Move to Trash on the con-textual menu. You can recover the document from the Trash until you empty the Trash or the Trash becomes so full that OS X empties part of it for you.

- **iOS.** On the document-management screen, tap and hold the document until the icons start jiggling, and then tap Delete (the Trash icon) on the toolbar. In the dialog that appears, tap Delete Document in Pages, Delete Spreadsheet in Numbers, or Delete Presentation in Keynote.

- **iCloud.** On the Pages for iCloud screen, Numbers for iCloud screen, or Keynote for iCloud screen, Control+click the document, and then click the Delete command on the contextual menu. (This command is called Delete Document in Pages, Delete Spreadsheet in Numbers, and Delete Presentation in Keynote.) In the confirmation dialog that opens, click Delete.

How Do I Work with Text in iWork Apps?

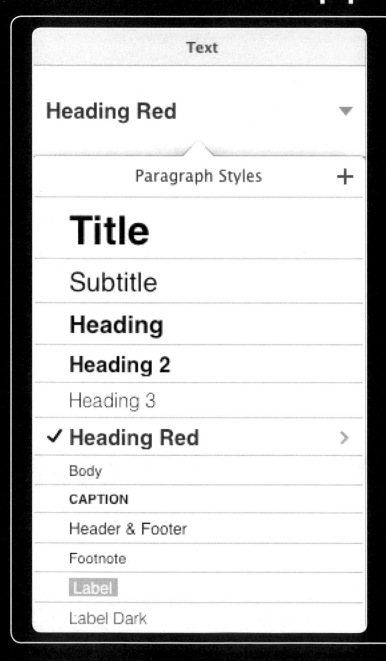

The iWork documents you create in Pages, Numbers, and Keynote will likely differ greatly from each other — but it's almost certain that each document will contain text and that you will want to format it so that it looks right. This chapter shows you how to input text as quickly and efficiently as possible in your documents by using the features and shortcuts that the apps offer. It also covers how to navigate through text and select it, as well as how to use the various means of formatting to save time, effort, and frustration.

Working Efficiently with Text

Whether you create your own documents or edit other people's, you almost certainly work extensively with text. This section shows you how to input text as quickly and accurately as possible by using text replacements on OS X and text shortcuts on iOS, how to insert special characters, and how to create hyperlinks in your documents.

Genius

OS X and iOS automatically sync your text replacements among your devices as long as you have the Documents & Data feature turned on in your iCloud preferences. So, you can create your text replacements on any of your Macs or iOS devices as you work. However, if you need to create many text replacements, you can normally do so more quickly on a Mac, and then have iCloud propagate them to your iOS devices.

Creating and using text replacements in OS X

OS X includes a system-wide feature for text replacement that can save you a lot of time and typing. To use your text replacements in the iWork apps, you must turn them on in the Substitutions feature, which also controls other substitutions the apps can make to help you input text quickly and easily.

Note

Earlier versions of the iWork apps on OS X had a feature called Auto-Correction. Apple has removed this feature and replaced it with the Text feature in Keyboard preferences.

Controlling substitutions in the iWork apps

The iWork apps on OS X have a Substitutions feature that can automatically insert smart quotes, smart dashes, smart links, and text replacements for you. Substitutions has four elements:

- **Smart Quotes.** When you turn on Smart Quotes, Substitutions replaces straight quotes (" and ") with smart quotes that curl in the appropriate direction ("and").

- **Smart Dashes.** When you turn on Smart Dashes, Substitutions replaces two hyphens with an em dash (a long dash, like this one: —).

- **Smart Links.** When you turn on Smart Links, Substitutions replaces any recognizable Internet address (such as www.apple.com) with a hyperlink.

- **Text Replacement.** When you turn on Text Replacement, Substitutions replaces any defined shortcut with its replacement text.

Note The Substitutions feature works at the app level rather than at the system level, so you can use different substitution settings in each app if you want. For example, you can turn on Smart Dashes in Pages but turn it off in Numbers. The text replacements are at the system level, so you cannot use the same shortcut for a different text replacement in different apps.

Here's how to control which substitutions an iWork app uses:

1. **Open the app.**

2. **Click Edit to open the Edit menu.**

3. **Click or highlight Substitutions to display the Substitutions submenu (see Figure 3.1).** A check mark indicates that a feature is on.

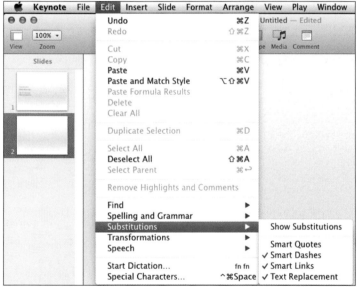

3.1 You turn individual substitutions on or off as needed in the Substitutions submenu.

4. **Click Smart Quotes, Smart Dashes, Smart Links, or Text Replacement to turn it on or off, as needed.**

5. **To choose further options, or to replace items (quotes, dashes, links, or text items) after you have been working with the features turned off, choose Edit ⇨ Substitutions ⇨ Show Substitutions.** The Substitutions window opens.

6. **Select or clear the Smart Dashes check box, the Smart Links check box, the Text Replacement check box, and the Smart Quotes check box, as needed (see Figure 3.2).**

7. **If the pop-up menus below the Smart Quotes check box show the wrong types of quotes, open each menu in turn and choose the right type.**

3.2 In the Substitutions window, you can choose which substitutions or type of smart quotes to use.

8. **Click the Close button (the red button at the left end of the title bar) to close the Substitutions window.** You can also press ⌘+W or choose Edit ➪ Substitutions ➪ Hide Substitutions if you prefer.

Opening the Text pane in System Preferences

Here's how to open the Text pane in System Preferences:

1. **Choose Apple ➪ System Preferences from the menu bar.**

Genius

If the System Preferences icon appears on the Dock, you can click it to open System Preferences. Alternatively, Control+click the System Preferences icon on the Dock to display its contextual menu, and then click Keyboard to go straight to the Keyboard pane.

2. **Click Keyboard to display the Keyboard pane.**

3. **Click the Text tab to display the Text pane.**

Working with text replacements and text shortcuts

With the Text pane in Keyboard preferences open, you can create a text replacement like this:

1. **Click the Add (+) button below the list of text replacements.** System Preferences selects the next unused line and displays an edit box in the Replace column.

2. **Type the shortcut in the Replace column (see Figure 3.3).**

3. **Press Tab to select the corresponding box in the With column.** If you prefer, you can click in the With column instead.

4. **Type the replacement text, and then press Return.**

3.3 You can quickly create one or more text replacements by working in the Text pane in Keyboard preferences on OS X.

Note To edit an existing text replacement, double-click it in either the Replace or With column in the Text pane in Keyboard preferences. Type the new shortcut or replacement text, and then press Return.

To delete a text replacement on OS X, click it in the Text pane, and then click the Remove (–) button. iCloud syncing causes the replacement to be removed from your other Macs and your iOS devices as well.

After creating your text shortcuts, you can put them to use immediately by following these steps:

1. **Open an app that accepts text input, such as Keynote.**

2. **Type the shortcut text for the item you want to insert.** The app displays a pop-up bubble containing the replacement text (see Figure 3.4).

3. **Type a space or punctuation character to input the replacement text.** If you don't want to input the replacement text, click the X button in the pop-up bubble.

3.4 To use a text shortcut, type its replacement text.

71

Choosing Settings for Spelling, Smart Quotes, and Smart Dashes

From the Text pane in Keyboard preferences, you can also choose the following settings for spelling, smart quotes, and smart dashes:

- **Correct spelling automatically.** Select this check box to enable automatic spell checking. This is usually helpful, but turn it off if you find the queries distracting.

- **Spelling pop-up menu.** Choose Automatic by Language if you want OS X to check the spelling automatically by the language it detects. This is usually worth trying first. If you don't like the results, open the pop-up menu and then click the language you want to use. You can also click Set Up at the bottom of the menu to display a dialog for choosing which languages to use. Clear the check box for any language you don't want to use, and drag the selected languages into your preferred order, and then click Done.

- **Use smart quotes and dashes.** Select this check box to enable automatic substitution of quotes and dashes. Use the "for Double Quotes" pop-up menu to choose which double quotes to use (your choices include regular double smart quotes, ". . .", and double guillemets, ». . .«) and the "for Single Quotes" pop-up menu to choose which single quotes to use (for example, regular single smart quotes, ' ').

Creating and using text shortcuts on iOS

iOS provides a full implementation of text shortcuts. To set them up, you navigate to the Keyboard screen in the Settings app and create the text shortcuts you need. You can then use them in just about any app that supports text input.

Genius If you use the same iCloud account with both a Mac and an iOS device, you may prefer to create your text shortcuts on the Mac and have iCloud sync them to your iOS device.

Displaying the Keyboard screen

To start setting up your text shortcuts, first display the Keyboard screen and make sure Auto-Correction is turned on. Follow these steps:

1. **Press the Home button to display the Home screen.**

2. **Tap Settings to display the Settings screen.**

3. **Tap General to display the General screen.**

4. **Tap Keyboard to display the Keyboard screen.**

5. **Make sure the Auto-Correction switch is set to On (see Figure 3.5).**

Working with text shortcuts

Here's how to create a new text shortcut from the Keyboard screen in the Settings app:

1. **Tap Add New Shortcut to display the Shortcut screen.**

2. **In the Phrase box, type the word or phrase you want the shortcut to input (see Figure 3.6).** For example, you might input your job title.

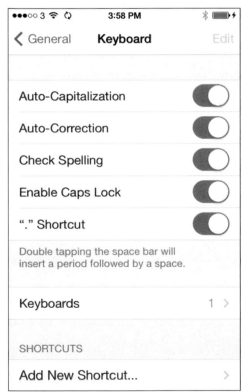

3.5 On the Keyboard screen in the Settings app, make sure the Auto-Correction switch is set to On.

3.6 On the Shortcut screen, type the word or phrase, the shortcut for it, and then tap Save.

3. **Press Return to move the focus to the Shortcut box.** You can also tap in the Shortcut box if you prefer.

4. **Type the shortcut you will use to input the text.** Normally, you want to use an abbreviation or non-word, rather than a real word you might use in your documents. Otherwise, you must refuse the automatic correction each time you type the word.

Genius On the Shortcut screen in iOS, you see that the Shortcut field is marked Optional. Normally, you want to create a shortcut so you can input the phrase quickly and consistently. If you omit the shortcut, iOS suggests the phrase when you've typed enough to identify it. iOS also doesn't query the spelling even if the phrase isn't in the dictionary.

5. **Tap Save.** Settings saves the shortcut and displays the Keyboard screen again. The new shortcut appears in the Shortcuts list.

Here's how to delete a text shortcut:

1. **On the Keyboard screen in the Settings app, tap Edit to switch the screen to Edit mode.**

2. **Tap the Delete icon to the left of the shortcut's name.** The shortcut's button slides partway to the left, revealing a Delete button on the right side of the button (see Figure 3.7).

3. **Tap Delete.** Settings deletes the shortcut.

4. **When you finish editing your text shortcuts, tap Done to return to the Keyboard screen.**

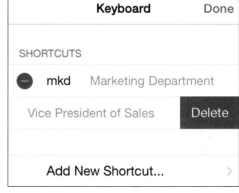

3.7 You can quickly delete any text shortcut you no longer need.

Genius When you need to delete a text shortcut quickly, navigate to the Keyboard screen, swipe left on the shortcut's button, and then tap the Delete button that appears.

After creating your text shortcuts, you can simply use them in almost any app that accepts text input. To do so, follow these steps:

1. **Open an app that accepts text input, such as Pages.**

2. **Type the shortcut text for the item you want to insert.** The app displays a pop-up bubble containing the replacement text (see Figure 3.8).

3.8 To use a text shortcut, type its replacement text.

3. **Type a space or punctuation character to input the replacement text.** If you don't want to input the replacement text, tap the pop-up bubble.

Inserting special characters and hyperlinks

Most likely, you can complete many documents using the regular characters that appear on the keyboard. However, occasionally, you may need special characters, such as accented letters (for example, á or ñ) or emoticons (the formal name for smileys). OS X provides a selection of special characters that you can insert easily using the Special Characters panel. iOS gives you access to various special characters directly from the keyboard; you can also activate an entire extra keyboard of graphical characters.

Inserting special characters on OS X

Here's how to insert special characters on OS X:

1. **Position the insertion point where you want the special character to appear.**

2. **Choose Edit ⇨ Special Characters or press Control+⌘+Space to display the Special Characters panel.**

3. **Click the tab button at the bottom (see Figure 3.9) to display the panel you want to see.** You have the following choices:

   • **Recents and Favorites.** This panel shows the characters you've used most recently or those you use most frequently.

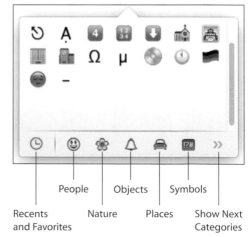

3.9 Use the Special Characters panel to insert characters in the iWork apps on OS X.

75

- **People.** This panel includes emoticons (smileys), items of clothing, and symbols such as hearts.

- **Nature.** This panel includes animals, plants, sun and moon symbols, and rainbows.

- **Objects.** This panel includes everything from Halloween pumpkins and CDs to weapons, musical instruments, and fruit.

- **Places.** This panel includes buildings, means of transport, traffic signs, and widely known flags.

- **Symbols.** This panel includes arrows, widely used symbols (such as Not Drinking Water), and clocks.

- **Show Next Categories.** Click this button to display the next batch of categories. Click the resulting Show Previous Categories button to go back to the original categories.

- **Letterlike Symbols.** This panel includes symbols such as °, ©, and ™.

- **Pictographs.** This panel (see Figure 3.10) includes sun symbols, card suits (hearts, diamonds, clubs, and spades), and chess pieces.

- **Bullets/Stars.** This panel offers a wide variety of bullet and star symbols.

- **Technical Symbols.** This panel includes symbols including the Apple Command key (⌘), Delete symbol, and technical symbols for illustrations.

- **Sign/Standard Symbols.** This panel includes telephone symbols, radioactive and danger symbols, and recycling symbols.

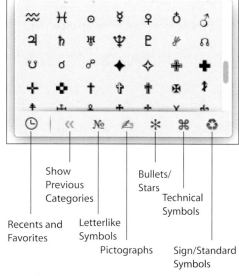

Show Previous Categories

Recents and Favorites

Letterlike Symbols

Pictographs

Bullets/Stars

Technical Symbols

Sign/Standard Symbols

3.10 Click the buttons at the bottom of the Special Characters panel to navigate to the set of characters you need.

4. **Hold the mouse pointer over a symbol to see its name or description.**

5. **Double-click the character you want to insert.** The Special Characters panel closes automatically.

If you need to work extensively with special characters, use these three advanced moves:

- **Search for a character.** Scroll up to the top of the Special Characters panel and type your search term in the Search box you find there. A list of results appears (see Figure 3.11). If you find the right character, double-click it to input it into your document.

3.11 Use the Search box at the top of the Special Characters panel to locate characters matching a keyword.

- **Display the large version of the Characters dialog.** Scroll to the top of the Special Characters panel, and then click the button to the right of the Search box. The large version of the Characters dialog opens (see Figure 3.12). This dialog enables you to browse more characters at once. This, together with a blown-up version of the selected character and a list of related characters, makes it easier to find exactly what you need. When you do, click Add to Favorites to add it to your favorites or simply double-click it to insert it in the document.

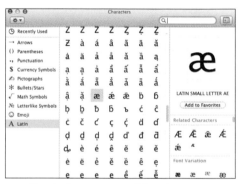

3.12 Use the large version of the Characters dialog when you need to work extensively with special characters.

- **Display the small version of the Characters dialog.** If you need to keep the Characters dialog open so you can quickly insert other characters, click the button in the upper-right corner of the large version of the Characters dialog. The app displays the small version of the Characters dialog (see Figure 3.13), which stays on-screen and enables you to input a special character by clicking it. Click the X button at the left end of the title bar when you want to close the Characters dialog.

3.13 Click a special character in the small version of the Characters dialog to insert the character in the document.

Genius

To search for a character, click the button to the right of the Search box to display the Characters dialog.

Inserting special characters on iOS

iOS enables you to insert special characters in two main ways: by inserting modified versions of characters that appear on the keyboard, and by using the Emoji keyboard. You may need to enable the Emoji keyboard before you can use it.

To insert special characters from the keyboard, tap and hold the base character on the keyboard, and then slide your finger to the the character you want on the pop-up panel. Only some characters have these pop-up panels. For example:

3.14 To input a special character, tap and hold the base character, and then slide your finger to the special character on the pop-up panel.

- **Vowels.** Each vowel key (a, e, i, o, and u) has a pop-up panel with accented and modified versions of the vowels. Figure 3.14 shows the pop-up panel for the letter *a*.

- **Punctuation.** Punctuation keys, such as the period (.) and question mark (?), provide alternate characters.

- **Symbols.** The hyphen key opens a pop-up panel containing the en dash (–), em dash (—), and a bullet character.

Here's how to input graphical characters using the Emoji keyboard:

1. **In an app that accepts text input, tap in a text area to display the on-screen keyboard.**

2. **Display the Emoji keyboard:**
   - Tap the globe icon toward the lower-left corner of the keyboard to cycle through your keyboards. If you've set up only your regular keyboard (for example, English) and Emoji, tapping this icon toggles between them, which is handy.

- If you've set up too many keyboards for toggling or cycling easily, tap and hold the globe icon to display the pop-up menu, and then tap Emoji (see Figure 3.15).

3. **Tap the tab button at the bottom of the keyboard to display the category you want (see Figure 3.16).**

3.15 Use the globe icon and the pop-up menu (if necessary), to switch to the Emoji keyboard.

3.16 Tap a tab button to display the appropriate Emoji category, and then swipe left or right through the icons to find the one you want.

4. **Swipe left or right to display the screen containing the icon you want.**

5. **Tap the icon to insert it.**

When you finish using the Emoji keyboard, tap the globe icon one or more times to toggle or cycle back to your regular keyboard. Alternatively, tap and hold the globe icon to display the list of keyboards, and then tap the one you want.

Enabling the Emoji Keyboard

Here's how to enable the Emoji keyboard so that you can input graphical characters:

1. **Press the Home button to display the Home screen.**
2. **Tap Settings to open the Settings app.**
3. **Tap General to display the General screen.**
4. **Tap Keyboard to display the Keyboard screen.**
5. **Tap Keyboards to display the Keyboards screen.**
6. **Tap Add New Keyboard to display the Add New Keyboard screen.**
7. **Tap Emoji.** iOS returns you to the Keyboards screen, where Emoji now appears on the list.

You can now input Emoji characters as explained in the main text.

Inserting hyperlinks

To enable people who open your documents to navigate to the Internet addresses in them, you can include hyperlinks. To insert a hyperlink, simply type or paste the address in the document and type a space or a punctuation character. The iWork app automatically creates a hyperlink to the address and displays an underline on the text to represent the hyperlink visually.

On OS X, you can take greater control of hyperlinks like this:

1. **Type the address for the hyperlink, and then press the spacebar or type a punctuation mark.** The iWork app automatically converts the address to a hyperlink.
2. **Click the hyperlink to display the Edit Link dialog.** You can also Control+click the hyperlink, and then click Edit Link on the contextual menu.
3. **In the Link to pop-up menu, select the link type: Webpage or Email.** Webpage is the default.
4. **In the Link box, edit the link if necessary.** If you've typed it correctly, you shouldn't need to change it.

5. **In the Display box, type the text you want to display for the link (see Figure 3.17).** For example, you may want to use text such as Visit Our Website instead of the address itself.

6. **Click Open if you want to open the link in your web browser or e-mail app to test it.** Otherwise, click in the document to close the Edit Link dialog.

3.17 Use the Edit Link dialog on OS X to change the link type, display different text for it, or remove it.

Note

If you create a link inadvertently, you can restore the text to normal by using the Undo command immediately; choose Edit ⇨ Undo or press ⌘+Z. After that, you need to remove the link. Control+click the link to display the Edit Link dialog, and then click Remove.

Using Find and Replace

The iWork apps include Find and Replace functionality that you can use to locate and change text in your documents. Find and Replace works in a similar way on the three platforms and has these features:

- **Find.** You can locate the next instance or previous instance of the text you input.

- **Replace.** You can locate the next instance or previous instance of text, replace an instance, or replace all instances.

- **Whole Words.** You can restrict the search to whole words. For example, turning on Whole Words enables you to find *art* without finding words such as *heart*, *partly*, and *cartwheel*. Click this item again, removing the check mark, when you need to turn this feature off. At this writing, the iPhone and iPod touch don't have this feature.

- **Match Case.** You can also restrict the search by making it case sensitive. Match Case is useful when you need to distinguish words by their capitalization — for example, when you need to find *Hospital* but not *hospital*. At this writing, the iPhone and iPod touch don't have this feature.

Using Find and Replace on OS X

Here's how to use Find and Replace in the iWork apps on OS X:

1. **Press ⌘+F or choose Edit ➪ Find ➪ Find.** Unless you're good with the menus, the keyboard shortcut is usually fastest. The Find & Replace window appears. Normally, this window shows just the Find field at first.

2. **Click the Action menu at the left end, and then choose any of the following options, as shown in Figure 3.18:**

   ● **Find.** Click this item to switch back to Find after using Find & Replace.

3.18 Open the Action menu at the left end of the Find & Replace window, and then choose the options you want.

   ● **Find & Replace.** Click this item to display the Replace field and command buttons so you can replace what you search for.

   ● **Whole Words.** Click this item, placing a check mark next to it, to restrict the search to whole words instead of searching for matches both within words and as whole words. Click the Whole Words item again, removing the check mark, when you're ready to turn this feature off.

   ● **Match Case.** Click this item, placing a check mark next to it, to make the search case sensitive. Match Case is useful when you need to distinguish words by their capitalization. Click the Match Case item again, removing the check mark, when you need to turn this feature off.

3. **To find text, follow these steps:**

   a. **Type the text in the text box.** The app searches for the text, and a readout appears at the right side showing the number of matches — for example, *4 found* (see Figure 3.19).

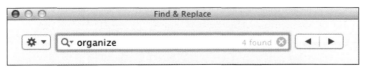

3.19 Type the text you want to find, and then use the left- and right- arrow buttons to navigate among the instances of the text in the document.

    b. **Click the right-arrow button on the right end of the Find & Replace window to move to the next instance, or click the left-arrow button to move to the previous instance.**

4. **To replace text, follow these steps:**

    a. **Click the Action menu at the left end of the Find & Replace window, and then click Find & Replace to display the Replace controls.**

    b. **Type the search text in the Find box.**

    c. **Type the replacement text in the Replace box (see Figure 3.20).**

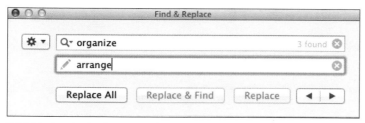

3.20 Display the Replace controls in the Find & Replace window when you need to replace text in a document.

    d. **Click the right-arrow button on the right end of the Find & Replace window to move to the next instance, or click the left-arrow button to move to the previous instance.**

    e. **Click Replace to replace this instance.** Click Replace & Find to replace this instance and find the next, or click Replace All to replace all instances.

5. **When you finish using the Find & Replace window, click its Close button (the red button at the left end of the title bar) to close it.**

Genius

On OS X, you can press ⌘+F to display the Find & Replace dialog, press ⌘+G to find the next instance of what you searched for last time, or press Shift+⌘+G to find the previous instance. You can also select text and press ⌘+E to use it as the Find text. For example, select a word, press ⌘+E, and then press ⌘+G to find the next instance of that word.

Using Find and Replace on the iPad

Here's how to use Find and Replace on the iPad:

1. **Tap the Tools button (the wrench icon) on the toolbar, and then tap Find.** The Find and Replace bar appears.

2. **Tap the Settings icon at the left end (see Figure 3.21), and then use the pop-up menu to set any of the following options:**

- **Find.** Tap this item to switch back to Find after using Find & Replace.

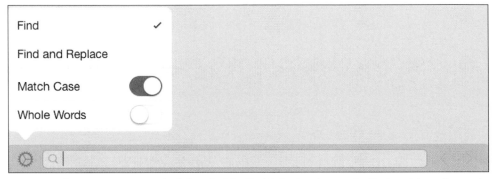

3.21 Open the pop-up menu at the left end of the Find & Replace bar on the iPad, and then choose the options you want.

- **Find and Replace.** Tap this item to display the Replace field and command button so you can replace the word or term for which you search.
- **Whole Words.** Set this switch to On to restrict the search to whole words instead of searching for matches both within words and as whole words.
- **Match Case.** Set this switch to On to make the search case sensitive.

3. **To search, type the search text in the Find box.** If the app finds the text, it highlights the first occurrence in yellow and the remaining occurrences (if any) in white. You can then tap the highlighted word and edit what you've found, or navigate among the instances by tapping the > and < buttons on the Find & Replace bar (see Figure 3.22).

3.22 You can navigate among instances of the search text by tapping the < and > buttons at the right end of the Find & Replace bar.

4. **If you want to use Replace rather than Find, tap the Action icon to the left of the Find box, and then tap Find and Replace on the pop-up menu.** Type the search text in the Find box, and then type the replacement text in the Replace box. The app searches automatically and highlights the instances it finds, using a yellow highlight for the first instance and a white highlight for the others. You can then tap Replace to replace the current instance and then tap the < button or > button to navigate to another instance, or tap the < button or > button to go to another instance without replacing this one.

5. **When you finish using Find and Replace, tap in the document to hide the Find & Replace bar.**

Using Find and Replace on the iPhone or iPod touch

Here's how to use Find and Replace on the iPhone or iPod touch:

1. **Tap the Tools button on the toolbar, and then tap Find.** The Find and Replace bar appears at the top of the screen.

2. **To search, type the search text in the Find box, and then tap the Search button on the keyboard (see Figure 3.23).** If the app finds the text, it highlights the first occurrence. You can then edit what you've found, or tap Previous or Next at the bottom of the screen (see Figure 3.24) to navigate to another instance.

3. **If you want to use Replace rather than Find, tap the Edit icon to the left of the Find box (see Figure 3.25).** Type the search text in the Find box, type the replacement text in the Replace box, and then tap Search. You can then use the four buttons that appear at the bottom of the screen:

    -   Tap < to go to the previous instance (see Figure 3.26).

    -   Tap > to go to the next instance.

    -   Tap Replace to replace the current instance.

    -   Tap Replace All to replace all instances in the document.

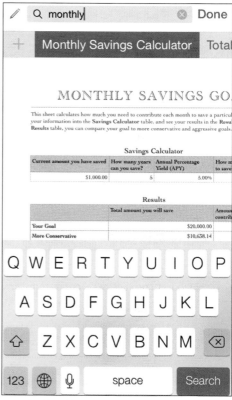

3.23 On the iPhone or iPod touch, type the text in the Find box, and then tap Search.

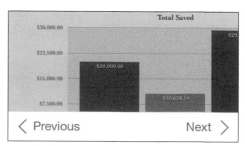

3.24 Tap Previous or Next at the bottom of the screen to navigate to another instance of the search text.

4. **When you finish using Find or Replace, tap Done in the upper-right corner of the screen to close the Find and Replace bar.**

Using Find and Replace in iCloud

Here's how to use Find and Replace in iCloud:

1. **Press ⌘+F or choose Tools ⇨ Show Find and Replace.** The Find & Replace bar appears across the bottom of the screen.

2. **Click the Action menu at the left end and choose any of the following options, as shown in Figure 3.27:**

   - **Find.** Click this item to switch back to Find after using Find & Replace.

   - **Find & Replace.** Click this item to display the Replace field and command buttons so you can replace what you search for.

   - **Whole Words.** Click this item (which places a check mark next to it) to restrict the search to whole words instead of also searching for matches within words. Click the Whole Words item again to remove the check mark when you're ready to turn off this feature.

   - **Match Case.** Click this item, placing a check mark next to it, to make the search case sensitive. Match Case is useful when you need to distinguish

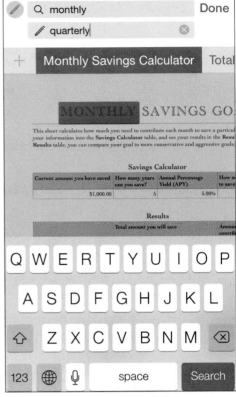

3.25 Tap the Edit icon to the left of the Find box to display the Replace box, type the replacement text, and then tap Search.

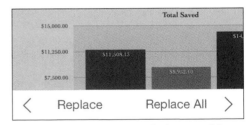

3.26 Tap Previous or Next at the bottom of the screen to navigate to another instance of the search text.

words by their capitalization. Click the Match Case item again, which removes the check mark, when you need to turn off this feature.

3.27 Open the Action menu at the left end of the Find & Replace bar, and then choose the options you want.

3. **To find text, follow these steps**:

   a. **Type the text in the text box.** The app searches for the text and selects the first instance.

   b. **Click the right-arrow button on the right end of the Find & Replace bar to move to the next instance, or click the left-arrow button to move to the previous instance.**

4. **To replace text, follow these steps**:

   a. **Click the Action menu at the left end of the Find & Replace window, and then click Find & Replace to display the Replace controls.**

   b. **Type the search text in the Find box.** The app automatically finds the first instance (if there is one) after the current position of the insertion point.

   c. **Type the replacement text in the Replace box (see Figure 3.28).**

3.28 Type the replacement text in the Replace box on the Find and Replace bar.

   d. **Click Replace to replace this instance.** Click the right-arrow button on the right end of the Find & Replace window to move to the next instance, or click the left-arrow button to move to the previous instance.

5. **When you finish using the Find & Replace bar, click Done to close it.** You can also press ⌘+F to close the bar.

Navigating and Selecting Text

To work effectively in your documents, you need to navigate around them. The iWork apps support standard means of navigation on each platform. You also need to be able to select text when you need to work with it — for example, to format or replace it. Selection is easy, but I review it here briefly to make sure you know the moves.

Navigating text

You can navigate on OS X or in the iCloud apps by using the pointing device (mouse, trackpad, or other device) or the keyboard:

- **Mouse**. Use the scroll bars as normal. Either click the thumb (the scroll box) and drag it, or click in the scroll bar above the thumb or below it. Click to place the insertion point.

- **Trackpad**. Swipe up, down, left, or right with two fingers. Click to place the insertion point.

- **Keyboard**. Use the keys and keyboard shortcuts explained in Table 3.1.

Table 3.1 Navigation Keys and Keyboard Shortcuts

Navigation Key or Shortcut	Effect
Left	Move one character to the left.
Control+B	Move back one character. This shortcut works with both left-to-right text and right-to-left text.
Right	Move one character to the right.
Up	Move up one line.
Down	Move down one line.
Option+Control+B	Move to the beginning of the current word (if in the word) or to the beginning of the previous word (if already at the beginning of the current word).
Option+Left	Move to the left edge of the current word. This shortcut works with both left-to-right text and right-to-left text.
Option+Control+F	Move to the end of the current word (if in the word) or to the end of the next word (if already at the end of the current word).
Option+Right	Move to the right edge of the current word. This shortcut works with both left-to-right text and right-to-left text.
⌘+Up	Move the insertion point to the beginning of the document, text box, table cell, or shape.
⌘+Down	Move the insertion point to the end of the document, text box, table cell, or shape.
Control+A	Move to the start of the current paragraph.
Control+E	Move to the end of the current paragraph.
Option+Up	Move to the start of the current paragraph.
Option+Down	Move to the end of the current paragraph.
⌘+Left	Move to the start of the current line.
⌘+Right	Move to the end of the current line.
Page Up	Scroll up by one screen of content.

Navigation Key or Shortcut	Effect
Page Down	Scroll down by one screen of content.
Option+Page Up	Scroll up by one screen and move the insertion point.
Option+Page Down	Scroll down by one screen and move the insertion point.
Home	Display the beginning of the document without moving the insertion point from its current location.
End	Display the end of the document without moving the insertion point from its current location.
Control+L	Display the insertion point's current location in the middle of the screen.

You can navigate in the iWork apps on iOS in the following ways:

- **Scroll.** Tap and drag to scroll up, down, left, or right.

- **Zoom.** Place two fingers (or a finger and thumb) on the screen and pinch outward to zoom in. Pinch inward to zoom out.

Selecting text

You can select text on OS X and in iCloud by using the keyboard, the pointing device (mouse, trackpad, or other), or both together.

To select text with the keyboard, move the insertion point to the beginning or end of what you want to select, hold down Shift, and then move the insertion point to the opposite end of the selection. Alternatively, use the keyboard shortcuts listed in Table 3.2.

To select text with the mouse or trackpad, you can simply click at the beginning of what you want to select, then keep holding down the mouse button or trackpad button as you drag to the end of the selection. If you prefer, you can click at the end and then drag back to the beginning.

You can also perform the following actions with your pointing device:

- **Double-click a word to select it.**

- **Triple-click anywhere in a paragraph to select it.** You can also triple-click to the left or right of the paragraph.

- **Use Shift.** Click at the start (or at the end) of the selection, navigate to the end (or to the start), then hold down Shift while you click.

Table 3.2 Keyboard Shortcuts for Selecting Text

Navigation Key or Shortcut	Effect
⌘+A	Select everything in the document or the item in which you're working.
Shift+⌘+A	Deselect everything that is selected.
Shift+Right	Extend the selection one character to the right.
Shift+Left	Extend the selection one character to the left.
Shift+Option+Left	Extend the selection to the beginning of the current word (if in a word) or to the beginning of the previous word (if not).
Shift+Option+Right	Extend the selection to the end of the current word (if in a word) or to the end of the next word (if not).
Shift+⌘+Left	Extend the selection to the start of the current line.
Shift+⌘+Right	Extend the selection to the end of the current line.
Shift+Up	Extend the selection up one line.
Shift+Down	Extend the selection down one line.
Shift+Option+Up	Extend the selection to the beginning of the current paragraph.
Shift+Option+Down	Extend the selection to the end of the current paragraph.
Shift+Home	Extend the selection to the beginning of the document, text box, table cell, or shape.
Shift+Option+Up	Extend the selection to the beginning of the document, text box, table cell, or shape.
Shift+End	Extend the selection to the end of the document, text box, table cell, or shape.
Shift+Option+Down	Extend the selection to the end of the document, text box, table cell, or shape.

Genius

You can select a bulleted paragraph easily by clicking its bullet. To rearrange a bulleted list, drag a bullet to move its paragraph. Any sub-bullets or numbered points move with the bullet.

Here's how to select text on iOS:

1. **Double-tap a word to select it.** iOS displays a highlight on the selection and selection handles around it.

2. **Drag the left selection handle to move the start of the selection to where you want it (see Figure 3.29).**

3. **Drag the right selection handle to move the end of the selection where you want it.**

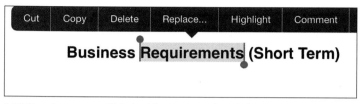

3.29 To select text on iOS, double-tap a word, and then drag the selection handles as needed.

Formatting Text

To make text in a document look the way you want, you apply formatting to it. The iWork apps provide three categories of formatting:

- **Direct formatting.** Direct formatting is formatting such as boldface or italics that you apply directly to text, rather than as part of a style (see the next item).

- **Styles.** Styles are collections of formatting that you can apply in a single move. A style typically contains font formatting (including the font, font size, font weight, and color) and paragraph formatting (including the alignment, space before, space after, and flow instructions such as keeping the paragraph with the next paragraph or putting a page break before it).

Note Each paragraph in a Pages document, each cell in a Numbers spreadsheet, and each text paragraph on a Keynote slide has a style applied to it. Even if you create a blank Pages document with apparently no style, the body text has a style such as Body Text applied.

- **List formatting.** List formatting is formatting for creating bulleted lists and numbered lists. You can apply list formatting on top of a paragraph's existing style.

Genius Make sure you understand the difference between direct formatting and styles. Direct formatting is useful for quick-and-dirty formatting, but you should use styles for most of your formatting. This is because styles enable you not only to format your documents quickly and consistently but also to make sweeping changes when needed.

Applying direct formatting

You can easily apply direct formatting to your documents on any of the iWork platforms by using the controls in the Format inspector on OS X or the Format panel in iOS or iCloud.

Here's how to apply direct formatting on OS X:

1. **Select the item you want to affect in the following ways:**

   - **Pages.** Click in the paragraph you want to format, or select multiple paragraphs.

   - **Numbers.** Click the cell you want to format, or select multiple cells.

   - **Keynote.** Click a placeholder to format all the text in it, or click in the paragraph you want to format. To format multiple paragraphs, select them.

2. **If the Format inspector isn't displayed, click the Format button on the toolbar to display it.** Figure 3.30 shows the Format inspector for Pages, but the Format inspectors for Numbers and Keynote work in similar ways.

3. **In Keynote or Numbers, click the Text tab at the top of the Format inspector to display the Text pane.**

4. **Click the button or control for the formatting you want to apply.** For example, click the Font pop-up menu and then click the appropriate font, or click the Bold button to apply boldface.

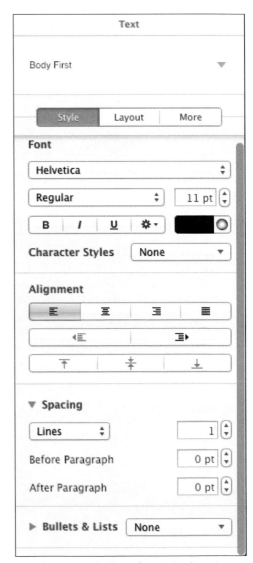

3.30 You can apply direct formatting by using the Format inspector in the iWork apps on OS X.

On OS X, you can press ⌘+B to toggle boldface on the current word or selection, press ⌘+I to toggle italic, or press ⌘+U to toggle underline.

Here's how to apply direct formatting in the iWork apps on iOS:

1. **Select the text you want to format.**

2. **Tap the screen to display the toolbar.**

3. **Tap the Format button to display the Format panel.**

4. **Tap the button or control for the formatting you want to apply.** For example, tap the Bold button to apply boldface, or tap the Center button to apply center alignment (see Figure 3.31).

3.31 Use the Format panel on iOS to apply direct formatting (such as boldface or center alignment) to the selection.

Here's how to apply direct formatting in iCloud:

1. **Select the item you want to affect in the following ways:**

   - **Pages.** Click in the paragraph you want to format, or select multiple paragraphs.

   - **Numbers.** Click the cell you want to format, or select multiple cells.

   - **Keynote.** Click a placeholder to format all the text in it, or click in the paragraph you want to format. To format multiple paragraphs, select them.

2. **If the Format panel isn't displayed, choose Tools⇨Settings⇨Show Format Panel to display it**.

3. **Click the button or control for the formatting you want to apply.** For example, click the Color swatch, and then click the color to apply (see Figure 3.32).

Applying styles

To format your documents quickly and consistently, you should use styles whenever possible. A style is a complete collection of formatting information that you can apply to a paragraph or selection in a single click. You can then apply direct formatting or list formatting (discussed next) on top of the style formatting as needed.

For example, say your document contains headings. By applying the Heading style to the top-level headings, the Heading 2 style to the second-level headings, and the Heading 3 style to the third-level headings, you can give your document a visible structure with consistent formatting. If a word in one of the headings needs extra emphasis, you can apply either a character style or direct italic formatting to it on top of the style formatting.

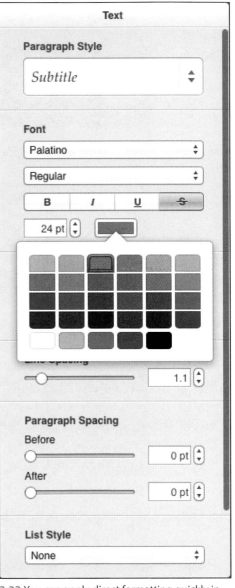

3.32 You can apply direct formatting quickly in iCloud by using the Format panel.

Note When you apply list formatting or direct formatting on top of a style in OS X, the app displays an asterisk (*) to the right of the style's name in the Format inspector to indicate that you have changed the style.

Genius

As well as paragraph styles, the iWork apps on OS X provide *character styles*: styles you can apply to particular words or characters within a paragraph or container to differentiate them from the rest of the style. For example, when you need to emphasize part of a paragraph, you can apply the Italic character style. The built-in character styles include Link (for hyperlinks), Bold, Italic, and Underline. You can create other character styles as needed.

Here's how to apply a style in the iWork apps on OS X:

1. **If the Format inspector isn't displayed, click the Format button on the toolbar to display it.**

2. **Click the Paragraph Styles list at the top of the panel (see Figure 3.33).** You can click either the drop-down button or the main part of the control, which shows the name of the current style.

3. **Click the style you want to apply.** The text or selection takes on the style formatting.

4. **If you want to apply a character style to part of the item, select that part, click the Character Styles pop-up menu, and then click the character style you want to apply (see Figure 3.34).**

Here's how to apply a style in the iWork apps on iOS:

1. **Tap the Format button on the toolbar to display the Format panel.**

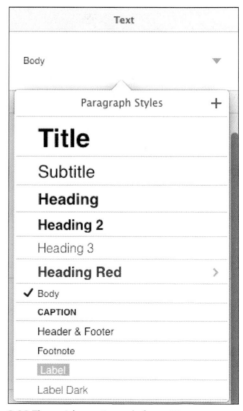

3.33 The quick way to apply formatting consistently is to apply a paragraph style from the Format inspector.

2. **Tap Style to display the Style pane (see Figure 3.35) if it's not displayed at first.**

3. **Tap the style in the Paragraph Style list.**

4. **Tap in the text to close the Format panel.**

3.34 You can apply a character style on top of the paragraph style when you need to make part of the item look different.

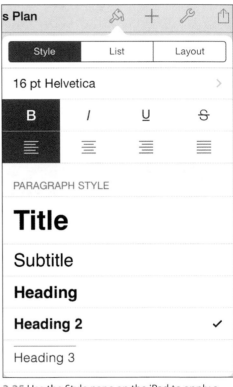

3.35 Use the Style pane on the iPad to apply a paragraph style.

Here's how to apply a style in the iWork apps in iCloud:

1. **If the Format panel isn't displayed, click the Tools button on the toolbar, and then choose Settings ⇨ Show Format Panel to display it.**

2. **Click the Paragraph Style pop-up menu to display the list of styles.**

3. **Click the style to apply.**

Working with styles on OS X

Each iWork template comes with a set of styles designed to work harmoniously together. However, to create documents that look exactly the way you want, you may need to customize the styles in a template. You can do so by updating existing styles or creating new styles. You can also rename an existing style or delete a style you don't need.

Genius

You can rearrange the style list by dragging styles up and down it. Put the styles you use most often near to the top for quick access even when a template contains many styles.

Updating a style

You can update an existing style by changing its formatting. Here's what to do:

1. **If the Format inspector isn't displayed, click the Format button on the toolbar or choose View ⇨ Inspector ⇨ Format to display it.**

2. **Apply the style to the paragraph or other item with which you will work.**

3. **Change the formatting of the style as needed.** For example, change the font and font size. The Style pop-up menu displays an asterisk (*) after the style's name to indicate you have overridden the default formatting. The Update button appears on the right side of the Style pop-up menu.

3.36 Click Update to update the style with the formatting override you've applied. The app updates each paragraph that uses the style.

4. **Click Update (see Figure 3.36).** The app redefines the style and updates the formatting of all the paragraphs that have the style applied.

Creating a new style

You can quickly create a new style in Pages, Numbers, or Keynote. Here's how to create a paragraph style; the moves for creating a character style are the same except that you use the Character Styles pop-up menu instead of the Style pop-up menu. Follow these steps:

1. **Select a paragraph of text.**

2. **If the Format inspector isn't displayed, click the Format button on the toolbar to display it.** You can also choose View ⇨ Inspector ⇨ Format.

3. **Click the Style pop-up menu at the top of the Format inspector, and then apply the style that's nearest to what you want.** You can start from any style, but usually it's easiest to start with something that's at least partly right.

4. **Click the Style pop-up menu again, and this time, click the plus sign (+) to the right of Paragraph Styles.** The app creates a new style based on the current style, gives it a

97

default name derived from the current style's name (for example, Body 1 for the new style if the current style is Body), and displays an edit box around the name (see Figure 3.37).

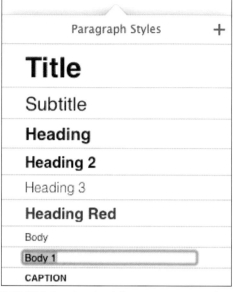

3.37 Click the plus sign (+) to create a new style based on the current one.

5. **Type the new name for the style, and then press Return, or click elsewhere to apply it.**

6. **Click the Style pop-up menu once more.** This time, click the new style to apply it to your sample paragraph.

7. **Format the paragraph the way you want the new style to appear.**

8. **Click Update on the right side of the Style pop-up menu.** The app updates the new style with the formatting you've given it.

Renaming a style

Each existing style comes with a predefined name that explains its role in the document: Title, Subtitle, Heading, Body, and so on. However, you can follow these steps to rename styles as needed to make the names more descriptive or more helpful:

1. **If the Format inspector isn't displayed, click the Format button on the toolbar or choose View ⇨ Inspector ⇨ Format to display it.**

2. **Click the Style pop-up menu to display the list of styles.**

3. **Move the mouse pointer over the style you want to rename.** The > mark appears to the right of the style's name.

4. **Click > to display the pop-up menu of actions.**

Note

To clear the override on a style, click the > button to display the pop-up menu of actions for the style, and then click Clear Override. The app removes from the styled item any formatting that doesn't belong to the style.

5. **Click Rename Style.** The app selects the name and displays an edit box around it.

6. **Type the new name for the style.**

7. **Press Return or click outside the name to apply it.**

Deleting a style

When you no longer need a style, you can follow these steps to delete it:

1. **If the Format inspector isn't displayed, click the Format button on the toolbar or choose View ➪ Inspector ➪ Format to display it.**

2. **Click the Style pop-up menu to display the list of styles.**

3. **Move the mouse pointer over the style you want to delete.** The > mark appears to the right of the style's name.

4. **Click > to display the pop-up menu of actions.**

5. **Click Delete Style.**

6. **If any paragraph in the document uses that style, a dialog opens prompting you to choose the style with which to replace the style you're deleting.**

7. **Click the pop-up menu, and then click the replacement style (see Figure 3.38).**

3.38 Choose the replacement style for the one you're deleting.

8. **Click OK.** The app applies the replacement style to the paragraphs and deletes the existing style.

Genius

If you're the only person who uses a particular template, you may prefer to leave in it any styles that you don't need now just in case you need them in the future. However, if you share the template with other people, you may find it better to remove any unneeded styles so that nobody can apply them.

Applying list formatting

To apply list formatting, select the text as described earlier in this chapter, and then apply the list formatting to it. Normally, you want to apply the right style to the text before applying list formatting.

Applying list formatting on OS X

Here's how to apply list formatting in the iWork apps on OS X:

1. **If the Format inspector isn't displayed, click the Format button on the toolbar to display it.**

2. **If the Bullets & Lists section is collapsed, click its disclosure triangle to expand the section.**

3. **Click the Bullets & Lists pop-up menu, and then click the list style you want to apply (see Figure 3.39).**

4. **If you want to change the type of bullet, click the second pop-up menu, and then click the bullet type to use.** Your choices are No Bullets, Text Bullets, Image Bullets, or Numbers.

5. **If you want to change the indent, use the spin-box controls on the Indent line.**

6. **To change the bullet character itself, open the pop-up menu on the Bullet line, and then click the character you want.** For example, if you have chosen Text Bullets in the second pop-up menu, you can choose among a bullet, a five-pointed star, an eight-pointed star, and similar characters.

7. **To change the size of the bullet character, click the Size spin-box control.** For example, you could set the Size to 125% to make the bullet larger.

8. **To change the alignment of the bullet, click the Align spin-box control.**

Applying list formatting on iOS or in iCloud

Here's how to apply list formatting in the iWork apps on iOS:

1. **Tap the Format button on the toolbar to display the Format panel.**

2. **Tap List to display the List pane (see Figure 3.40).**

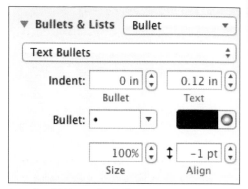

3.39 On OS X, use the Bullets & Lists section of the Format inspector to apply list formatting and adjust its details.

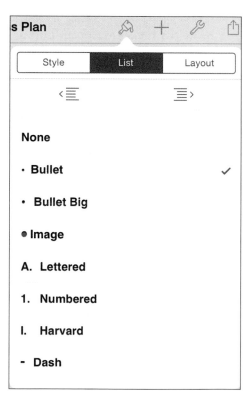

3.40 Use the List pane on the iPad to apply list formatting.

3. Tap the list type you want.

4. If you want to change the indentation on the list, tap the Indent button (the right button at the top of the pane) or the Unindent button as needed.

5. Tap in the text to close the Format panel.

Here's how to apply list formatting in the iWork apps in iCloud:

1. If the Format panel isn't displayed, click the Tools button on the toolbar, and then choose Settings ⇨ Show Format Panel to display it.

2. Click the List Style pop-up menu, and then click the list style to apply (see Figure 3.41).

3. If you want to change the indentation on the list, tap the Indent button (the right button at the top of the pane) or the Unindent button as needed.

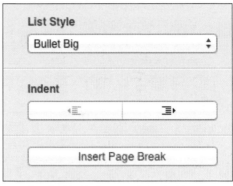

3.41 Use the List Style controls in the Format panel to apply a list style in iCloud.

101

How Do I Use Common Features in iWork Apps?

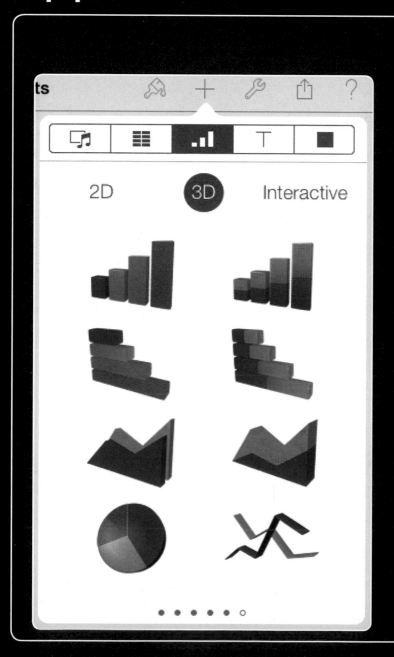

To help you create documents quickly and easily, the three iWork apps have many features in common. This chapter shows you how to insert pictures and shapes in your documents, add tables and make them look good, and create compelling charts from your data. This chapter also covers how to share and print your documents, collaborate on them, lock them so they cannot be changed, and how to choose preferences in Pages, Numbers, and Keynote. First, there's a quick overview of objects and how the iWork apps handle them.

Understanding Objects

Text-based documents can easily appear dull, no matter how compelling their content may be. To illustrate, decorate, and otherwise enliven your documents, you can add objects to them. The iWork apps enable you to add a wide range of objects, including pictures in various formats, movies, audio files, tables for laying out data, and charts for visualizing data.

Note
At this writing, you cannot insert objects (such as pictures or shapes) in table cells. This is something you could do in earlier versions of the iWork apps for OS X, and many longtime iWork users are hoping Apple will restore this functionality.

These object types are very different from each other, but the iWork apps make them easy to work with by handling them all in much the same way. These are the general steps for working with objects:

1. **Insert the object.** You learn the details of inserting the various types of objects in the following sections. For example, you can open the Shape panel, as shown in Figure 4.1, and click a shape to insert it in a document.

2. **Reposition the object as needed.** You can move the object freely around the area of the iWork document, which is called the *document canvas*. The app displays any helpful information available, such as a pop-up showing its absolute position or alignment guides showing its position relative to other objects. Here is how to reposition objects:

   - **OS X or iCloud.** Click the object and drag it (see Figure 4.2).

   - **iOS.** Tap and hold the object, and then drag it.

3. **Resize the object in one of the following ways by dragging one of the selection handles:**

   - **Resize in one dimension.** Drag a side handle.

   - **Resize proportionally.** Drag a corner handle (see Figure 4.3).

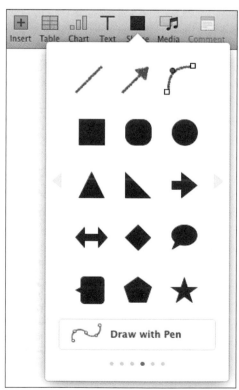

4.1 You can easily insert any of a variety of objects in an iWork document.

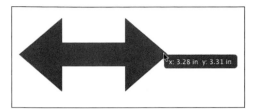

4.2 After inserting an object, drag it to reposition it where you want.

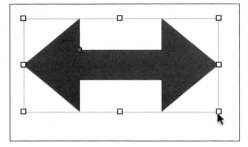

4.3 Drag a corner handle to resize an object proportionally.

4. **Format the object to look the way you want.** To format the object in one of the following ways, use the controls in the Format panel or on the Format screen:

  - **OS X.** Click the Format button on the toolbar or choose View ⇨ Inspector ⇨ Format.

  - **iOS.** Tap the Format button (the button with the paintbrush icon) on the toolbar. You can then tap the Style button to display the Style pane, which contains options for formatting the object's style. Figure 4.4 shows the Format panel on the iPad, in which you can quickly change the color of the selected shape.

  - **iCloud.** Choose Tools ⇨ Settings ⇨ Show Format Panel if the Format panel is currently hidden.

5. **If necessary, arrange the shape's position relative to other shapes in one of the following ways by using the tools in the Arrange pane or on the Arrange screen:**

  - **OS X.** With an object selected, click the Arrange button in the Format inspector to display the Arrange pane (see Figure 4.5).

  - **iOS.** With an object selected, tap the Arrange button in the Format panel to display the Arrange pane (see Figure 4.6). Here, you can drag the Move to Back/Front slider to move the selected object forward or back

4.4 Use the Format panel to apply formatting to the shape.

105

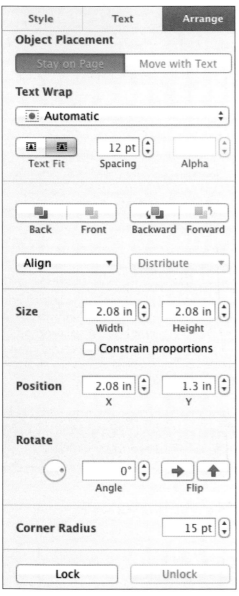

4.5 On OS X, the Arrange pane in the Format inspector enables you to control placement, text wrapping, front-to-back placement, and other settings for objects.

4.6 The Arrange pane in the iWork apps on the iPad enables you to move the object forward and back, change its vertical alignment, and set its margins.

relative to the other objects in the document, change its vertical alignment, and set its margins. You can also tap Lock to lock the object against unintentional changes. (To unlock the object, tap the Format button, and then tap the Unlock button that appears on the Format panel.)

- **iCloud.** With an object selected, click the Arrange button in the Format panel to display the Arrange pane. As you can see in Figure 4.7, this pane contains controls for moving the object forward and backward, changing its size and position, and rotating or flipping it.

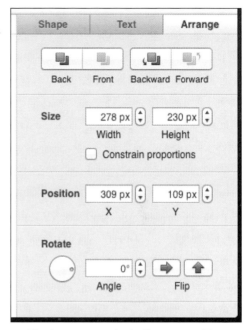

4.7 The Arrange pane in the Format panel in iCloud enables you to move the selected object forward and back, resize and reposition it, or rotate and flip it.

Note In iOS, touch an object with two fingers, and then rotate them to rotate the object.

Inserting Pictures, Shapes, Audio, and Movies

A great way to give your documents punch is to insert photos, images, and shapes in them. The iWork apps let you quickly add photos from your available sources, such as your Mac's media library or your iPad's Photos collection. The apps share a library of shapes that you can easily insert in your documents and customize to look the way you want.

Inserting a picture

You can quickly insert a picture in a Pages document, a Numbers spreadsheet, or a Keynote presentation. Depending on which platform you're using, you can access various sources of pictures in the following ways:

- **OS X.** You can access your Media Library through the Media Browser, or you can simply drag photos from iPhoto. iPhoto offers your Photo Stream photos as well as your local photos. You can also drag photos from the Finder or your Desktop.

- **iOS.** You can access any photo in the Photos app or your Photo Stream. The Camera Roll album in the Photos app contains the photos you take with your iOS device's camera and any photos you save to the device from sources such as incoming e-mail messages, incoming instant messages, or web pages.

- **iCloud.** You can access any photo from the file system of the computer you're using.

Here's how to insert a picture in the iWork apps on OS X:

1. **In the app you're using, click the Media button on the toolbar to display the Media Browser.**

2. **If the Photos pane isn't displayed at first, click the Photos button to display it (see Figure 4.8).**

4.8 The Photos pane in the Media Browser gives you direct access to the main photo collections on your Mac.

3. **In the left column, click the source of photos you want to display.** For example, click Photos to see the photos in your iPhoto library, or click My Photo Stream to display the photos in your Photo Stream.

4. **Click the photo you want to insert.** The app inserts the photo in the document and displays selection handles around it so you can resize or reposition it, as discussed later in this chapter.

Here's how to insert a picture in the iWork apps on iOS:

1. **Position the insertion point where you want the picture to appear.**

2. **Touch the + button on the toolbar to display the Insert panel (on the iPad) or the Insert screen (on the iPhone or iPod touch).**

3. **Touch the Media button (to the left of the tab bar) to display the Photos pane shown in Figure 4.9.**

Note

The first time you try to access your photos from an iWork app, iOS displays a dialog telling you that the app would like to access your photos. Tap OK to continue. If you need to revoke this permission later, open the Settings app, tap Privacy, and then tap Photos. On the Photos screen, set the app's switch to Off instead of On.

4. **Tap the collection of photos you want to display.** The photos in the collection appear.

5. **Tap the photo you want to insert.** The app inserts the photo in the document and displays selection handles around it so you can resize or reposition it, as discussed later in this chapter.

Here's how to insert a picture in the iWork apps on iCloud:

1. **Click the Image button on the toolbar to display the Image pop-up panel.**

2. **Click Choose Image (see Figure 4.10) to display the Choose Image sheet.**

3. **Navigate to and select the file you want to insert.**

4. **Click Choose.** The app inserts the image in the document and displays selection handles around it so you can resize or reposition it, as discussed later in this chapter.

4.10 To insert an image on iCloud, click the Image button, click Choose Image, and then use the Choose Image sheet to select the file.

4.9 Use the Insert panel on the iPad (shown here), or the Insert screen on the iPhone or iPod touch to insert a photo in a document on iOS.

Note

At this writing, the iWork for iCloud apps have a maximum file size of 2.4MB for images. If you choose an image larger than this, the app gives you an error message, recommending you reduce the image size and try again. Use an image editor such as Preview (on OS X) or Paint (on Windows) to create a smaller version of the image, and then insert it.

Inserting a shape

The iWork apps provide a selection of shapes you can easily insert and then customize to suit your documents. To insert a shape, you use the Shape panel or screen.

Note On OS X and iOS, the Shape panel contains six sets of shapes. Each set contains the same shapes but with a different color or look. In iCloud, the Shape panel has a single set with a default color; after inserting a shape, you use the Shape pane in the Format panel to change the color and other attributes as needed.

Here's how to insert a shape in the iWork apps on OS X:

1. **Click the Shape button on the toolbar to display the Shape pane.**

2. **Navigate to the set of shapes you want (see Figure 4.11) in any of the following ways:**

   - **Click the Previous arrow on the left side of the pane or the Next arrow on the right side.**

   - **Swipe left or right on the trackpad.**

   - **Click one of the dots at the bottom of the pane.**

3. **Click the shape you want to insert.** The app inserts the shape at a standard size and displays selection handles around it so that you can immediately resize it.

Here's how to insert a shape in the iWork apps on iOS:

1. **Tap the + button on the toolbar to display the Shape pane (on the iPad) or the Shape screen (on the iPhone or iPod touch).**

2. **Navigate to the pane or screen that contains the shape color you want (see Figure 4.12).** You can swipe left or right or touch the dots at the bottom of the pane.

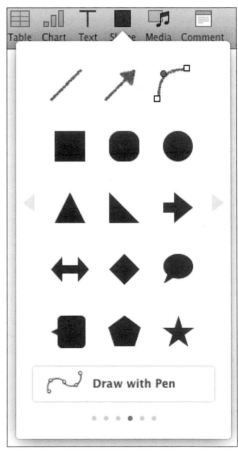

4.11 On OS X, click the Shape button on the toolbar, navigate to the appropriate set of shapes, and then click a shape to insert it in the document.

111

3. **Touch the shape you want to insert.**
The app inserts the shape at a standard
size and displays selection handles
around it so that you can immediately
resize it.

Here's how to insert a shape in the iWork apps
in iCloud:

1. **Click the Shape button on the toolbar
to display the Shape panel.** On iCloud,
the Shape panel contains only one
color, so you insert the shape you want
and then change its color as needed.

2. **Click the shape you want to insert.**
The app inserts the shape at a standard
size and displays selection handles
around it, as shown in Figure 4.13.

3. **If the Shape pane in the Format panel
isn't displayed automatically, click
the Shape button to display it.**

4. **Click the color you want to apply to
the shape.** For more options, click the
Fill color swatch and pick a color fill, a
gradient fill, or an image fill from the
Color pop-up panel.

4.12 On iOS, swipe left or right to navigate to the
appropriate color, and then touch the shape you
want to insert.

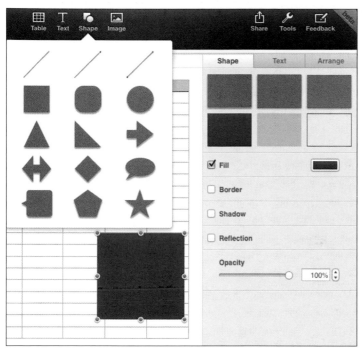

4.13 After you click the shape you want to insert, use the controls in the Shape panel to format the shape the way you want it.

Inserting audio and movies on OS X

On OS X, you can insert audio items and movies into your iWork documents. At this writing, you cannot insert audio items and movies on iOS or in iCloud. Audio items and movies do appear in your iWork documents on iOS and in iCloud. On iOS, you can play these items and perform some minimal formatting, such as setting an audio item to loop (in other words, to play repeatedly). On iCloud, audio items and movies appear as placeholders that you cannot edit — but at least you can see them, so you can avoid deleting them accidentally.

Inserting and formatting an audio item

Here's how to insert an audio item in an iWork document on OS X:

1. **Display the part of the document to which you want to add the audio item.** For example, in Numbers, click the appropriate sheet.

2. **Click the Media button on the toolbar to display the Media panel.**

3. **Click the Music button at the top of the panel to display the Music pane.**

4. **In the left column, click the source of the audio track.** For example, click Music to display all the songs in your iTunes library (see Figure 4.14).

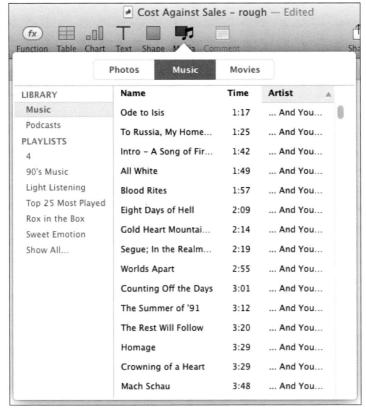

4.14 To add an audio item, click the track in the Music pane of the Media panel.

5. **Click the track you want to insert.** The app inserts it as an audio object and selects it.

6. **If the Format panel isn't displayed, click the Format button on the toolbar to display it.**

7. **Click the Audio tab in the Format panel to display the Audio pane (see Figure 4.15).**

Genius

The Replace button at the top of the Audio pane in the Format panel enables you to replace the audio item with another item but retain its position and whatever formatting you've applied. The Movie pane has a similar button for replacing a movie that you've added to the document.

8. **In the Controls area, use the playback controls to play the audio.** Drag the Volume slider to set the initial volume to a suitable level.

9. **If you need to trim the beginning or end of the audio, drag the Start or End box on the Trim control.** Play the audio back to make sure you have exactly what you need.

10. **If you want the audio item to loop, click the Repeat pop-up menu, and then choose Loop or Loop Back and Forth, as needed.** Choose None to turn off looping.

4.15 Use the controls in the Audio pane of the Format panel to set the volume for the audio item, trim its length, or set it to repeat.

Inserting and formatting a movie

Here's how to insert a movie in an iWork document on OS X:

1. **Display the part of the document to which you want to add the movie.** For example, in Keynote, click the slide on which you want to place the movie.

2. **Click the Media button on the toolbar to display the Media panel.**

3. **Click the Movies button at the top of the panel to display the Movies pane.**

4. **Click the movie you want to insert.** The app inserts it at a standard size.

Note

If the iWork app prompts you to optimize the movie for iOS, click Optimize if you want to optimize the movie now. Optimization may take some time. If you prefer to leave optimization until later, click Not Now. You can then click the movie and choose Format ➪ Movie ➪ Optimize Movie for iOS when you want to optimize the movie.

5. **Drag the movie where you want it to appear.**

6. **Resize the movie by dragging either a side or corner handle.** Dragging either type of handle resizes the movie proportionally.

7. **If the Format panel isn't displayed, click the Format button on the toolbar to display it.**

8. **Click the Movie tab in the Format panel to display the Movie pane (see Figure 4.16).**

9. **In the Controls area, use the playback controls to play the audio.** Drag the Volume slider to set the initial volume to a suitable level.

10. **If you need to trim the beginning or end of the movie, drag the Start or End box on the Trim control.** As you drag, the movie displays the current frame, so it's easy to see when you've reached the right place.

11. **To set the poster frame for the movie, drag the slider until the movie displays the frame you want.** The poster frame is the frame that appears for the movie until you start playing the movie.

4.16 Use the controls in the Movie pane of the Format panel to set the volume and poster frame for the movie, trim its length, or set it to repeat.

12. **If you want the movie item to loop, click the Repeat pop-up menu, and then choose Loop or Loop Back and Forth, as needed.** Choose None to turn off looping.

Adding Tables to Your Documents

To lay out your documents neatly, you can create tables. Tables are fundamental to spreadsheets, so most Numbers templates include one or (usually) more tables. Some Keynote slide masters also contain tables, as do some Pages templates — but you can insert a table at any other point when you need one.

Note At this writing, Pages and Keynote for iCloud don't enable you to create or edit tables, but this functionality is supposedly coming soon. Numbers does enable you to create and edit tables.

Genius At this writing, the iWork apps have some restrictions as to the content you can place in tables. For example, you cannot place pictures in table cells. These restrictions aren't much of a problem when you're creating new documents, because you can work around them, but you need to pay attention when opening documents from earlier versions of iWork, because the new apps may strip out such content without warning.

Inserting and working with tables

Inserting a table works in almost exactly the same way on OS X as on iOS. Here's what to do:

1. **Display the part of the document where you want the table to land.** For example, in Pages, go to the appropriate page in the document.

2. **Display the Table panel in one of the following ways:**

   - **OS X.** Click the Table button on the toolbar.

   - **iOS.** Tap the + button, and then tap the Table button (the second button from the left) at the top of the panel.

3. **Scroll left or right to display the set of table designs that contains the one you want to use.** You can also click or tap the dots at the bottom of the panel to move among the sets.

4. **Click or tap the table you want to insert (see Figure 4.17).** The app inserts a table of the default size with that table style.

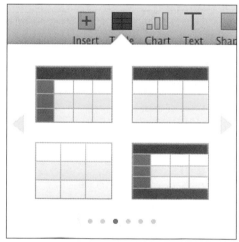

4.17 On the Table panel, navigate to the appropriate set of table designs, and then click the table you want to insert.

Here are the moves you need to work with a table you've inserted:

- **Select a cell.** Click or tap the cell. You can then type content in it.

- **Select a column or row.** Click or tap the table to select it, and then click or tap the column or row heading. Figure 4.18 shows an example of selecting a column on the iPad.

<table>
<tr><td colspan="2">Use this calculator to d
number of units you ne</td><td>Cut</td><td>Copy</td><td>Paste</td><td>Insert...</td><td>Sort...</td><td>Fit</td><td>Create Chart</td></tr>
<tr><td></td><td></td><td></td><td></td><td></td><td></td><td></td><td>0</td><td>$0</td></tr>
<tr><td></td><td></td><td></td><td></td><td></td><td></td><td></td><td>15</td><td>$1,155</td></tr>
<tr><td>Fixed Costs</td><td>$8,140</td><td></td><td></td><td></td><td></td><td></td><td>30</td><td>$2,310</td></tr>
<tr><td>Variable Cost per Unit</td><td>$13</td><td></td><td></td><td></td><td></td><td></td><td>45</td><td>$3,465</td></tr>
<tr><td>Unit Price</td><td>$77</td><td></td><td></td><td></td><td></td><td></td><td>60</td><td>$4,620</td></tr>
<tr><td>Unit Increments</td><td>15</td><td></td><td></td><td></td><td></td><td></td><td>75</td><td>$5,775</td></tr>
<tr><td>BREAK-EVEN POINT</td><td>127</td><td></td><td></td><td></td><td></td><td></td><td>90</td><td>$6,930</td></tr>
</table>

4.18 Click or tap the column or row heading to select a column or row.

- **Move the table.** Click or tap the table to select it, and then click or tap the blue circle.

- **Resize the table.** Click and drag a side handle to resize the table in one dimension. Click and drag a corner handle to resize the table proportionally in both dimensions.

- **Add rows or columns to, or delete rows or columns from, the table.** Click or tap the table to select it. Then, on OS X, move the mouse pointer over the round button to the right of the column headings or below the row headings; on iOS, tap this button. When the button changes to a spin button, click or tap the up button to add rows or columns or the down button to delete them.

- **Add rows or columns within the table.** On OS X, move the mouse pointer over the row heading or column heading, click the pop-up button that appears, and then click the appropriate command on the pop-up menu — for example, click Add Column Before or Add Column After (see Figure 4.19). On iOS, tap the heading of the row or column before which you want to insert the new item, and then tap Insert on the pop-up control bar.

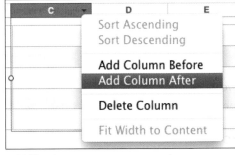

4.19 Use the pop-up menu on a column or row heading to insert or delete columns or rows.

- **Delete rows or columns within the table.** On OS X, move the mouse pointer over the row heading or column heading, click the pop-up button that appears, and then click Delete. On iOS, tap the row heading or column heading and then tap Delete on the pop-up control bar.

In iWork for OS X, you can use the keyboard shortcuts shown in Table 4.1 to manipulate tables.

Table 4.1 Keyboard Shortcuts for Manipulating Tables on OS X

Keyboard Shortcut	Effect
Tab	Select the next cell in the table.
Shift+Tab	Select the previous cell in the table.
Return	Open the selected cell for editing.
⌘+Return	Stop editing the open cell and select it.
⌘+Return twice	Stop editing the open cell, and select the table.
⌘+A	Select the entire table (click in the table first).
Option+Up Arrow	Insert a row above the selected row.
Option+Down Arrow	Insert a row below the selected row.
Option+Left Arrow	Insert a column to the left of the selected column.
Option+Right Arrow	Insert a column to the right of the selected column.
Option+⌘+C	Copy the style of the selected cell.
Option+⌘+V	Paste the copied cell style into the selected cell.
Control+Shift+⌘+V	Paste into a cell but preserve its existing style.
Option+⌘+U	Auto-align the content of the selected cell.
Left, Right, Up, or Down	Move the selected table by one point.
Shift+Left, Right, Up, or Down	Move the selected table by 10 points.
Option+Tab	Insert a tab in the cell you're editing.
Control+Return	Insert a line break in the cell you're editing.
Return	Insert a paragraph break in the cell you're editing.

Formatting a table

To make a table look the way you want, you format it. Normally, you apply a table style to set the overall look of the table. You can then choose options such as displaying the table name, displaying the table border, and shading alternate rows.

Formatting a table on OS X

Here's how to format a table on OS X:

1. **Click the table to select it.** You need to select the table to make the Table pane appear in the Format panel.

2. **If the Format panel isn't displayed, click the Format button on the toolbar to display it.**

3. **Click the Table button to display the Table pane (see Figure 4.20).**

4. **In the Table Styles area at the top, click the table style you want to apply.**

5. **In the Headers & Footer area, use the three pop-up menus to set the number of header columns (the first menu), header rows (the second menu), and footer rows (the third menu).**

6. **Select the Table Name check box if you want the table name to appear.** Select the default name on the table and type the name you want.

7. **Click the buttons in the Table Font Size area to decrease or increase the overall size of the table's fonts.**

8. **Use the controls in the Table Outline area to set the style, color, and width of the outline (the border) around the table.**

9. **Select the Outline table name check box if you want the outline to include the table name.**

10. **In the Grid Lines area, click the buttons to toggle on or off the display of particular gridlines in the table.**

11. **To shade alternate rows in a different color, select the Alternating Row Color check box, and then use the color swatch to pick the color to use.** Shading alternate rows can make tables easier to read, especially for large tables that are densely packed with information.

4.20 The Table pane in the Format panel provides the commands for applying table-wide formatting.

12. **In the Row & Column Size area, set the default height of rows in the Row box and the default width of columns in the Column box.** Click the Fit button for rows to adjust row height to fit the tallest cell. Click the Fit button for columns to adjust the column width to fit the widest cell.

Sorting by Multiple Columns

When you have complex data, sorting by multiple columns is often useful. For example, in a table that contains customer records, you might want to sort first by the State column, then by the City column, and finally, by the Last Name column.

At this writing, you can sort only by a single column in the iWork apps. So, if you sort by the State column, and then sort by the City column, the app sorts your data only by the City column.

With some data, you can work around this limitation by concatenating the data in the cells in an extra column, and then sorting by that column. For example, if your table uses column headings, such as State and City, input the formula =State&City&Last Name in an extra column to concatenate the contents of the State, City, and Last Name columns, giving results such as AZPhoenixSmith and TXDallasJones. (If your table doesn't have descriptive column headings, use the column letters instead — for example, =D&E&C.) You can then sort by the extra column to get the data in the order you want.

Genius

Using the Fit buttons to adjust row height and column width can be handy, but you normally want to use these buttons only after inputting most (or all) of the content for the table — or you can use them as often as needed. After using these buttons, you may need to reduce column width manually for any column that contains cells with contents much longer than most other cells in that column.

13. **Select the Resize rows to fit cell contents check box if you want the table to adjust row height automatically.**

Formatting a table on iOS

Here's how to format a table on iOS:

1. **Tap the table to select it.** Selecting the table adds the Table pane to the Format panel.

2. **If the Format panel isn't displayed, tap the Format button on the toolbar to display it.**

3. **Tap the Table button to display the Table pane (see Figure 4.21).**

4. **Tap the table style you want to apply.**

5. **Tap Table Options to display the Table Options panel.**

6. **Set the Table Name switch to On (see Figure 4.22) if you want the table name to appear.**

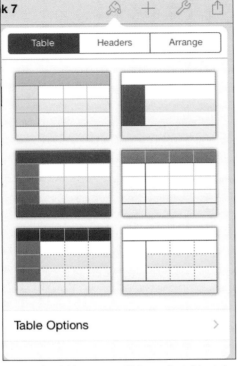

4.21 In the Table pane on iOS, tap the table style you want, and then tap Table Options.

4.22 In the Table Options panel, you can control the table name, border, alternate-row shading, and font.

7. **Set the Table Border switch to On if you want the table border to appear.**

8. **Set the Alternating Rows switch to On if you want to shade alternate rows to make the table easier to read.**

9. **Use the Table Font controls to set the font for the table.** Tap the Table Font button to display the Table Font panel, and then tap the font to use. You can tap the Info (i) button for a font to display the available styles; tap Table Font when you're ready to return to the Table Font panel. After choosing the font, tap Table Options to display the Table Options panel again.

10. **Tap Grid Options to display the Grid Options panel, in which you can configure the table grid.**

11. **Set the Horizontal Lines switch to On (see Figure 4.23) if you want to display horizontal gridlines.**

12. **Set the Header Column Lines switch to On if you want to display lines around the header column.**

13. **Set the Vertical Lines switch to On if you want to display vertical gridlines.**

14. **Set the Header Row Lines switch to On if you want to display lines around the header row.**

15. **Tap Table Options to return to the Table Options panel.**

16. **Tap Table to return to the Table panel.**

17. **Tap Headers to display the Headers panel.**

18. **Tap the + and − buttons on the Header Rows row (see Figure 4.24) to set the number of header rows.**

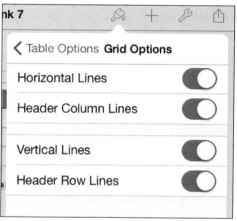

4.23 In the Grid Options panel, choose which gridlines to display on the table.

4.24 Use the Headers panel to set up the table header rows, header columns, and footer rows.

19. **Tap the + and − buttons on the Header Columns row to set the number of header columns.**

20. **Tap the + and − buttons on the Footer Rows row to set the number of footer rows.**

21. **Tap outside the Headers panel to close the panel.**

Sorting a table

To make a table display its data in the order you want, you can sort it by a column in one of the following ways:

⦿ **OS X.** Click the table, move the mouse pointer over the heading of the column by which you want to sort, and then click Sort Ascending or Sort Descending.

- **iOS**. Follow these steps:

  1. **Tap the table to select it.**

  2. **Tap the heading of the column by which you want to sort.** The pop-up control bar appears.

  3. **Tap Sort on the pop-up control bar to display the sort commands.**

  4. **Tap Sort Ascending or Sort Descending.**

Adding Charts to Your Documents

A chart is a great way of adding detail, impact, and persuasion to a document. While Numbers is the main charting app in the iWork suite, you can easily add charts to your Pages documents and Keynote presentations as well.

Note

At this writing, the iWork for iCloud apps do not support adding or editing charts, but Apple says this feature is coming soon.

Choosing the right chart for your data

To make your chart convey your interpretation of the data most clearly, you need to choose the right chart type. Table 4.2 lists the main chart types in detail and explains when each type is effective.

Table 4.2 iWork Chart Types

Chart Type	Explanation	When to Use It
Column	Each value appears as a separate vertical column.	To show how the values compare to each other.
Stacked Column	Each category appears as a separate vertical column, divided into separate colored sections that represent each value.	To show the contribution each item makes in a category. For example, to show how different products contribute to your company's revenues.
Bar	Each value appears as a separate horizontal bar.	To show how the values compare to each other, using a horizontal orientation rather than a vertical orientation.
Stacked Bar	Each category appears as a separate horizontal bar, divided into separate colored sections that represent each value.	To show the contribution each item makes in a category.

Chart Type	Explanation	When to Use It
Area	Each category appears as a line connecting the points (values), but the area below the line is shaded.	To show the contribution of each series over time.
Stacked Area	Like an area chart, but with the areas stacked on top of each other to make them more visible.	As with the area chart, to show the contribution of each series over time, but to provide extra visual clarity.
Pie	Each value in a single series of data appears as a slice of a round pie.	To show how each value contributes to the whole (the pie).
Line	Each value appears as a point, with a line connecting the points and representing the category as a whole.	To show changes over time — for example, to chart temperature or fluctuations in a currency's value.
Mixed	The chart presents two data series together on a single chart. For example, you can combine a line chart and a column chart.	When you need to show two separate sets of data that can use the same axes.
2-axis	The chart represents each of its two data series as a separate chart. The two charts share an X axis but have separate Y axes, one on the left and one on the right.	To show two separate sets of data that require different Y axes but can share an X axis (for example, showing years or departments).
Scatter	Each value appears as a separate point.	To show how two different sets of numbers are related, either without drawing a line through the data points or by drawing a *best-fit* line. Often used for representing medical or scientific studies.
Bubble	Each value appears as a separate bubble, with the size of the bubble corresponding to its value.	To show how three data series are related — like a scatter chart but with an extra data series.

Note For many of the chart types, iWork also offers a 3-D version that works the same way but adds greater visual impact — sometimes at the expense of clarity. For the Column, Bar, Scatter, and Bubble chart types, iWork provides an interactive version of the chart as well.

Inserting a chart

You insert a chart in Pages and Keynote using a different technique than in Numbers. In Pages and Keynote, you use the Chart Data Editor, a mini spreadsheet window, to input and edit the chart data, while in Numbers you input the chart data in a table in a spreadsheet.

Inserting a chart in Pages or Keynote

Here's how to insert a chart in Pages or Keynote:

1. **Open the Chart panel in one of the following ways:**

   - **OS X.** Click the Chart button on the toolbar (see Figure 4.25).

   - **iOS.** Tap the + button on the toolbar, and then tap the Chart button.

2. **Select the chart category you want by clicking or tapping 2D, 3D, or Interactive.**

3. **Select the chart color in one of these ways:**

   - **Drag or swipe left or right.**

   - **Click or tap the row of dots at the bottom of the Chart panel.**

4. **Click or tap the chart type to insert.** The app adds a chart of that type to the document, populating it with sample data so there's something to see. Figure 4.26 shows a new chart added on OS X.

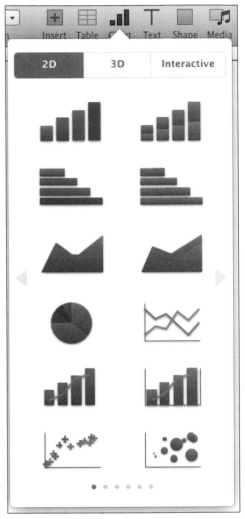

4.25 On OS X, click the Chart button on the toolbar to start inserting a chart in Pages or Keynote.

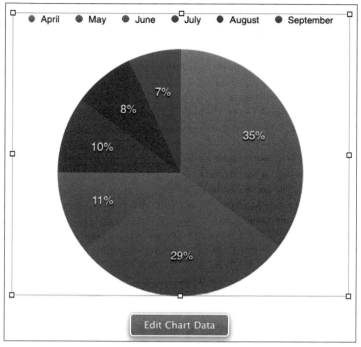

4.26 On OS X, click Edit Chart Data to start editing.

5. **Reposition or resize the chart if you want to.** If the chart has landed on another element, you may want to move it now. Otherwise, it may be better to finish creating the chart, and then reposition and resize it in the following ways:

   - **Reposition the chart.** Drag the chart to reposition it.
   - **Resize the chart.** Drag a handle to resize the chart.

6. **Open the Chart Data Editor in one of the following ways:**

   - **OS X.** Click the Edit Chart Data button below the chart.
   - **iOS.** Tap the chart to display the pop-up control bar, and then tap Edit Data (see Figure 4.27).

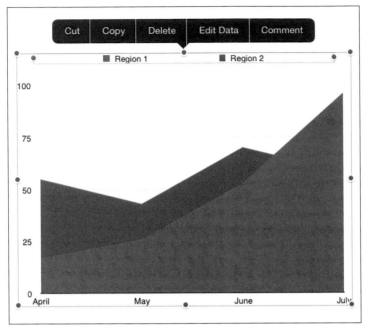

4.27 On iOS, open the Chart Data Editor by tapping the chart, and then tapping Edit Data on the pop-up control bar.

7. **Input the data for the chart.** Figure 4.28 shows the Chart Data Editor on OS X. Here is how to input the data:

- **Replace the sample data.** Click or tap a column label or row label, and then type the label you want to use. Similarly, click or tap a sample value, and then type your real value in its place.

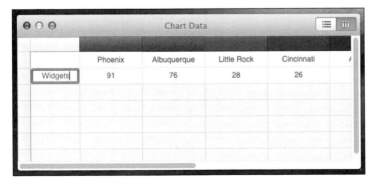

4.28 In the Chart Data Editor, replace the sample data with the real data for the chart.

- **Paste in data from another app, such as Numbers or Excel.** In the other app, select the data, and then copy it (for example, press ⌘+C on OS X). In the Chart Data Editor, select the upper-right cell where you want to paste the data, and then press ⌘+V (on OS X) or tap Paste on the pop-up control bar (in iOS) to paste in the data.

- **Insert or delete a row or column.** On OS X, move the mouse pointer over the row heading or column heading, click the pop-up button that appears, and then click the appropriate command — for example, click Insert Column Before to insert a new column before the current column (see Figure 4.29), or click Delete Column to delete the column. On iOS, tap the row heading or column heading, and then tap Insert or Delete on the pop-up control bar.

4.29 You can quickly insert a column from the pop-up menu on the column heading or a row from the pop-up menu on the row heading.

- **Move a row or column.** Click or tap the row heading or column heading, and then drag it to where you want it to appear. The Chart Data Editor moves the other rows or columns to accommodate the one you dragged. Figure 4.30 shows an example on the iPad.

8. **Return from the Chart Data Editor to the chart in one of the following ways:**

   - **OS X.** Click the Close button (the red button at the left end of the window's title bar) to close the Chart Data Editor. If you prefer, you can leave the Chart Data Editor open while you work with the chart.

4.30 To move a column or row, select it, and then drag it to its new position.

- **iOS.** Tap Done to close the Chart Data Editor. Because iOS implements the Chart Data Editor as a screen, not a window, you must close the Chart Data Editor to return to the chart. However, you can reopen the Chart Data Editor in a moment when you need to edit the chart's data again.

Your chart reappears, showing the latest data.

Inserting a chart in Numbers

Here's how to insert a chart in Numbers:

1. **In your spreadsheet, select the cells that contain the data you want to chart.** If the data includes series labels, such as the names of salespeople or the years shown by the data, select those cells, too.

2. **Open the Chart panel in one of the following ways:**
   - **OS X.** Click the Chart button on the toolbar.
   - **iOS.** Tap the + button on the toolbar, and then tap the Chart button.

3. **Select the chart category you want by clicking or tapping 2D, 3D, or Interactive.**

4. **Select the chart color in one of these ways:**
   - **Drag or swipe left or right.**
   - **Click or tap the row of dots at the bottom of the Chart panel.**

5. **Click or tap the chart type to insert.** Numbers creates a chart of that type using the data you selected.

6. **Reposition or resize the chart as needed:**
   - **Reposition the chart.** Drag the chart to reposition it.
   - **Resize the chart.** Drag a handle to resize the chart.

You can now format the chart as described in the next section.

Formatting a chart

After creating a chart, you can format it so that it looks the way you want it to. To format the chart, you use the Format panel. The Format panel works differently on OS X than on iOS, so I cover the platforms separately.

Formatting a chart on OS X

Here's how to format a chart on OS X:

1. **Click the chart to select it.** Selecting the chart makes the chart-formatting tools available in the Format panel.

2. **If the Format panel isn't displayed, click the Format button on the toolbar to display it.**

3. **Click the Chart button to display the Chart pane (see Figure 4.31).**

4. **If you need to change the chart type, click the Chart Type pop-up menu at the bottom of the pane, and then click the chart type you want.** Usually, you want to change the chart type only if the type you first chose really doesn't work with the data — but if you do need to make this change, it's best to make it before changing the chart's formatting.

5. **To give the chart a different look (but keep the current type), click the style in the Chart Styles box at the top of the Chart pane.** Scroll or swipe left or right to move through the available sets of styles.

6. **In the Chart Options area, select the Title check box if you want to give the chart a title.** Double-click the title on the chart and type the text for the title.

7. **Also in the Chart options area, select or deselect the Legend check box to control whether a legend appears for the chart.** Depending on the data you're using, the app may or may not have turned on the legend by default.

8. **To change the font used, use the controls in the Chart Font area.** Open the upper pop-up menu and choose the font, then open the lower pop-up menu and choose the style — for example, Regular or Bold Oblique. Click the left button to make the font size smaller; click the right button to make it bigger.

4.31 In the Chart pane, you can change a wide range of settings, including the chart type and style, the title and legend, and the font and colors.

9. **To change the chart colors, click the Chart Colors swatch, and then make your choice on the pop-up panel that opens (see Figure 4.32).** Click Colors, Images, or Textures at the top of the panel to choose the category, and then scroll or swipe left or right to move through the sets of styles.

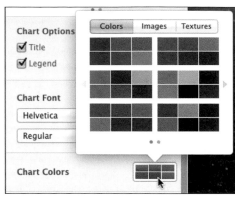

10. **To change the chart background, click the Background & Border Style disclosure triangle to expand the Background & Border Style area, and then choose the fill from the pop-up menu.** Your

4.32 Click the Chart Colors swatch to choose the colors, images, or textures for filling the chart.

choices are Color Fill, Gradient Fill, Advanced Gradient Fill, Image Fill, or Advanced Image Fill. After you make this choice, controls appear that you can use to set up the fill you want.

11. **To apply a shadow to the chart or elements in it, click the Shadow disclosure triangle to expand the Shadow area.** Choose the element in the pop-up menu, and then use the controls to set up the shadow you want.

12. **To format the individual parts of the chart, click the button(s) that appear between the Chart and Arrange buttons in the Format pane when the chart is selected.** These buttons, and the panes they display, depend on the chart type you're formatting. For example, a pie chart has the Wedges pane, whereas a column chart has the Axis pane (see Figure 4.33) and the Series pane.

Formatting a chart on iOS

Here's how to format a chart on iOS:

1. **Tap the chart to select it.** Selecting the chart makes the chart-formatting tools available in the Format panel.

2. **If the Format panel isn't displayed, tap the Format button on the toolbar to display it.**

3. **Tap the Chart button to display the Chart pane (see Figure 4.34).**

4. **If you want to change the chart style, tap the style to apply.**

5. **Tap Chart Options to display the Chart Options pane.**

6. **If you need to change the chart type, tap Chart Type.** In the Chart Type pane that appears, scroll down as needed, and then tap the chart type to apply. Tap Chart Options to return to the Chart Options pane.

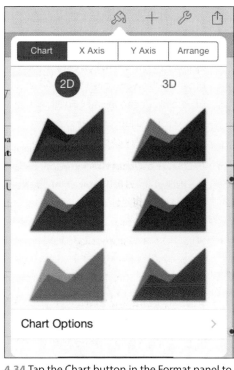

4.34 Tap the Chart button in the Format panel to change the chart style and options in the Chart pane.

4.33 Use the chart's panes in the Format panel to format the individual elements of the chart.

7. **To control the chart title, tap Chart Title (see Figure 4.35).** In the Chart Title pane that appears, set the Chart Title switch to On or Off. If you set it to On, tap the button for the alignment you want: Left, Center, Right, or Justified. Tap Chart Options to return to the Chart Options pane.

8. **Set the Legend switch to On if you want the legend to appear, or to Off if you don't.**

9. **Set the Border switch to On or Off, as needed.**

10. **In Numbers, set the Show Hidden Data switch to On to display any rows or columns hidden in the range of cells used for the chart, or to Off if you want to keep the data hidden.**

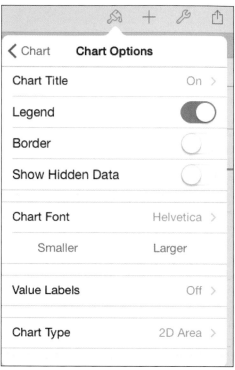

4.35 Use the controls in the Chart Options pane to choose which elements to display, to set the font, or to switch the chart type.

Genius

Numbers enables you to hide columns or rows in your spreadsheets. By hiding data, you can prevent anomalous or awkward data points from appearing in a table or in a chart derived from it. The Show Hidden Data switch in the Chart Options pane enables you to include data in the chart even though it is hidden in the table.

11. **To change the font size, tap Smaller or Larger.** To change the font, tap the Chart Font button. In the Chart Font pane that appears, tap the font you want. To choose the font style, tap the Info button (the *i*) to the right of the font's name. Tap the Chart Options button when you're ready to return to the Chart Options pane.

12. **To control whether and where value labels appear, tap Value Labels.** In the Value Labels pane that appears, tap Off if you want to turn off value labels; otherwise, tap the position for the value labels, such as Above Right. Tap Chart Options to return to the Chart Options pane.

13. **To control whether the number format in the chart is the same as in the source, tap Number Format.** (This setting appears only for some chart types.) In the Number Format

pane, set the Same as Source switch to On or Off, as needed. Tap Chart Options to return to the Chart Options pane.

14. **When you finish choosing chart options, tap outside the Chart Options pane to close the pane.**

Laying Out Objects

After inserting objects in your documents, you can control their layout by resizing and repositioning them, moving them forward and backward in the vertical stack, or aligning and distributing them. You can also change an object's orientation by rotating or flipping it, group objects together so you can work with them as a single unit, and lock objects so they can't be changed.

Repositioning, moving, and resizing objects

On any of the iWork platforms, you can reposition an object by dragging it to its new location, or resize an object by dragging its handles. You can also use these two moves:

- **Resize an object proportionally.** On OS X or in iCloud, Shift+drag a handle.

- **Constrain an object's movement.** On OS X or in iCloud, press Left Arrow, Up Arrow, Right Arrow, or Down Arrow to move the object straight in that direction. Hold Shift, and then press the appropriate arrow key to move 10 pixels instead of one pixel. On iOS, tap and hold the object you want to move, and then tap and hold another finger anywhere else on the screen. You can now drag the object vertically, horizontally, or diagonally.

Each iWork document uses a vertical stack on which you can move objects forward and backward to control which parts of which objects are visible. For example, say you place a square on top of a circle, and each shape has the same width. When the square is on top, the circle is invisible. However, if you move the square backward down the vertical stack, the circle appears in front of it, so the circle appears on top of the square, with the uncovered parts of the square visible.

Here's how to move objects forward and backward in the vertical stack:

- **OS X.** Control+click the object, and then click Send to Back or Bring to Front on the contextual menu. For more precise control, open the Arrange pane in the Format inspector, and then click Backward, Forward, Back, or Front.

- **iOS.** Tap the object, tap the Format button on the toolbar to display the Format pane, and then tap the Arrange button. In the Arrange pane, drag the Move to Back/Front slider to move the object forward or back as needed.

Note At this writing, you cannot move objects forward or backward in the vertical stack on iCloud. The only work-around is to create the objects in the order in which you want them to appear, starting with the one that is the farthest back.

Aligning and distributing objects

To help you arrange objects neatly, OS X provides commands for arranging and distributing objects, whereas iOS and iCloud offer alignment guidelines. To arrange selected objects on OS X, open either the Arrange or contextual menu, choose Align Objects, and then click Left, Center, Right, Top, Middle, or Bottom. The Center command centers the objects horizontally; the Middle command centers the objects vertically.

To distribute objects on OS X, open either the Arrange or contextual menu, choose Distribute Objects, and then select Horizontally, Vertically, or Evenly. To align objects on iOS or iCloud, drag an object and watch the guidelines that appear when it nears another object.

Note If iOS doesn't display the guidelines, tap the Tools icon on the toolbar, tap Settings, and then set the appropriate switches — Center Guides, Edge Guides, and Spacing Guides — to On. In iCloud, click the Tools button on the toolbar, click settings, and then click to place a check mark next to Center Guides, Edge Guides, or Spacing Guides.

Rotating and flipping objects

If an object is the wrong way around, you can rotate or flip it in one of the following ways:

- **OS X.** Use the Angle controls in the Arrange pane in the Format inspector to rotate an object. To flip an object, click the appropriate Flip arrow in the Arrange pane.

- **iOS.** Tap and hold the object with two fingers, and then turn the fingers to rotate the object. After you start the rotation, you can continue it with only one finger, which is often easier.

- **iCloud.** Either ⌘+click an object and rotate it manually, or use the Angle controls in the Arrange pane in the Format panel. To flip an object, click the appropriate Flip arrow in the Arrange pane.

Locking and unlocking objects

When you need to prevent an object from moving, you can lock it in place on OS X or iOS in one of the following ways:

- **OS X.** Select the object, and then choose Arrange ⇨ Lock. You can also press ⌘+L or click the Lock button in the Arrange pane of the Format inspector.

- **iOS.** Select the object, and then tap the Format button on the toolbar to display the Format panel. Tap the Arrange button to display the Arrange pane, and then tap Lock.

When you need to change the object again, unlock it like this:

- **OS X.** Select the object, and then choose Arrange ⇨ Unlock. You can also press Option+⌘+L or click the Unlock button in the Arrange pane of the Format inspector.

- **iOS.** Select the object, tap the Format button on the toolbar, and then tap Unlock on the Format panel.

Grouping and ungrouping objects

When you need to move or format several objects together, you can group them in one of the following ways:

- **OS X.** Select the objects, and then choose Arrange ⇨ Group. You can also Control+click in the selection, and then click Group on the contextual menu. Alternatively, press Option+⌘+G or click the Lock button in the Arrange pane of the Format inspector.

- **iOS.** Select the objects, tap one of them, and then tap Group on the pop-up command bar.

- **iCloud.** Select the objects, and then click Group in the Arrange pane of the Format panel.

Genius

In Pages for iOS, you cannot group objects if any of them is set to move with text. To change this setting, tap the object, tap the Format button on the toolbar, and then tap the Arrange button to display the Arrange pane. Tap Wrap to display the Wrap pane, and then set the Move with Text switch to Off.

To ungroup grouped objects, select the group, and then give the Ungroup command in the same way that you gave the Group command. On OS X, you can also press Option+Shift+⌘+G.

Creating Styles and Placeholders

As you've seen earlier in this book, the easiest way to format your documents quickly and consistently is to use styles. As discussed in Chapter 3, you can customize the iWork apps' existing styles for text and create your own styles. In the iWork apps on OS X, you can also create custom styles for objects such as charts and tables, define placeholder text in Pages, and define other types of placeholders.

Creating an object style

To make objects of a particular type appear consistently in your documents, you can create a style for them. For example, you can create a style for charts and then apply it to each chart that needs that look.

Here's how to create an object style:

1. **Insert an object of the appropriate type.** For example, insert a chart.
2. **Format the object to give it the look you want the style to have.**
3. **Select the object if it's not already selected.**
4. **Choose Format ⇨ Advanced ⇨ Create *Object* Style, where *Object* is the name of the object.** For example, for a chart, choose Format ⇨ Advanced ⇨ Create Chart Style. (The menu command automatically shows the name of the object you've selected — you don't have to pick the command from a long list of other objects.)

After creating a style, you can apply it from the Styles area at the top of the pane for that object in the Format panel. For example, you can apply a chart style from the Chart Styles area at the top of the Chart pane in the Format panel.

Defining placeholder text in Pages

If you create templates in Pages, you may want to add placeholder text to provide instructions on what the template's user should type or to provide sample text. You can do so by defining placeholder text like this:

1. **Type the text you want to create as a placeholder.**
2. **Select the text and format it the way you want it to appear.**
3. **Select the text of the placeholder, but don't select the paragraph mark at the end of the text.** Turn on the display of invisibles (choose View ⇨ Show Invisibles or press Shift+⌘+I) so that you can see the paragraph mark if necessary.

Genius

The reason you must not select the paragraph mark at the end of the text when defining placeholder text is that Pages deletes the placeholder text when the user starts typing over it. If the paragraph mark is part of the placeholder, it is deleted, and what the user types takes on the formatting of the next paragraph.

4. **Choose Format ⇨ Advanced ⇨ Define as Placeholder Text or press Control+Option+Shift+T.** Pages marks the text as placeholder text.

Defining text placeholders in Numbers and Keynote

In Numbers and Keynote, you can define text placeholders — formatted text boxes that contain placeholder text for the user to replace when creating a document. Here's how to define a text placeholder:

1. **Insert the text box in the document.** Choose Insert ⇨ Text Box.

2. **Type any placeholder text in the text box.**

3. **Format the text box as you want it to appear.**

4. **Choose Format ⇨ Advanced ⇨ Define as Text Placeholder or press Control+Option+Shift+T.** Numbers or Keynote marks the text box as a placeholder. You can then replace the placeholder text with live text that picks up the formatting you applied to the text box.

Defining media placeholders

In all three iWork apps for OS X, you can define media placeholders. Here's how to do this:

1. **Insert the appropriate media file in the document.** This can be an image, an audio file, or a movie.

2. **Position and format the media file as you want the media placeholder to appear.**

3. **Click the media file to select it.**

4. **Choose Format ⇨ Advanced ⇨ Define as Media Placeholder.** The app marks the file as a placeholder. You (or anyone else) can then replace the file with another file but retain the formatting applied to the placeholder.

Sharing and Printing Your Documents

The iWork apps give you various ways of sharing your documents with others. You can share a link to a document, e-mail a document, or print it. On iOS devices, you can also open a document in another app, copy a document to iTunes, or copy it to a WebDAV server.

Sharing and printing a document on OS X

The iWork apps on OS X give you access to the sharing commands via the Share button on the toolbar. After you share a link to a document, the people with whom you share it can collaborate on the document with you in real time. Here's how to share a link via iCloud:

1. **Click the Share button on the toolbar to display the Share pop-up menu.**

2. **Click or highlight Share Link via iCloud to display the submenu.**

3. **Click the means of sharing on the submenu.** For example, click Email (see Figure 4.36).

4.36 Open the Share Link via iCloud submenu, and then click the means of sharing you want to use.

4. **Take the actions needed to complete the sharing.** For example, address the e-mail message, add any explanation needed, and then send it.

When someone is sharing the document, the Share button shows green figures instead of the blue rectangle with an arrow. To see the document's sharing status, click the Share button on the toolbar, and then click View Share Settings. In the View Share Settings dialog (see Figure 4.37), you can see how many people are editing the document, turn off sharing, or send the document's link to other people.

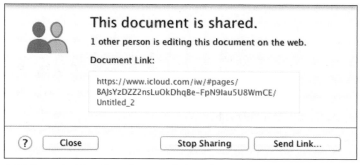

4.37 Open the View Share Settings dialog when you need to find out how many people are editing a document.

Sharing Documents in Other Ways on OS X

On OS X, you can also share documents in the following standard ways:

- **E-mail a document.** Start a message in Mail (or reply to an existing message). Click the Attach button (the paperclip icon) on the toolbar, select the file, and then click Choose File. Alternatively, drag the file into the message window from a Finder window or your desktop. You can use similar techniques in other e-mail apps.

- **Send a document via Messages.** In a chat, choose Buddies ➪ Send File, select the file, and then click Send. You can also drag the file into the chat window from a Finder window or your desktop.

- **Share a document via AirDrop.** Open a Finder window and click AirDrop in the sidebar to activate AirDrop. Open another Finder window, navigate to the document you want to share, and then drag it to the recipient's icon in the AirDrop window.

Here's how to send a copy of a document on OS X:

1. **Click the Share button on the toolbar to display the Share pop-up menu.**
2. **Click or highlight Send a copy to display the submenu.**
3. **Click the means of sharing on the submenu.** For example, click Messages.
4. **Take the actions needed to send the copy of the document.** For example, choose the contact to whom you want to send the document, and then click Send.

Sharing documents on iOS

On iOS, you can share the open document quickly and easily from within the iWork apps.

Sharing a link via iCloud

When you want others to be able to view your document online (and work on it if they have permission to do so), use the Share Link via iCloud command. Follow these steps:

1. **Open the app for the document you want to share.**
2. **Open the document in the app.**

3. **Tap the Share Link via iCloud command in one of the following ways:**

   - **iPad**. Tap the Share button on the toolbar and then tap Share Link via iCloud.

   - **iPhone or iPod touch.** Tap the Tools button on the toolbar, tap Share and Print, and then tap Share Link via iCloud.

Note

The first time you tap Share Link via iCloud on the Share and Print screen, the First Time Sharing? dialog opens. Tap Learn More if you want to learn more about the Share Link via iCloud feature. Otherwise, tap Continue and follow the remaining steps in the list.

4. **On the Share sheet, tap the means of sharing, such as Message.**

5. **Take any actions necessary to send the link.** For example, address the message and send it.

Sending a copy of a document

When you need to provide someone with an actual copy of a document rather than a link to a document on iCloud, use the Send a Copy command. Follow these steps:

1. **Open the app for the document you want to share.**

2. **Open the document in the app.**

3. **Choose the Send a Copy command in one of the following ways:**

   - **OS X.** Click the Share button on the toolbar, click or highlight Send a Copy, and then click the means of sharing on the submenu — for example, Email.

   - **iPad.** Tap the Share button on the toolbar, then tap Send a Copy. On the Share sheet that opens, touch the means of sharing, such as Message (see Figure 4.38).

   - **iPhone or iPod touch.** Tap the Tools button on the toolbar, then tap Share and Print. On the Share and Print screen, tap Send a Copy. On the Share sheet that opens, tap the means of sharing — for example, AirDrop.

   - **iCloud.** Click the Tools button on the toolbar, and then click Send a Copy. In the Choose a format to send via iCloud Mail dialog (see Figure 4.39), tap the format you want to use. Your choices are the app's native format

4.38 Touch the means of sharing on the Share sheet.

(such as Pages), PDF, or the equivalent Microsoft Office format (such as Word format for a Pages document).

4. **Take the actions needed to complete sending the copy of the document.** For example:

   • **E-mail.** Address the message and send it.

   • **Messages.** Choose the recipient.

   • **AirDrop.** Click or tap the icon for the recipient.

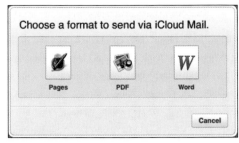

4.39 When sending a copy of a document from an iCloud app, click the format in the Choose a format to send via iCloud Mail dialog.

Opening a document in another app

On iOS, you can open the document in another app. This form of sharing is for getting around the separate storage areas that iOS provides for its apps to prevent them from trampling each other's documents.

Here's how to open a document in another app:

1. **Open the app for the document.**

2. **Open the document in the app.**

3. **Choose the Open in Another App command in one of the following ways:**

   • **iPad.** Tap the Share button on the toolbar, and then tap Open in Another App to display the Open in Another App dialog.

   • **iPhone or iPod touch.** Tap the Tools button on the toolbar, then tap Share and Print. On the Share and Print screen, tap Open in Another App to display the Open in Another App screen.

4. **Tap the format you want to use (see Figure 4.40).** The format you choose controls which apps will be available for receiving the document.

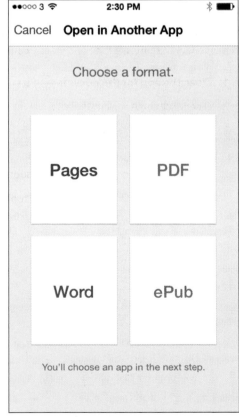

4.40 Tap the format to use for the document you will open in another app.

143

5. **Tap the appropriate format.** The iWork app exports the document in that format and then displays another screen or dialog with a preview of the document and its name.

6. **Tap Choose App (see Figure 4.41).** The Share sheet opens, showing the available apps for the document type.

7. **Tap the app you want to use (see Figure 4.42).** The app opens and displays the document.

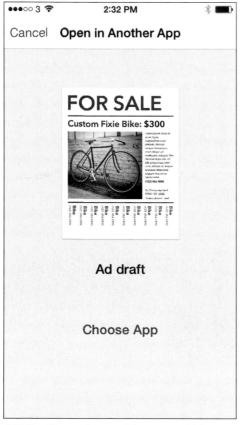

4.41 Tap Choose App on this screen, which shows the document ready for opening in another app.

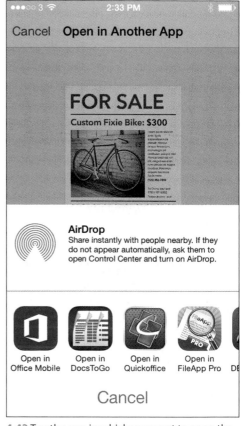

4.42 Tap the app in which you want to open the document.

Printing documents on iOS

If you have an AirPrint-compliant printer, you can print documents straight from your iPad, iPhone, or iPod touch. Here's how to print:

1. **Open the document you want to print.**

2. **Display the Printer Options dialog or Printer Options screen:**

   ● **iPad.** Tap the Tools button on the toolbar and then tap Print.

   ● **iPhone or iPod touch.** Tap the Tools button on the toolbar, tap Share and Print, and then tap Print.

3. **Tap Printer (see Figure 4.43) to display the Printer dialog or screen, and then tap the printer.**

4. **Tap the + button or − button to adjust the number of copies as needed.**

5. **Tap Print.**

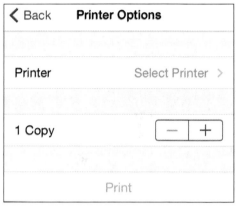

4.43 On the Printer Options screen, choose the printer, set the number of copies, and then tap Print.

Genius

If you don't have an AirPrint-capable printer, look at apps such as Printer Pro and handyPrint, which enable you to print to non-AirPrint printers. Printer Pro comes from the App Store and runs on your iOS device; there's a Lite version you can download for free to make sure it works for your iOS device and printer. handyPrint (www.netputing.com/handyprint/) runs on a Mac and is donationware.

Copying a document to a WebDAV server

If your company uses a WebDAV server for sharing documents, you can copy a document to it from your iOS device. Here's how to do this:

1. **Open the app for the document.**

2. **Open the document in the app.**

3. **Choose the Open in Another App command in one of the following ways:**

   ● **iPad.** Tap the Share button on the toolbar, then tap Send a Copy. On the Share sheet that opens, tap WebDAV (see Figure 4.44). The WebDAV Sign In dialog opens.

●   **iPhone or iPod touch.** Tap the Tools button on the toolbar, then tap Share and Print. On the Share and Print screen, tap Send a Copy. On the Share sheet that opens, tap WebDAV. The WebDAV Sign In screen appears.

4. **Type the server name (see Figure 4.45).**

4.45 Type the login details for the WebDAV server, and then tap Sign In.

4.44 Tap WebDAV on the Share sheet to start sharing a document from your iOS device to a WebDAV server.

5. **Type your username.**

6. **Type your password.**

7. **Tap Sign In to sign in to the server.**

8. **Navigate to the folder in which you want to save the document.**

9. **Tap Save.**

Copying a document to iTunes

When you need to get an iWork document off your iOS device and onto your computer, you can connect the device to your computer and use the Copy to iTunes command. This command lets you choose between transferring the document in its native format (for example, as a Numbers spreadsheet) and exporting the document to a different format (such as Microsoft Excel or PDF).

Here's how to use the Copy to iTunes command:

1. **Connect your iOS device to your computer, either via USB or via Wi-Fi.**

2. **On the iOS device, open the app for the document.**

3. **Open the document in the app.**

4. **Choose the Open in Another App command in one of the following ways:**

    - **iPad.** Tap the Share button on the toolbar, then tap Send a Copy. On the Share sheet that opens, tap iTunes. The Send to iTunes dialog opens. Like the Open in Another App dialog (look back to Figure 4.40), this dialog lets you choose the format in which to export the document.

    - **iPhone or iPod touch.** Tap the Tools button on the toolbar, then tap Share and Print. On the Share and Print screen, tap Send a Copy. On the Share sheet that opens, tap iTunes. The Send to iTunes screen appears, giving you a choice of formats in which to export the document.

5. **Tap the appropriate format.** The iWork app exports the document in that format.

6. **On your computer, open iTunes if it's not already open.**

7. **Click the iOS device's button on the navigation bar or in the sidebar (depending on which you're using) to display the management screens for the iOS device.**

8. **Click the Apps tab to display the Apps screen.**

9. **Scroll down to display the File Sharing area.**

10. **Click the iWork app from which you gave the Copy to iTunes command.** The list of its files appears.

11. **Click the file.**

12. **Click Save To.** The Save To dialog opens.

13. **Navigate to the appropriate folder.**

14. **Click Save To.** iTunes copies the file to the folder you chose.

Collaborating on Documents

If you store your iWork documents on iCloud, you can work on a document at the same time as other people. This can be a great way of finishing your documents more quickly and eliminating time-consuming review stages.

To enable your colleagues to collaborate on a document with you, share a link to the document, as described in the previous section. A colleague can then click the link in the message to open the document and start working on it with you. Similarly, a colleague can send you a link to a shared document, and you can click the link to open the document.

Working in a shared document

After opening a shared document, you can simply start working on it. To see who else is using the document, click the Share button on the toolbar and look at the Collaborator List panel (see Figure 4.46). The colored circle to the left of each collaborator's name shows the color in which their activities appear. The Show Activity check box controls whether you see the Collaborator Cursor and highlight (discussed in a moment).

The Collaborator Cursor, an upward-pointing triangle, indicates where a collaborator's insertion point is currently located (see Figure 4.47). A color highlight shows the selection a collaborator has made.

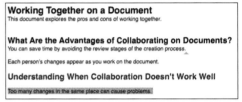

4.47 The Collaborator Cursor and color highlight help you see where your collaborators are working.

4.46 Click the Share button on the toolbar to display the Collaborator List. Each collaborator has a different color.

Genius The iWork apps are pretty smart about enabling two or more people to change the same part of a document at the same time, but in general, it is best to avoid any area you can see someone else is currently using. To this end, keep the Show Activity check box in the Collaborator List panel selected.

Using comments

When you collaborate with others on documents, the iWork apps' Comments feature is often useful. Comments are notes you can add to a document without directly affecting its text and other contents. When the time comes to review the document, you can go through the comments, deal with them one by one, and remove them from the document.

Caution At this writing, the iWork for iCloud apps do not support comments. Existing comments in iWork documents don't appear in the iWork for iCloud documents, so you can accidentally delete comments you can't see.

You can quickly insert a comment like this on OS X:

1. **Select the text or object to which you want the comment to refer.** To comment on text, you can simply click in a word.

2. **Click the Comment button on the toolbar to open a comment box.**

3. **Type the text of the comment (see Figure 4.48).**

4. **Click outside the comment box to collapse it to a yellow comment marker.**

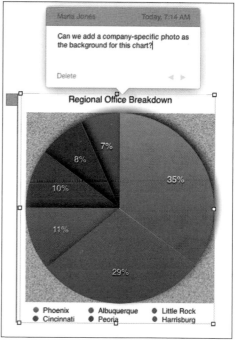

4.48 Type the text of the comment in the comment box on OS X.

Genius For comments, each iWork for OS X app uses the name set in the Author text box in its General preferences pane. You can use a different name in each iWork app if you want. To change the name, open the application menu, click Preferences, and then click the General button.

Here's how to insert a comment on iOS:

1. **Tap to select the text or object on which you are commenting.** For text, you can position the insertion point within a single word, but it is usually clearer to select all of the text to which the comment refers.

2. **Tap to display the pop-up control bar.**

3. **Tap Comment to insert a comment (see Figure 4.49).** On the iPhone or iPod touch, you may need to tap the right-arrow button one or more times to display the next set of controls on the control bar in order to reach the Comment button.

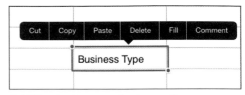

4.49 Tap the Comment button on the pop-up control bar to insert a comment on iOS.

Genius

To change the name shown for comments on iOS, tap the Tools button on the tool-bar, tap Settings, and then tap Author Name. Type the name to use for the com-ments, and then tap Done on the iPhone or iPod touch. On the iPad, tap outside the Author Name panel to close the panel.

4. **Type the text of the comment (see Figure 4.50).**

5. **Tap outside the comment box to collapse it to a yellow comment marker.**

When reviewing a document, you can easily go through the comments and delete each one with which you've finished. Follow these steps to do so:

1. **Click or tap the comment marker to open the comment.**

2. **Click or tap the Next (>) button or the Previous (<) button to navigate from comment to comment.**

3. **Click or tap Delete to delete the current comment.**

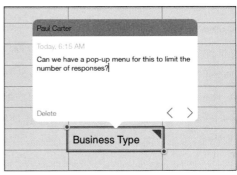

4.50 Type the text of the comment in the comment box on iOS.

Locking and Unlocking Documents on OS X

If you want to prevent a document from being changed, you can lock it against changes. Locking is useful for documents that you share with others but over which you want to maintain control. When you need to make changes to the document, you unlock it again.

Caution At this writing, locking does not work effectively on iCloud. Even if you lock a document using one of the iWork apps on OS X, the corresponding app on iOS or in iCloud can unlock the document and save changes to it.

Here's how to lock a document:

1. **Move the mouse pointer over the document's title bar.** A pop-up button appears to the right of the document's name or the Edited readout that appears if the document contains unsaved changes.

2. **Click the pop-up button to display the document details pane (see Figure 4.51).**

3. **Select the Locked check box.**
   The word *Locked* appears to the right of the document's name in the title bar.

4. **Click outside the document details pane to close it.**

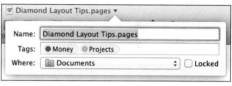

4.51 Select the Locked check box to lock a document and prevent any changes.

To unlock a document, move the mouse pointer over the title bar, click the pop-up button to the right of the name, and then deselect the Locked check box in the document details pane.

If you try to edit a locked document, the iWork app displays a dialog telling you that the docu-

4.52 Click Unlock to unlock the locked document or Duplicate to create a copy. Alternatively, click Cancel.

ment is locked. Click Unlock (see Figure 4.52) if you want to unlock the document for editing; click Duplicate if you want to create a copy that you can edit without changing the original; or click Cancel if you want to take neither action.

Choosing Preferences and Settings

Like most other apps, the iWork apps on OS X have preferences you can set to control how the apps behave. The iWork apps on iOS and iCloud also have preferences, but they refer to them as *settings*. This section shows you how to choose preferences and settings.

Choosing iWork preferences on OS X

On OS X, the three iWork apps share many preferences for things such as creating new documents, detecting lists, and controlling the rulers and alignment guides. I explain how to open the Preferences window, and then go through the common preferences before exploring those that are unique to the individual apps.

To start choosing preferences, open the Preferences window by pressing ⌘+, (⌘ and the Comma key) or choosing Pages ⇨ Preferences, Numbers ⇨ Preferences, or Keynote ⇨ Preferences.

Each Preferences window has two tabbed panes, the General pane and the Rulers pane. I start with the General pane, so if the Rulers pane is displayed, click the General button to display the General pane (see Figure 4.53).

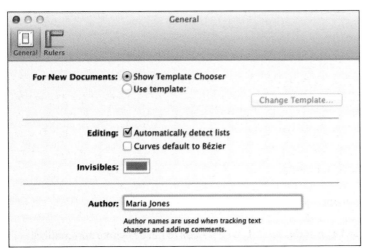

4.53 In the General pane, you can choose how to create new documents, set editing options, and specify your author name for tracking changes and adding comments.

Choosing common General preferences

The apps have the following four common preferences in the General pane:

- **For New Documents.** In this area, choose whether to display the Template Chooser window (in Pages and Numbers) or the Theme Chooser window (in Keynote) when you start creating a new document by choosing File ⇨ New or pressing ⌘+N. If you want to use the same template or theme for each new document, click the Use template or Use theme option button, click Change Template or Change Theme, and then pick the template or theme. Choose the Blank template to create a blank document in Pages or Numbers.

- **Automatically detect lists.** Select this check box if you want the app to detect when you are creating a list of items automatically. For example, if you type 1, followed by a space and some text, when you press Return, Pages applies list formatting, because the numbering looks like a list. If you don't want this automatic formatting, deselect the Automatically detect lists check box.

- **Curves default to Bézier.** Select this check box if you want to use Bézier curves for your shapes. With Bézier curves, you drag the handles at the ends of a curve to adjust the curve.

- **Author.** In this text box, type the author name you want to appear for comments. Pages also uses this name for tracked changes (also called revision marks).

Choosing app-specific General preferences

Pages has one app-specific preference in the General pane called Invisibles. Click the color swatch to set the color Pages uses for *invisibles*, which are characters that normally have no visible marker in the document, such as spaces and carriage returns.

Note

To display invisible characters in a Pages document, choose View ▷ Show Invisibles or press Shift+⌘+I. To hide invisible characters again, choose View ▷ Hide Invisibles or press Shift+⌘+I again.

Numbers also has only one app-specific preference in the General pane called Use header names as labels. Select this check box to refer to a cell by the names of its column header and row header (in that order). For example, in a table that has a column named 2014 and a row named Indianapolis, you can refer to the cell at their intersection by using "2014 Indianapolis" instead of its standard name (for example, A15). It can be faster and more convenient to use header cell names as labels, so you probably want to experiment with it.

Keynote has the following four app-specific preferences in the General pane:

- **Scale placed images to fit on slide.** Select this check box to have Keynote automatically resize (scale) images to fit on slides when you place them. This feature is usually helpful, because it saves you from having to resize many images manually. If Keynote gets the sizing wrong, you can adjust it in moments.

- **Outline View Font.** In this pop-up menu, select the font size to use for outline view.

- **Copy audio and movies into document.** Select this check box if you want Keynote to copy audio and movie files into the document when you add those items to your slides. Copying the files into the document gives you a self-contained presentation that you can work on with another computer or device. The disadvantage is that including the audio and movies increases the document size.

- **Optimize Movies for iOS.** Open this pop-up menu and choose Automatically, Always Ask, or Never Ask, as needed. If you plan to use iOS to work with the presentation or to deliver it, choose Automatically. If you want Keynote to prompt you, choose Always Ask; if you do not want to optimize movies for iOS, choose Never Ask.

Choosing common Rulers preferences

Pages, Numbers, and Keynote share the following five preferences in the Rulers pane (see Figure 4.54):

- **Ruler Units.** Choose the measurement units you want to use for the ruler. Your choices are Inches, Centimeters, or Points.

153

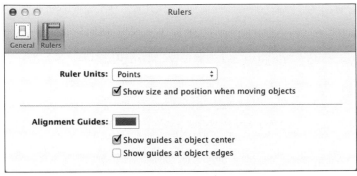

4.54 Choose preferences in the Rulers pane to control the ruler units the app uses and the alignment guides it displays.

Note A point is a typesetting measurement equivalent to 1/72 inch.

- **Show size and position when moving objects.** Select this check box to make the app display the size and position of an object you are moving. Usually this information is helpful for positioning an object precisely. If your Mac lags while you move objects, try deselecting this check box.

- **Alignment Guides color.** Click the color swatch and then use the Colors window to select the color of the alignment guides that the app displays.

- **Show guides at object center.** Select this check box to make the app display alignment guides at the center of an object. These guides are useful for aligning objects by their centers.

- **Show guides at object edges.** Select this check box to make the app display alignment guides at the edges of an object. These guides are useful for aligning objects by their edges.

Choosing Keynote-specific Rulers preferences

In addition to the five common Rulers preferences, Keynote also has these three:

- **Show guides for relative sizing.** Select this check box to make Keynote display guides for sizing objects relative to each other.

- **Show guides for relative spacing.** Select this check box to make Keynote display guides for spacing objects relative to each other.

- **Master Guides color.** Click this color swatch and then use the Colors window to select the color for the guide lines on slide masters.

154

Note

Besides these extra Rulers preferences, Keynote also has two extra whole panes of preferences: the Slideshow pane and the Remote pane. These panes are covered in the chapters on Keynote.

Choosing iWork preferences on iOS

The iWork apps on OS X have only a few preferences, so it doesn't take long to set them. First, open the Settings app and navigate to the app's screen like this:

1. **Press the Home button to display the Home screen.**

2. **Tap Settings to display the Settings screen.**

3. **Tap the app's name to display the app's screen.** Figure 4.55 shows the Keynote screen, which offers more settings than the Pages screen and the Numbers screen.

Pages has only one setting (which Numbers and Keynote have, as well) called Use iCloud. Set this switch to On to allow the app to use iCloud. Normally, you want to do this to get the most out of the app.

Numbers has the following two preferences, both of which Keynote also has:

- **Ask to Open Copies.** Set this switch to On to make the app prompt you, when opening a document created in the '09 version of the app, to create a copy of the document instead of opening the original. Numbers and Keynote must convert these documents when opening them, so if you need to keep the original documents in their '09 formats, set this switch to On.

- **Restore.** Set this switch to On if you want Numbers or Keynote to display the Getting Started screen each time you launch the app. Normally, this screen is helpful only at first launch (if then), but you can display it every time if you choose.

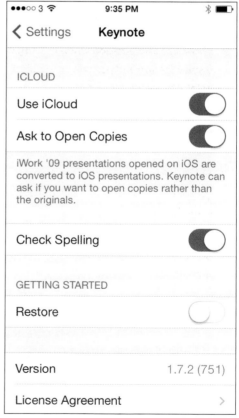

4.55 To choose iWork preferences in iOS, display the app's screen in the Settings app.

Keynote also has one other preference called Check Spelling. Set this switch to On to check the spelling in your presentations automatically.

Choosing iWork settings on iCloud

On iCloud, each iWork app has some settings you can adjust to control how the app appears and how it behaves. Here's how to choose settings in an iWork for iCloud app:

1. **Click the Tools button on the Toolbar to display the Tools menu.**

2. **Click or highlight Settings to display the Settings submenu.**

3. **Choose the command you want to use.** For example, on the Settings submenu for Pages, you can click Show Format Panel (see Figure 4.56) to display the Format panel.

4.56 To choose settings in the iWork for iCloud apps, choose Tools ⇨ Settings.

Each app has the following five settings:

● **Show Format Panel/Hide Format Panel.** Choose this command to display or hide the Format panel. If you have plenty of space on screen, you may want to keep the Format panel displayed all the time. If you're short of space, hide the Format panel when you're concentrating on content.

● **Check Spelling.** Choose this command to turn spell checking on or off, whichever you find most helpful.

- **Center Guides.** Choose this command to turn on or off the display of center guides on objects. Center guides are helpful when you have a need for aligning objects by their centers.

- **Edge Guides.** Choose this command to turn on or off the display of edge guides on objects. Edge guides are helpful for aligning objects by their edges.

- **Spacing Guides.** Choose this command to turn on or off the display of spacing guides on objects. Spacing guides are helpful for getting objects evenly spaced.

How Do I Create Attractive Documents in Pages?

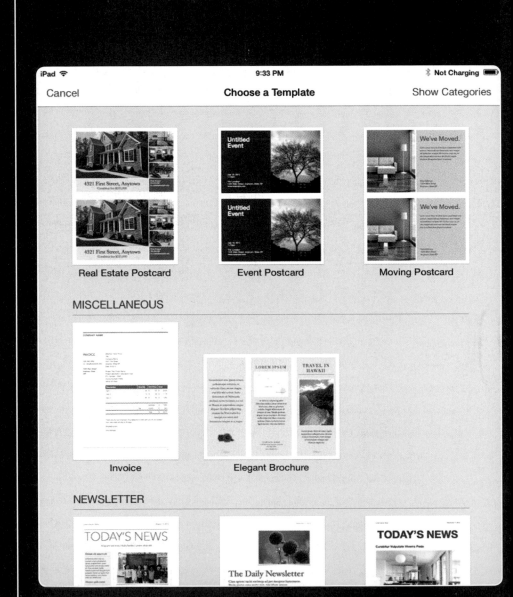

With Pages, you can create attractive documents using your Mac, PC, and iOS devices. To do so, you have to know the types of documents you can create and pick a suitable template for them. You can then set the page size, orientation, and margins, type and format the text, and add headers or footers. For complex documents, you can create columns of text, lay out text using tables, and insert footnotes or endnotes. Also, when collaborating with others on documents, you can track changes so that you can review each insertion or deletion with care.

Understanding the Types of Documents You Can Create

Pages enables you to create both word-processing and page-layout documents. Here's the difference:

- **Word-processing document.** This type of document uses a body area that causes the text to flow automatically from one page to the next. If you create a multicolumn layout, as explained later in this chapter, the text flows automatically from the bottom of one column to the top of the next column, and from the bottom of the last column on one page to the top of the first column on the next page. You can use the text-flow features that Pages offers to force text to the next line or next page, prevent a paragraph from breaking across pages, and suppress typesetting widows and orphans.

- **Page-layout document.** In this type of document, you turn off the body area of the document and place objects on the document canvas, positioning them as needed. For the text of the document, you can place text boxes as needed; you can also make text flow along a series of text boxes on the same page.

A document based on one of Pages' templates has its body area or text boxes and other objects already set up, so all you need to do is type the text and other content. In documents you create yourself in Pages on OS X, you can turn the body area on or off in the same way as the header and footer. Follow these steps:

1. **Click the Setup button on the toolbar to display the Document Setup inspector.** You can also choose View ⇨ Inspector ⇨ Document Setup.

Caution Turning off the body area removes any text in the body area and any inline objects placed there. If the body area contains any text or other objects you want to keep, copy or move them before turning off the body area.

2. **If the Document pane isn't displayed, click the Document button at the top of the inspector to display it.**

3. **Select the Document Body check box to turn on the body area, or deselect this check box to turn off the body area (see Figure 5.1).**

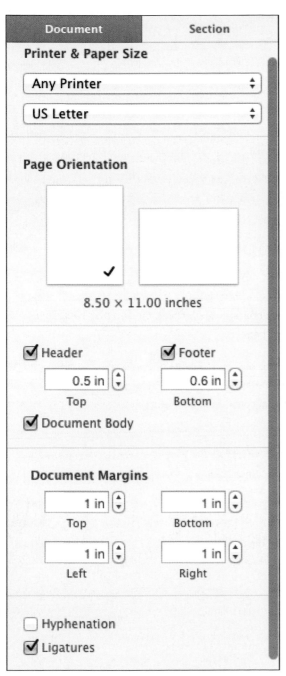

5.1 Deselect the Document Body check box in the Document Setup inspector to turn off the body area of a document.

4. **When you turn off the body area, Pages displays the Are you sure you want to remove the body of the document? dialog (see Figure 5.2).** Click Remove if you're sure you want to do this.

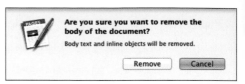

Are you sure you want to remove the body of the document?

Body text and inline objects will be removed.

Remove   Cancel

5.2 Click Remove to remove any body text and inline objects from your document when you turn off the body area.

Note

At this writing, you cannot turn off the body area in Pages for iOS or Pages for iCloud.

Choosing a Suitable Template

To create your documents quickly and effectively, base each of them on a suitable template. This can be a Pages template, one that you create, or a template you add from another source. For example, various companies sell packs of iWork templates, some concentrating on document design, some on content and functionality, and some combining the two.

Genius

In earlier versions of Pages, the Template Chooser dialog presented the templates in two main categories, Word Processing and Page Layout, but also gave an All view that enabled you to view all the templates at once. Apple has removed this distinction, perhaps because people found it confusing.

To choose a template, open the Template Chooser in one of the following ways:

- **OS X.** Choose File ➪ New or press ⌘+N.
- **iOS.** On the Pages screen, tap the + button in the upper-left corner, and then tap Create Document.
- **iCloud.** On the Pages for iCloud screen, click the Create Document button.

You can then select the template in the Template Chooser. Figure 5.3 shows the Choose a Template screen on the iPad. If you want to see the templates in a single category instead of having them all displayed in a single list, tap Show Categories, and then tap the appropriate category.

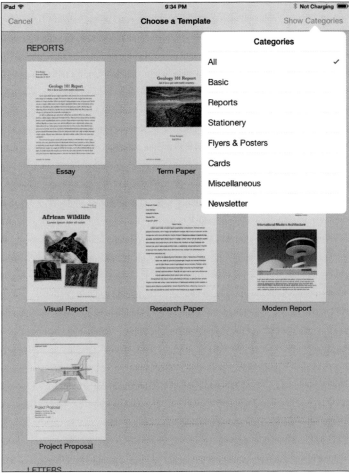

5.3 To narrow down the templates on the Choose a Template screen on iOS to a single category, tap Show Categories, and then tap the category.

Inserting Text, and Line and Page Breaks

After creating your documents, your next move will often be to input the text it needs. Even when you are creating a highly graphical page-layout document, its textual contents will normally be essential to help the reader understand the document's purpose and importance.

Inputting text

If the document uses a body area, you can input text using the following standard methods for the platform:

- **Type the text.** Use text replacements on OS X or shortcuts on iOS to input boilerplate text more quickly and accurately.

- **Paste the text.** You can paste from other Pages documents or other sources as needed.

- **Dictate the text.** On OS X, use the Dictation pane in Dictation & Speech preferences in System Preferences to choose your input source, enable dictation, and choose the language and shortcut. On iOS, tap the microphone button on the keyboard, speak at the tone, and tap Done when you finish.

Genius

If you plan to use OS X's Dictation feature, download the Enhanced Dictation pack, which enables you to dictate text while your Mac is offline. In Dictation & Speech preferences, click the Dictation button, and then select the On radio button on the Dictation line. Select the Use Enhanced Dictation check box to make OS X download the Enhanced Dictation pack.

You can also use these methods to input text in text boxes and other objects that accept text. When entering text in a text box, you don't need to select the placeholder text first — just select the text box and start typing.

Inserting line and page breaks

Pages automatically wraps text at the right edge of the body area and of each text box or table cell, but you can also break lines manually as needed. Similarly, Pages automatically flows the text from the end of one page in a word-processing document to the start of the next, but at times, you may need to break pages manually. Here's how to insert line and page breaks on OS X:

- **Line break.** Press Shift+Return.

- **Page break.** Choose Insert ➪ Page Break or press ⌘+Enter. Press Enter on the numeric keypad, not the Return key.

On iOS, you use the Insert panel to insert line and page breaks in the following ways:

- **iPad.** Tap the + button at the upper-right corner of the keyboard to display the Insert panel (see Figure 5.4), and then tap Line Break or Page Break, as needed.

iPhone or iPod touch. Follow these steps:

1. **Tap and hold the point in text where you want to insert a break.** The pop-up control bar appears.

2. **Tap Insert to display the Insert panel.**

3. **Tap Line Break or Page Break.**

To insert line breaks and page breaks in iCloud, Control+click where you want to place the break, and then click Line Break or Page Break, as appropriate.

5.4 Use the Insert panel to insert line and page breaks on iOS.

Formatting Text

To make your documents look good, you probably need to format the text they contain. I say probably because if you base the document on a template, and that template is fully set up with formatting, all of the formatting happens automatically, and you may not need to change any of it.

Deciding how to format your documents

As covered in Chapter 3, the best way to format your documents is like this:

1. **Start with paragraph styles.** Apply a paragraph style to each paragraph. For example, apply the Heading style to a paragraph that contains a main heading, or apply the Body style to a body paragraph.

2. **Apply character styles.** Apply a character style to any text unit smaller than a paragraph — a character, a word, a phrase, a sentence, or whatever — that you need to distinguish from the paragraph style. For example, apply the Italic style to text that needs emphasis.

3. **Apply list formatting.** If the paragraph is a list, apply list formatting such as Bullet or Numbered.

4. **Apply direct formatting for special effects.** For example, if you need to change the color of a word, or apply a shadow to it, use direct formatting.

Genius

You can apply any formatting as direct formatting — all of the formatting that goes to make up a style is available as direct formatting. However, using styles to apply the vast majority of a document's formatting and using direct formatting only for finishing touches saves time and effort. If you find yourself applying the same direct formatting to multiple items, consider creating a style instead.

Working with text on OS X

When you do use direct formatting, you can reuse it quickly in Pages on OS X by using the following commands:

- **Copy a style.** Select the text with the appropriate formatting and choose Format ⇨ Copy Style.

- **Paste a style.** Select the text to which you want to apply the formatting and choose Format ⇨ Paste Style.

To enable you to make your documents appear the way you want them to, Pages for OS X provides settings for controlling text flow and pagination.

Genius

You can use the text-flow and pagination features either via direct formatting or by incorporating them into your styles. Normally, you want to use both approaches, depending on the circumstances. For example, you might turn on Keep Lines on Same Page manually to prevent a particular paragraph from breaking across pages. If the problem occurs frequently, you might create a style with this setting so you could apply it quickly and consistently.

Here's how to adjust these settings:

1. **Click in the paragraph you want to affect, or select multiple paragraphs.**
2. **If the Format inspector isn't displayed, click the Format button on the toolbar to display it.**
3. **Click the More button to display the More pane.**
4. **Select the Keep lines on same page check box if you want to keep the lines of a paragraph together on one page instead of allowing it to break across pages.**

5. **Select the Keep with next paragraph check box if you want to keep a paragraph with the next paragraph, preventing a page break from falling between them.** For example, you might use this setting to keep a heading on the same page as the paragraph that follows it.

Caution It's best to use the Keep with next paragraph setting only for a couple of paragraphs at a time. While you *can* set a whole sequence of paragraphs to stay together, be careful — you may end up with a short page because Pages has moved a large block of text to the next page. For this reason, it's usually best not to apply this setting to body text styles, because it's normal to have several body text paragraphs in sequence.

6. **Select the Start paragraph on a new page check box if you want this paragraph to start a page.** This setting is often useful for headings.

7. **Select the Prevent widows and orphans check box to suppress the following type-set errors:**

   - **Orphan lines.** An *orphan line* is a paragraph's first line that appears alone at the bottom of a page.

   - **Widow lines.** A *widow line* is a paragraph's last line that appears alone at the top of a page.

For fine-tuning the layout of words in your documents, you can choose settings for hyphenation and ligatures. The following settings are located in the More pane in the Layout pane of the Format inspector:

- **Remove paragraph hyphenation.** Select this check box to remove hyphens that Pages has inserted to break lines of text more neatly.

- **Remove ligatures.** Select this check box to remove typeset ligatures (such as œ) in the document.

Setting the Document's Page Layout

Each of Pages' templates includes a full-page layout, so you may simply be able to choose the template you need and use it without making any further adjustments. However, if you need to create a custom document, you may need to change the page size and orientation, adjust the margins, add headers and footers, or insert page numbers. At this writing, you can set page layout for a document on OS X and iOS but not on iCloud.

Setting the document's page layout on OS X

To set the page layout for a document, you use the Document Setup inspector like this:

1. **Click the Setup button on the toolbar to display the Setup panel.**

2. **Click Document to display the Document Setup inspector (see Figure 5.5).** You can also choose View ➪ Inspector ➪ Document Setup.

3. **In the Printer & Paper Size section, open the upper pop-up menu and choose the printer you plan to use when you print the document.** If you don't know which printer you use, or the printer isn't available at the moment, choose Any Printer.

4. **In the Printer & Paper Size section, click the lower pop-up menu and choose the paper size.**

5. **In the Page Orientation section, click the left icon for portrait (upright) orientation or the right icon for landscape (wide) orientation.**

6. **To include a header area, select the Header check box.** Set the value in the Top box to control the distance between the header and the top of the page.

7. **To include a footer area, select the Footer check box.** Set the value in the Bottom box to control the distance between the footer and the bottom of the page.

8. **Make sure the Document Body check box is selected if you want to use a body area in the document.** As explained earlier in this chapter, you'd normally use a body area for a word-processing document such as a report or a letter but turn off the body area for a page-layout document such as a newsletter.

9. **In the Document Margins section, use the Top box, Bottom box, Left box, and Right box to set the distance between the document margins and those edges of the paper.**

10. **Select the Hyphenation check box if you want Pages to hyphenate the text in your document automatically to make the right edge of the text area less uneven.**

11. **Select the Ligatures check box if you want Pages to insert typeset ligatures (such as œ) in the document automatically.**

12. **Click the Setup button on the toolbar if you want to close the Document Setup inspector.**

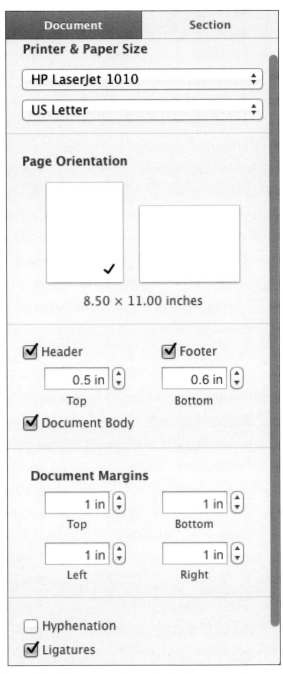

5.5 Click the Document button in the Setup panel to display the Document Setup inspector.

If you selected the Header check box or the Footer check box in the Document Setup inspector, the header area or footer area appears in the document when you move the mouse pointer over it. You can then add content to the header or footer by clicking in one of its sections and typing or pasting text. To insert page numbers, click the Insert Page Number button (see Figure 5.6), and then click the page-number format you want.

5.6 To create a header or footer, click in the header or footer area, and then type or paste the content.

Setting the document's page layout on iOS

Here's how to set the page layout for a document on iOS:

1. **Tap the Tools button on the toolbar to display the Tools panel (on the iPad) or the Tools screen (on the iPhone or iPod touch).**

2. **Tap Document Setup to display the Doc Setup screen.** Figure 5.7 shows the Doc Setup screen on the iPad, but the Doc Setup screen on the iPhone and iPod touch is almost identical.

Note The Doc Setup screen works only in portrait orientation. If you're holding your iOS device in landscape orientation, you must rotate the device to portrait orientation when using Doc Setup.

3. **To change the paper size, tap the Change Paper Size button, and then tap the size you want on the resulting screen.**

4. **Drag the margin lines to adjust the margins. You can either drag the arrows on the lines or simply drag the lines themselves.**

5. **To add a header or footer, follow these steps:**

   a. **Touch Tap to edit header to open the header area, or touch Tap to edit footer to open the footer area.**

   b. **Tap in the section of the header or footer that you want to change.** The pop-up control bar appears (see Figure 5.8).

5.7 On the Doc Setup screen, you can adjust the margins, add a header or footer, or change the paper size.

    c. Tap the item you want to insert. For example, tap Page Numbers to display the Page Numbers panel (see Figure 5.9), and then tap the page-number format to insert.

    d. Tap in the document body when you're ready to stop editing the header or footer.

6. **Tap the Done button to finish editing the document setup and return to the document.**

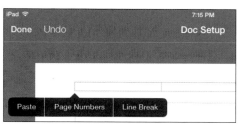

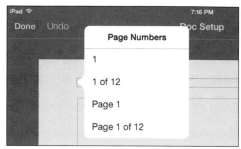

5.8 Tap the header or footer section you want to edit, and then tap the appropriate button on the pop-up control bar.

5.9 Use the Page Numbers panel to insert page numbers in the header or footer.

Creating Multicolumn Layouts

Newspaper-style columns of text are great for documents such as newsletters. When you reach the bottom of the first column, Pages flows the text to the top of the second column, and so on.

Pages makes it simple to use different numbers of columns in different parts of your documents. You can use multiple columns either within the body of a word-processing document or within a text box in either a word-processing document or a page-layout document.

At this writing, you can use columns in Pages on OS X and iOS but not on iCloud. You can open documents containing columns in Pages for iCloud. The columns display correctly, and you can edit their contents, but you cannot change the columns themselves.

Genius

The key to using columns successfully is to use sections. A *section* is a part of a document that has particular layout characteristics — for example, two columns and 1-inch layout margins. The whole of a section must have the same number of columns, so when you need to change the number of columns, you must create a new section.

Working with columns in Pages on OS X

In Pages for OS X, you can quickly create multiple columns from existing text. You can then customize those columns by inserting column breaks. Here's how to set up multiple columns:

1. **Choose the part of the document for which you want to change the number of columns in one of the following ways:**

   - To affect the whole document, just click anywhere in it.
   - To affect just part of a document, select it.

Genius

When you change the number of columns for a text selection within the document, Pages automatically turns that selection into a separate section, putting a section break before it and another section break after it. If you prefer to create your sections manually, choose Insert ⇨ Section Break to insert section breaks where you want them. Then, click in the section in which you want to change the number of columns.

2. **If the Format inspector isn't displayed, click the Format button on the toolbar to display it.**

3. **Click the Layout button to display the Layout pane.**

4. **If the Columns section is collapsed, click its disclosure triangle to expand it (see Figure 5.10).**

5. **Click the arrows in the Columns box to set the number of columns.**
   Alternatively, type the number.

6. **If you want the columns to have different widths from each other, deselect the Equal column width check box.** Normally, this check box is selected by default, so Pages automatically gives each column the same width. After deselecting the check box, you can select a column in the list box, change its width in the column named Column, and change its gutter in the Gutter column.

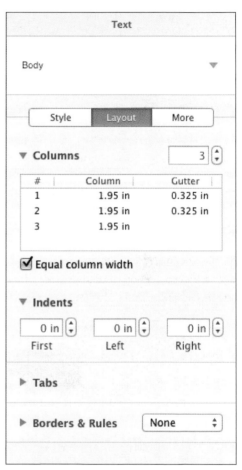

5.10 Use the Columns section of the Layout pane in the Format Inspector to set up multiple columns in a Pages document on OS X.

Note

The *gutter* is the space between columns. You can reduce the gutter to nothing by setting zero measurement units (for example, 0 inches) for special effects. To make your documents readable, it's usually best to have at least 0.25 inches between columns. The document shows your changes in real time, so you can easily see what looks best.

173

Now that you've set up the columns, type the text in them. When the text reaches the bottom of one column, it flows automatically to the next.

To remove columns from a section of a document, click in that section, open the Layout pane of the Format inspector, and then set the Columns box to 1. If the preceding section and following section also use a single column and the same page layout, you may want to remove the section breaks and turn the sections into a single section.

If you need to end a column before the bottom of a section (for example, so that a particular paragraph appears at the top of the next column), insert a column break. Position the insertion point and choose Insert ⇨ Column Break.

Column breaks are invisible characters, so you don't see them unless you've set Pages to display invisibles. (Click the View pop-up menu button on the toolbar and choose Show Invisibles or press ⌘+Shift+I.) When you do display invisibles, a column break appears as a horizontal blue line with a box at its right end.

Working with columns in Pages on iOS

As on OS X, Pages on iOS enables you to create columns quickly and easily. Follow these steps:

1. **Select the text to which you want to apply multiple columns.** If you've broken your document up into sections, you can simply tap in the appropriate section.

2. **Tap the Format button on the toolbar to display the Format panel.**

3. **Tap the Layout button to display the Layout tab.**

4. **On the Columns line, tap the + button to increase the number of columns (see Figure 5.11).** The label on the left changes to show the number of columns: 2 Columns, 3 Columns, and so on.

5. **To change the line spacing for the selection, tap the up button or down button on the Line Spacing control.**

6. **Tap in your document to close the Format panel.**

5.11 Use the Layout pane in the Format panel to create multiple columns on OS X.

To insert a column break on iOS, use the Insert panel in one of the following ways:

- **iPad.** Tap the + button at the upper-right corner of the keyboard to display the Insert panel, and then tap Column Break.

- **iPhone or iPod touch.** Tap and hold the appropriate point in the text, tap Insert on the pop-up control bar, and then tap Column Break.

Laying Out Objects in Pages

You can lay out objects with Pages using the techniques discussed in Chapter 4. For example, you can move objects forward and backward in the vertical stack to change what's visible, resize and reposition objects as needed, group objects you want to handle as a single unit, and lock objects in place to avoid unwanted changes. However, Pages also provides other commands for controlling object placement on your document pages and for customizing your text boxes.

In the Arrange pane of the Format inspector for Pages, you also find these extra options:

- **Object Placement buttons.** Click the Stay on Page button to keep the table on its current page. Click the Move with Text button to allow the table to move with the text, including moving to another page if necessary. (These buttons oppose each other; clicking one deselects the other.)

- **Text Wrap pop-up menu.** Click this pop-up menu and choose the text wrapping style you want for the body text near the object:

  - **Automatic.** Click this option to wrap the text squarely around the object.

  - **Around.** Click this option to wrap the text to the object's shape.

  - **Above and Below.** Click this option to make the text go above and below the object, with no text to the left and right.

  - **None.** Click this option to use no wrapping at all. The text appears right through the object. This effect can work well with near-transparent objects.

- **Text Fit buttons.** Click the left button for a loose fit; click the right button for a tight fit.

- **Spacing box.** Set the distance in points to use between the text and the object.

- **Alpha box.** Use this box to control the alpha setting for the object.

Working with Text Boxes

When you need text to appear in a particular place on a page, you can use a text box to put it there. Text boxes tend to be essential in page-layout documents, which have no body area, but they can be very useful in word-processing documents as well. Pages' templates make extensive use of text boxes, but you can easily insert your own custom text boxes as needed.

Inserting text boxes

You can quickly insert, resize, and reposition a text box on any of the iWork platforms. Here's how to insert a text box in Pages on OS X:

1. **Choose Insert ⇨ Text Box.** Pages inserts a default-size text box containing the text placeholder *Text*.

2. **Drag the text box to where you want it to appear.**

3. **Resize the text box as necessary:**

   - Drag a corner handle to resize the text box in both dimensions at once.

   - Drag a side handle to resize the text box in a single dimension.

4. **Type or paste the text into the text box.**

Genius For some layouts, you may need to make text flow from one text box to another. You can do this on OS X, but not on iOS or in iCloud. I cover flowing text later in this chapter.

Here's how to insert a text box in Pages on iOS:

1. **Tap the + button on the toolbar to display the Add panel.**

2. **Tap the T button to display the Text Box pane.**

3. **Tap the style of text box you want to insert.** Pages inserts a default-size text box containing the text placeholder *Text*.

4. **Tap the text box and drag it to where you want it to appear.**

5. **Resize the text box as necessary:**

   - Drag a corner handle to resize the text box in both dimensions at once.

   - Drag a side handle to resize the text box in a single dimension.

6. **Type or paste the text into the text box.**

Here's how to insert a text box on iCloud:

1. **Click the Text button on the toolbar.** Pages inserts a default-size text box containing the text placeholder *Text*.

2. **If the Format panel isn't displayed, click the Tools button on the toolbar, and then choose Settings ⇨ Show Format Panel to display it.**

3. **In the Shape pane of the Format panel, click the format you want to apply to the text box.**

4. **Drag the text box to where you want it to appear.**

5. **Resize the text box as necessary:**
   - Drag a corner handle to resize the text box in both dimensions at once.
   - Drag a side handle to resize the text box in a single dimension.

6. **Type or paste the text into the text box.**

Formatting a text box on OS X

The quick way to format a text box is by applying a style to the text box as a whole. You can also apply formatting separately to the text within a text box.

Here's how to format a text box on OS X:

1. **Click the text box to select it.** To format two or more text boxes at once, click the first text box, and then Shift+click each of the others.

2. **If the Format panel isn't displayed, click the Format button on the toolbar to display it.**

3. **Click the Style button to display the Style pane.**

4. **Click the style you want to apply.**

5. **If necessary, use the Fill controls, Border controls, Shadow controls, Reflection check box, and Opacity slider to change the way the style appears.** See Chapter 4 for details on using these controls to format objects.

6. **Click the Text button to display the Text pane.**

7. **Click the Style button to display the Style pane within the Text pane.**

8. **Use the Style list at the top of the pane to apply a style to each paragraph in the text box that needs to be formatted differently from the text-box style.**

9. **Use the remaining controls in the Text pane to apply any other formatting needed.** For example, you may need to use character styles to pick out specific words or phrases in the text box.

10. **Click the Layout button to display the Layout pane.**

11. **Choose any Columns, Text, Indents, Tabs, or Borders & Rules settings needed for the text box.**

12. **Click the More button to display the More pane.**

13. **Choose any Pagination & Breaks settings or Hyphenation & Ligatures settings needed.** I cover both of these categories of settings later in this chapter.

14. **Click the Arrange button to display the Arrange pane.**

15. **In the Object Placement area, click the Stay on Page button if you want to keep the text box on its current page.** Click the Move with Text button if you want the text box to move with the text to which it is anchored.

16. **Open the Text Wrap pop-up menu and choose the text wrapping for the text box:**

    - **Automatic.** Click this option to wrap the text squarely around the text box.

    - **Around.** Click this option to wrap the text to the shape of the text box.

    - **Above and Below.** Click this option to make the text go above and below the text box, with no text to the left and right.

    - **None.** Click this option to use no wrapping at all. The text appears right through the text box. This effect can be useful when you need to position some text over other text.

17. **Click the left Text Fit button to fit the body text loosely around the text box.** Click the right Text Fit button to fit the body text tightly around the text box.

18. **In the Spacing box, set the distance in points to use between the body text and the text box.**

19. **Use the remaining controls in the Arrange pane to adjust the text box's position, size, and rotation as needed.** You can also lock the text box in place until you need to unlock it, or group the text box with other objects.

Formatting a text box on iOS

Here's how to format a text box on iOS:

1. **Tap the text box to select it.**

Genius

You can select multiple text boxes at once and format them all together. Either tap two or more text boxes at the same time, or tap and hold one while you tap each of the others you want to select.

2. **Tap the Format button on the toolbar to display the Format panel.**

3. **In the Style pane, tap the style you want to apply.** If you choose a suitable style when inserting the text box, you may want to keep that style.

4. **To choose options for the style, tap the Style Options button, and then work in the Style Options panel.** From here, you can set the fill, border, and effects for the text box.

5. **Tap the Text button to display the Text pane.**

6. **Use the Paragraph Style list at the top of the pane to apply a style to each paragraph in the text box that needs to be formatted differently from the text-box style.**

7. **Use the controls in the upper part of the Text pane to adjust the font, font formatting, and alignment as needed.**

8. **Tap the Arrange button to display the Arrange pane.**

9. **Drag the Move to Back/Front slider to move the text box backward or forward vertically among the other objects in the document.**

10. **To change the wrapping, tap the Wrap button, and then work in the Wrap panel.** Here, you can change three settings:

    - **Wrap type.** In the main part of the panel, tap Automatic, Around, Above and Below, Inline with Text, or None, as needed.

    - **Move with Text.** Set this switch to On to make the text box move with the document's text. Set the switch to Off to keep the text box in place when the text moves.

    - **Extra Space.** Drag this slider to increase or decrease the amount of extra space around the text box. For example, you can increase the extra space to give a looser wrap.

11. **Set the vertical alignment by tapping the Top button, the Middle button, or the Bottom button.**

12. **If you need to change the number of columns in the text box, tap the + button or – button on the Column line.**

13. **If you need to change the internal margin between the text box's border and the text itself, tap the + button or – button on the Margin line.**

14. **When you finish formatting the text box, tap in the document to close the Format panel.**

Formatting a text box on iCloud

Here's how to format a text box on iCloud:

1. **Click the text box to select it.** To format two or more text boxes at once, click the first text box, and then Shift+click each of the others.

2. **If the Format panel isn't displayed, click the Format button on the toolbar and choose Settings ⇨ Show Format Panel to display it.**

3. **Click the Shape button to display the Shape pane.**

4. **At the top of the Shape pane, click the text box style to apply.**

5. **Use the Fill, Border, Shadow, Reflection, and Opacity controls to adjust the text box as needed.**

6. **Click the Text button to display the Text pane.**

7. **Use the Paragraph Style list at the top of the pane to apply a style to each paragraph in the text box that needs to be formatted differently from the text-box style.**

8. **Use the remaining controls in the Text pane to apply any other formatting needed.** For example, you may need to apply direct formatting to pick out specific words or phrases in the text box.

9. **Click the Arrange button to display the Arrange pane.**

10. **Use the controls in the Arrange pane to adjust the text box's position, size, and rotation as needed.** You can also group the text box with other objects or ungroup it from them.

Flowing text and arranging text boxes on OS X

On OS X, Pages provides four commands that enable you to flow text from one text box to another on a page and to create complex shapes by placing text boxes so that they overlap. These buttons for these commands appear at the bottom of the Arrange pane in the Format inspector when you select two or more text boxes; at other times, the buttons simply don't appear.

These are the four commands and how to use them:

- **Unite.** Select two or more text boxes and click this button to unite the text boxes so that text flows along them. Flowing text like this can save a huge amount of time over adjusting the text in a series of text boxes manually, and it can save you from mistakes such as extra words or missing words.

- **Intersect.** Arrange two or more text boxes so that their intersection covers the area you want to keep. Then click the Intersect button to remove all parts of the text boxes except for the intersection.

● **Subtract.** Create a text box and position it where you want it to appear. Create another text box and position it overlapping the first text box to indicate the part you want to remove from the first text box. Click this button to cut out the overlapped part. The remainder of the second text box disappears. If the first text box has a border, it runs along the part you've cut out.

● **Exclude.** Arrange two or more text boxes with an overlap. Click the Exclude button to exclude the overlapping parts. This is a handy way of creating more complex shapes using text boxes.

The Unite, Intersect, Subtract, and Exclude features are clever and can be helpful in creating document layouts. However, at this writing, these features are limited, suffering from the following main problems:

● **You can only use these commands with text boxes that appear on the same page.** If there is a page break between the text boxes, you can select them, and the commands appear to be available; but clicking the buttons has no effect. This limitation makes sense for Intersect, Subtract, and Exclude, but it is a big loss for Unite, because it means that you cannot flow text from a text box on one page to a text box on another.

● **After you choose the Unite, Intersect, Subtract, or Exclude command, you cannot resize or move the individual text boxes; instead, the text boxes work as a single unit that you can move or resize.** So, to make this feature work, you must size and place your text boxes correctly before giving the command.

● **There is no way to remove the effect of these commands on text boxes except by choosing the Undo command while it is still available in the Undo buffer.**

Inserting Footnotes and Endnotes

If you need to provide references to the material your document cites, you can add notes to it. Pages for OS X enables you to create footnotes and endnotes in your word-processing documents. At this writing, Pages for iOS currently supports creating only footnotes but can display endnotes. Pages for iCloud supports creating neither footnotes nor endnotes, but displays both.

Genius

Pages doesn't let you insert footnotes in page-layout documents. If you need to add notes to a page-layout document, use this workaround: Add a superscript number (or a symbol) to mark the note, and then add a text box containing the note text at the bottom of the page. If you want to create an endnote rather than a footnote, place the note text at the end of the document.

Choosing between footnotes and endnotes

On OS X, Pages enables you to create either of the following in a document:

- **Footnotes.** A footnote appears at the bottom of the page that includes the text to which the note refers. (Sometimes a footnote may need to be continued to the next page of the document.) Footnotes are great for providing reference information the reader can find easily, without having to turn pages, but if you have many footnotes, long footnotes, or both, page layout can become difficult.

- **Endnotes.** An endnote appears at the end of the document that includes the text to which the note refers. If the document is broken up into sections, you can place the endnotes at the end of each section instead. Choose endnotes when you don't want to shorten your pages with notes, when you are including notes that you think many readers will not bother to read (for example, academic citations), or when the document contains enough notes to make page layout tricky.

Unlike most word-processing applications, Pages doesn't let you use both footnotes and endnotes in the same document. This saves confusion, because once you've started using one type of note, you cannot accidentally use the other type. However, you can convert all footnotes to endnotes, or all endnotes to footnotes, so starting with the wrong type of note isn't a disaster.

Genius

To choose which type of notes a document uses on OS X, you use the Footnotes pane in the Format panel. Pages makes the Footnotes pane available only when a document contains footnotes or endnotes, so to be able to choose between the types of notes, you must first insert a footnote.

Working with footnotes and endnotes on OS X

This section shows you how to insert footnotes in your documents in Pages on OS X, choose between footnotes and endnotes, and format your footnotes. Here's how to insert a footnote on OS X:

1. **Place the insertion point where you want the footnote to appear.** Normally, you want to place the insertion point after the word, or the last word in the phrase, to which the footnote refers.

2. **Choose Insert ⇨ Footnote.** Pages inserts a footnote number at the position of the insertion point, displays the bottom of the current page (if it's not already visible), and inserts the corresponding footnote number to start the footnote.

3. **Type the text of the footnote.**

Once your document contains one or more footnotes, you can choose among footnotes and endnotes, and set the format, numbering, and spacing for them. Follow these steps:

1. **Position the insertion point in a footnote.**

Genius

You can double-click a footnote mark in the document body to go to that footnote in the footnote area or endnote area.

2. **If the Format panel isn't displayed, click the Format button on the toolbar to display it.**

3. **Click the Footnotes button to display the Footnotes pane.**

4. **Click the Type pop-up menu (see Figure 5.12), and then click Footnotes, Document Endnotes, or Section Endnotes, as needed.** Pages changes the existing notes to the type you select.

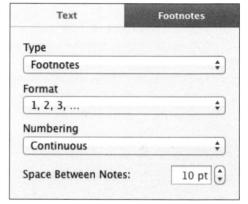

5.12 Use the controls in the Footnotes pane to choose which type of notes your document has, how to number them, and whether the numbering is continuous.

5. **In the Format pop-up menu, choose one of the following number formats:**

   - Your choices are 1, 2, 3; i, ii, iii; or symbols (the asterisk, or the dagger, double-dagger, and section-mark characters, and so on).

   - Symbols can be effective for footnotes but are highly confusing for endnotes because the reader must know the page number as well as the symbol.

6. **In the Numbering pop-up menu, choose how to number the notes.** Your choices are:

   - **Continuous.** Pages increases the numbers throughout the document or section. This is the best choice when your document contains many notes.

   - **Restarts on Each Page.** Choose this option when you're using symbols to identify footnotes. Don't use this option for endnotes — it's a recipe for confusion.

   - **Restarts for Each Section.** Choose this option when your document is divided into sections and you're placing endnotes at the end of each one rather than the end of the document.

7. **In the Space Between Notes box, you can adjust the amount of space to leave between notes.** The default value, 10 points, works well for many documents.

Note

> To delete a footnote or endnote, select its number or mark in the text, and then press Delete.

Working with footnotes on iOS

This section shows you how to insert footnotes in your Pages documents on iOS and how to format your footnotes. Here's how to insert a footnote on iOS:

1. **Place the insertion point where you want the footnote to appear.** For example, place the insertion point after the last word to which the footnote refers.

2. **Open the Insert panel in one of the following ways:**
   - **iPad.** Tap the + button in the upper-right corner of the on-screen keyboard (see Figure 5.13).
   - **iPhone or iPod touch.** Touch and hold after the word to display the pop-up control bar, and then tap Insert. In portrait mode, you may need to tap the right-arrow button to reach the part of the control bar that contains the Insert button.

3. **Tap Footnote (see Figure 5.14, which shows the iPhone).** Pages inserts a footnote and displays the footnote area.

4. **Type the text for the footnote.**

5.13 On the iPad, tap the + button in the upper-right corner of the keyboard to display the Insert panel.

Once your document contains one or more footnotes, you can set the format, numbering, and spacing for them. Follow these steps:

1. **Tap to position the insertion point in a footnote.**

2. **Tap the Format button to display the Footnotes panel (on the iPad) or the Footnotes pane (on the iPhone or iPod touch).**

3. **To apply font formatting, tap the Bold, Italic, Underline, or Strikethrough buttons (see Figure 5.15).**

4. **To change the font size, tap the arrow buttons on the Size control.**

5. **To change the color, tap the Color swatch.**

6. **To change the font, tap the Font button, and then choose the font in the Fonts panel or Fonts pane.** As usual, you can tap the Info (i) button to choose a font style, such as Oblique or Bold.

7. **Return to your document by tapping outside the Footnotes panel or the Footnotes pane.** On the iPhone or iPod touch, you can also tap the Done button.

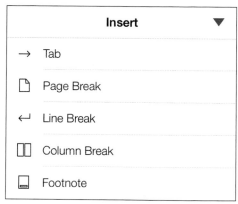

5.14 On the iPhone or iPod touch, tap Footnote in the Insert panel to insert a footnote.

5.15 Format your footnotes with the controls in the Footnotes panel on the iPad (shown here), or the Footnotes pane on the iPhone or iPod touch.

Note

To delete a footnote on iOS, place the insertion point after it, and then press Delete.

Tracking Changes

When you're editing a document on your own, you can usually make changes freely without needing to show what they are. However, when you're editing a document with other people, it's often helpful to track your changes so anyone else editing the document can review them. When you're the one reviewing changes your colleagues have made to a document, the review goes much more quickly if the changes are tracked so they're easy to find.

Without markup, comparing an edited version of a document to the original is slow, laborious work, even for a seasoned editor. Pages' Track Changes feature makes it easy for you to see exactly which changes your colleagues have made to a document.

Note

At this writing, Track Changes works on OS X and iOS but not on iCloud, but Apple is likely to add Track Changes to iCloud before long. OS X has a more full-featured implementation of Track Changes than iOS.

Understanding Track Changes

After you turn on Track Changes for a document, Pages tracks text you insert and text you delete. For example, if you type a new word, Pages marks it as an insertion; if you select a sentence, and then press Delete, Pages marks it as a deletion.

Genius

When you move text by cutting it from one point in a document and pasting it into another point, Pages marks the cut as a deletion and the paste as an insertion. This makes sense, but some other word-processing applications (for example, Microsoft Word) mark a move operation within the same document using different formatting than deletions and insertions, enabling you to see that moved text has come from within the document.

When Track Changes is turned on, Pages marks the changes anyone makes in the document. Pages uses these markings:

- **Change bar.** A vertical bar appears to the left of any changed line (see Figure 5.16). The color of the change bar shows which author made the change.

- **Color text.** Inserted text appears in a different color from the regular text font.

- **Strikethrough color text.** Deleted text appears in strikethrough.

Pages automatically assigns a different color to the first seven people who edit a document with Track Changes on. To change the color used for the changes you're making, click the Markup View

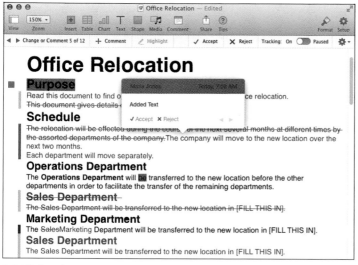

5.16 Deleted text appears in color strikethrough and inserted text appears in color.

button at the right end of the tracking bar, highlight Author Color, and then click the color you want to use. Your choices are Yellow, Green, Blue, Pink, Purple, Teal (blue-green), Orange, and Gray.

By default, Pages displays all the markup (the tracked changes) on the screen, enabling you to see each insertion, deletion, and comment. However, when you need to focus on the text rather than the changes, you can view the markup without deletions or simply view the final version of the text. These are your options for viewing the text:

- **Markup.** Choose this setting to view all the markup. This is the default.

- **Markup Without Deletions.** Choose this setting to see insertions and comments but not deleted text. This setting is useful for reading through the revised text and making sure it is complete. Having the deleted text visible can make it hard to read the remaining text, especially when there are many deletions.

- **Final.** Choose this setting to see how the final document will look if you accept all the revisions. By looking at the document without any of the markup, you can focus on the content and identify any remaining problems.

Caution At this writing, Track Changes does not track changes to formatting or to objects. This is limited compared to the Track Changes feature in Pages '09 (the previous version of Pages for OS X) and to change-tracking features in Microsoft Word, OpenOffice.org, or LibreOffice.

After you turn on Track Changes for a document, you cannot turn off Track Changes unless you accept or reject all the changes in the document. However, you can pause Track Changes if you need to make some changes without having Pages track them.

Working with Track Changes on OS X

Pages implements Track Changes differently on OS X than on iOS. In this section, you learn how to turn on Track Changes on OS X, review tracked changes, and turn off Tracked Changes. To turn on Track Changes, choose Edit ⇨ Track Changes. You can then start editing the text of the document, and Pages tracks the insertions and deletions you make.

When you turn on Track Changes, Pages displays the tracking bar below the toolbar (if it's displayed). Figure 5.17 shows the tracking bar, which provides controls for what you see, navigating among the tracked changes, and accepting or rejecting changes.

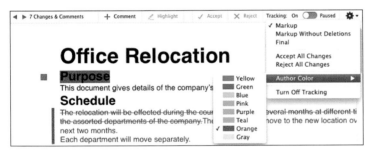

5.17 The tracking bar appears below the toolbar and gives you easy-to-reach control of Track Changes.

These are the controls on the tracking bar, from left to right:

- **Previous Change button.** Click this button to move to the previous tracked change.

- **Next Change button.** Click this button to move to the next tracked change.

- **Changes & Comments readout.** View this readout to see how many tracked changes and comments the document contains (for example, 7 Changes & Comments). When you select a change or comment, the readout shows which one it is — for example, Change or Comment 4 of 7.

- **Comment button.** Click this button to add a comment at the current position of the insertion point or at the current selection.

- **Highlight button.** Click this button to turn on highlighting.

- **Accept button.** Click this button to accept the selected change.

- **Reject button.** Click this button to reject the selected change.

Tracking Your Own Changes in Different Colors

Sometimes you may need to set up Pages to track some of your own changes in a different color so that you can identify them easily. For example, if you revise a document in two stages, you may want to distinguish the first stage from the second.

To do this, save and close the document, change your Author name, and then reopen the document. Pages then tracks the changes using the new author name and a different color. If you simply change the author name without closing the document, Pages also assigns your existing changes to the new author name.

To change your Author name on Pages for OS X, choose Pages ➪ Preferences, click General, and then type the name in the Author box. To change your Author name on iOS, tap the Tools button on the toolbar, tap Settings, and then tap Author Name.

Remember to restore your original author name after you finish working with this document.

● **Tracking switch.** Move this switch to Paused to turn off tracking temporarily. Move the switch back to On when you want to resume tracking.

● **Track Changes pop-up menu.** Use this menu to take other actions with Track Changes. You can switch among viewing the markup, viewing the markup without deletions, and viewing the final text without the markup or deletions. You can also accept or reject all changes in the document, pick the color used for an author's changes, or turn off tracking.

To turn off Track Changes for a document, you must accept or reject all the tracked changes. You cannot turn Track Changes off and leave tracked changes in the document the way you can with other apps, such as Microsoft Word.

Normally, it is best to review the tracked changes as described in the previous section before choosing Edit ➪ Turn Off Tracking to turn off Track Changes. If the document still contains tracked changes when you choose this command, Pages displays the Turn Off Change Tracking dialog (see Figure 5.18). Click Accept All Changes to accept all the remaining changes, click Reject All Changes to reject them, or click Cancel to close the dialog and return to the document so you can review the changes individually.

5.18 In the Turn Off Change Tracking dialog, you can click Accept All Changes, Reject All Changes, or Cancel.

Working with Track Changes on iOS

On iOS, you can easily turn Track Changes on and off and review changes. On the iPad, you can also choose which tracked changes to display. Here's how to turn on Track Changes on iOS:

1. **Tap the Tools button to display the Tools panel (on the iPad) or the Tools screen (on the iPhone or iPod touch).**

2. **Tap Change Tracking to display the Change Tracking panel (on the iPad) or the Change Tracking screen (on the iPhone or iPod touch).** Figure 5.19 shows the Change Tracking panel on the iPad, which includes controls for configuring Track Changes; the Change Tracking screen on the iPhone and iPod touch contains only the Tracking switch at this writing.

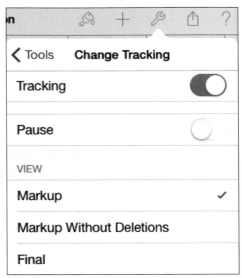

5.19 Set the Tracking switch to On to turn on Track Changes on iOS.

Note On the iPad, you can set the Pause switch on the Change Tracking panel to On to pause Track Changes while you make any changes you do not want to have tracked. In the View section of the panel, choose your Track Changes view by touching Markup, Markup Without Deletions, or Final, as needed.

3. **Set the Tracking switch to On.**

4. **Return the focus to the document:**
   - **iPad.** Tap outside the Change Tracking panel to close the panel.
   - **iPhone or iPod touch.** Tap Done to close the Change Tracking screen.

To accept and reject changes on iOS, touch a change. On the iPad, a pop-up window appears containing the details of the change; on the iPhone or iPod touch, the change appears in a pane at the bottom of the screen (see Figure 5.20).

Tap Accept to accept the change or Reject to reject it. Tap the Previous (<) button or Next (>) button to navigate from change to change. When you finish reviewing changes, tap Done on the iPhone or iPod touch. On the iPad, simply tap outside the current pop-up window.

elocation

find out what you need to do during the offi
~~etails of the company's office relocation.~~

~~ffected during the~~ |course of the next sever~~a~~
~~its of the company.~~The company will move

ove separately.

partment

~~tment~~ will **be** transferred to the new locatio
facilitate the transfer of the remaining dep

ent

~~will be transferred to the new location in [F~~

artment

Maria Jones	Done

Today, 7:06 AM

Deleted: The relocation will be effected during
the course of the next several months at
different times by the assorted departments of...

Accept   Reject

5.20 On iOS, you can quickly review, accept, and reject changes by using
the changes pane on the iPhone or iPod touch (shown here),
or the pop-up window on the iPad.

To turn off Track Changes for a document, you must accept or reject all the tracked changes. Normally, it is best to review the tracked changes individually, accepting or deleting each as necessary, before turning off tracked changes. However, if the level of changes is light, you may be comfortable accepting (or rejecting) them all in a single move. Here's how to turn off Track Changes on iOS:

1. **Tap the Tools button to display the Tools panel (on the iPad) or the Tools screen (on the iPhone or iPod touch).**

2. **Tap Change Tracking to display the Change Tracking panel (on the iPad) or the Change Tracking screen (on the iPhone or iPod touch).**

3. **Set the Tracking switch to Off.** If the document contains no tracked changes, Pages turns Track Changes off without comment. However, if the document contains any tracked changes, Pages displays the Turn Off Tracking dialog.

4. **Tap the appropriate button (see Figure 5.21):**

   - **Accept All Changes.** Tap this button to accept all the remaining changes without reviewing them.

   - **Reject All Changes.** Tap this button to reject all the remaining changes without reviewing them.

   - **Cancel.** Tap this button to close the dialog without accepting or rejecting the changes. You can then review the changes individually.

> **Turn Off Tracking**
> To turn off change tracking, you must accept or reject all changes.
>
> Accept All Changes
>
> Reject All Changes
>
> Cancel

5.21 In the Turn Off Change Tracking dialog, tap Accept All Changes, Reject All Changes, or Cancel, as needed.

Exchanging tracked changes with Microsoft Word

Pages' Track Changes feature is compatible with Microsoft Word's Track Changes feature for insertions and deletions, but Pages doesn't accurately show the other changes that Word marks. When you import a Word document that contains tracked changes into Pages, you lose tracking for other items, such as these:

- **Moved text.** Pages shows the moved text in its destination as inserted text, but the source text doesn't appear at all.

- **Formatting.** Pages shows the changed formatting, but does not retain the change tracking.

- **Objects.** Pages doesn't show change tracking on inserted objects.

When you export a Pages document containing tracked changes to Word format, all the changes — insertions, deletions, and comments — appear correctly in Word.

What Extra Features Do I Get Using Pages on OS X?

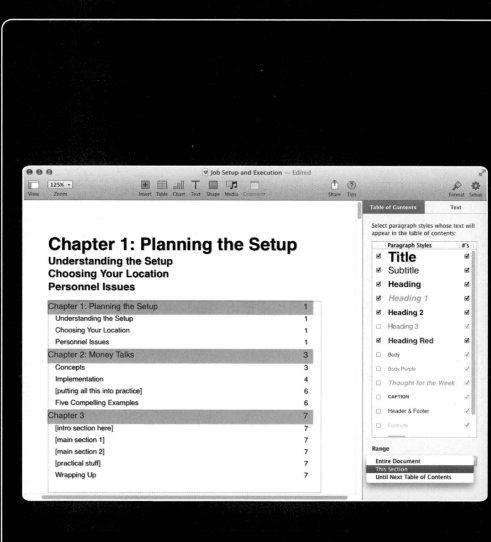

As covered in Chapters 4 and 5, Pages is a great app for creating good-looking documents on your Mac, your iOS device, or on iCloud. However, if you're using Pages mostly on your Mac, you can take advantage of extra features in the OS X version of Pages that the iOS and iCloud versions don't have. This chapter explains how to use these features, which include creating sections and tables of contents, customizing and creating styles, and building your own templates. This chapter also digs into considerations for working extensively with Microsoft Word documents.

Customizing the Pages Window

To work most effectively in Pages, you most likely want to customize the app's window to suit your needs. Compared to Pages '09, Pages 5 offers only a small amount of customization — but you can still control the zoom, use page thumbnails for quick navigation, and control the display of invisible characters.

Zooming in and out

You can zoom in and out on your documents on any of the iWork platforms, but Pages for OS X also gives you more flexible zoom. The Zoom pop-up menu on the toolbar gives you three main ways to zoom:

- **Fixed zoom increments.** Click 25%, 50%, 75%, 100%, 125%, 150%, 200%, 300%, or 400%, as needed.
- **Fit Width.** Click this menu item to zoom to fit the page's width in the Pages window.
- **Fit Page.** Click this menu item to fit the entire page in the Pages window.

The Zoom pop-up menu on the toolbar is often the easiest way to zoom, but you can also choose View ➪ Zoom and use the commands on the Zoom submenu. If you prefer to keep your hands on the keyboard, you can use the keyboard shortcuts explained in Table 6.1.

Table 6.1 Keyboard Shortcuts for Zooming in Pages for OS X

Keyboard Shortcut	Effect
⌘+>	Zoom in by one step
⌘+<	Zoom out by one step
⌘+0	Zoom to actual size (100%)
Shift+⌘+0	Zoom to fit the selected object or objects.

Navigating your documents with page thumbnails

When you work in a long document, take advantage of the page thumbnails feature for navigating quickly to the different parts of the document. The page thumbnails appear in a pane on the left side of the document window. You can display the page thumbnails in any of these ways:

- **Toolbar.** Click the View button and then click Show Page Thumbnails on the pop-up menu. Choose Hide Page Thumbnails when you want to hide the thumbnails again.

- **Menu bar.** Choose View ➪ Show Page Thumbnails or View ➪ Hide Page Thumbnails.
- **Keyboard.** Press Option+⌘+P to toggle the display of the thumbnails.

After displaying the page thumbnails pane (see Figure 6.1), simply click the page you want to display.

6.1 Use the page thumbnails pane to navigate quickly among the pages in a long document.

Note You can drag the right border of the page thumbnails pane to widen it (and enlarge the thumbnails) or narrow it (and shrink the thumbnails). Drag the border all the way to the left to hide the page thumbnails pane quickly.

Working with invisible characters and viewing a layout

As well as the regular letters, numbers, and other characters that you can see, each Pages document contains characters, such as spaces and tabs, which normally have no visible presence. Apple calls such characters *invisibles* and provides a command for displaying them, which can help you clear up layout problems in your documents: Seeing where extra spaces, tabs, or breaks appear makes it much easier to delete them or move them.

To display invisible characters, choose View ⇨ Show Invisibles from the menu bar or press Shift+⌘+I. Figure 6.2 shows a document with invisible characters displayed.

When you work on the layout of a document (as opposed to the content), you may find it helpful to view the layout boundaries. To do so, choose View ⇨ Show Layout from the menu bar or press Shift+⌘+L. You can then rearrange the layout boxes (see Figure 6.3) as needed. Choose View ⇨ Hide Layout from the menu bar or press Shift+⌘+L when you want to hide the layout boundaries again.

Spaces·appear·as·blue·dots·between·words.¶

A·nonbreaking·space·appears·as·a·blue·dot·with·a·caret·over·it,·like·this:character.¶

A·tab·appears·as·an·arrow: → ¶

A·line·break·appears·as·an·arrow:·↵
¶

A·paragraph·break·appears·as·a·pilcrow·character:¶

A·page·break·appears·as·a·blue·line·with·a·page·symbol:

6.2 Choose View ⇨ Show Invisibles from the menu bar when you want to see normally invisible characters, such as spaces, tabs, and paragraph marks.

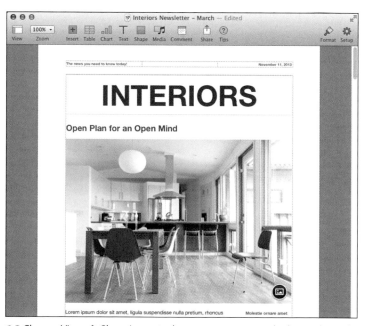

6.3 Choose View ⇨ Show Layout when you want to see the layout boundaries in a document.

Breaking Your Document into Sections

To create documents with different layouts, you can use sections. A section is an invisible division that makes it easier to implement different layouts in different parts of a document. Some of Pages' templates include multiple sections, so even if you haven't created any sections manually, you may already be using sections.

Genius

Each section in a document can have different page numbers, headers and footers, or background images. So, if you want to implement different headers or footers on different pages, or have page numbers in some parts of the document but not in others, you need to use separate sections.

Viewing and combining existing sections, or creating a new one

The easy way to see where the existing sections in a document are is to use the page thumbnails pane. Press Option+⌘+P or click the View button on the toolbar, and then click Show Page Thumbnails to open the page thumbnails pane. You can also choose View ⇨ Show Page Thumbnails from the menu bar. Then, click a thumbnail to make Pages display a yellow outline around the pages in the section (see Figure 6.4).

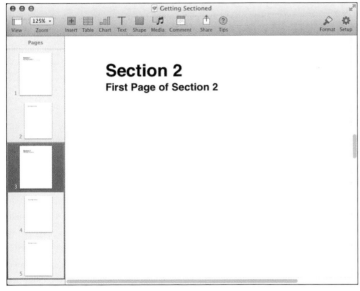

6.4 Click a page thumbnail to display a yellow outline around all the pages in a section.

Genius

In the page thumbnails pane, the first page of each section has a larger thumbnail than the other pages.

If you want to move the pages from two separate sections into a single section, delete the section break that separates them. Normally, it's easiest to delete the section break by displaying invisibles so you can see what you're doing, but you can also simply place the insertion point at the beginning of the second section and press Delete to delete the section break.

Note

To see where the section breaks are in a document, turn on the display of invisibles by choosing View ⇨ Show Invisibles or pressing Shift+⌘+I.

To create a new section, insert a section break. Place the insertion point on the page before or after which you want to start the new section, and then choose Insert ⇨ Section. Pages inserts a section break and places the insertion point in the new section.

Note

Instead of inserting a section break, you can insert a new section in the document at the position of the insertion point. Place the insertion point, and then choose Insert ⇨ Section.

Controlling the headers, footers, and page numbers in a section

To control the headers, footers, and page numbers in a section of a document, work in the Section pane of the Document Setup inspector like this:

1. **Click the Setup button on the toolbar to display the Document Setup inspector.** You can also choose View ⇨ Inspector ⇨ Document Setup from the menu bar.

2. **If the Document pane is displayed at first, click the Section button to display the Section pane.**

3. **In the Headers & Footers area, select the Hide on first page of section check box if you want to suppress the header and footer on the first page.**

4. **Deselect the Match previous section check box if you want to give this section a different header and footer.** Once you make this change, you can create a new header or footer in this section without affecting the header or footer in the previous section.

Caution

Don't create a new header or footer in a section before you deselect the Match previous section check box in the Section pane of the Document Setup inspector. If you do, it overwrites the previous section's existing header or footer, which you presumably want to keep.

5. **Click the Page Numbering pop-up menu, and then choose the page number format you want (see Figure 6.5).**

6. **If you've finished working with the Document Setup inspector, click the Setup button on the toolbar or press Option+⌘+I to hide it.** If you prefer, leave the inspector open for future use.

Creating a Table of Contents

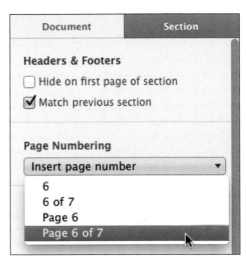

6.5 Use the Section pane in the Document Setup inspector to control the headers, footers, and page numbers in a section.

When you create a long document, it's a good idea to provide an easy means of navigation. Pages enables you to insert a table of contents and customize it to contain the elements you want. Pages identifies the paragraphs to pick up for the table of contents by their styles, which is another argument for using styles as your primary means of formatting — and for applying them consistently.

Here's how to insert a table of contents:

1. **Place the insertion point where you want the table of contents.** For most documents, you probably want to place the table of contents near the beginning of either the document or the section.

2. **Choose Insert ⇨ Table of Contents to display the Table of Contents submenu.**

3. **Click the type of table of contents you want:**
    - **Document.** Click this item to create a table of contents for the entire document.
    - **Section.** Click this item to create a table of contents for just this section of the document.
    - **To Next Occurrence.** Click this item to create a table of contents from here to wherever you place the next table of contents. This is useful for a long document that needs more than one table of contents, but isn't broken up into long sections.

4. **After Pages inserts the table of contents, use the Table of Contents pane (which Pages displays automatically) to choose which styles to include.** Select a style's check box to include it (see Figure 6.6), and deselect all the other check boxes.

201

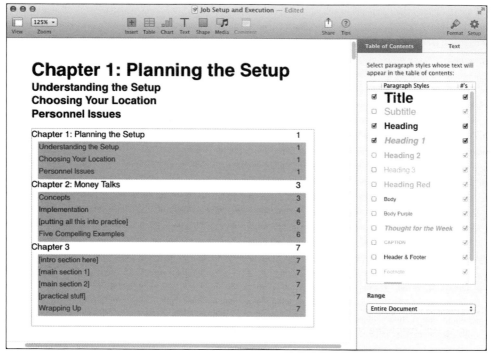

6.6 Use the Table of Contents pane to control which styles and page numbers appear in the table of contents.

5. **For each style you include in the table of contents, select the check box in the #'s column on the right if you want to include the page number.** Clear the check box to exclude the page number.

Note

Pages updates the table of contents automatically as you work. If you need to change the styles or page numbers included, click in the table of contents, display the Format inspector, and then work in the Table of Contents pane. Use the Range pop-up menu if you need to change the table of contents' type among Document, Section, and To Next Occurrence.

Working with Styles

As covered in Chapter 3, a *style* is a collection of formatting that you can apply in a single click. Pages provides *paragraph styles* for formatting entire paragraphs and *character styles* for formatting anything from a single character up.

The best way to format your documents is by applying a paragraph style to each paragraph, and then using either a character style or direct formatting to add any extra formatting needed on top of the paragraph style. For example, to create a first-level heading in a document, you would normally apply the Heading style. If a word in that heading needs emphasis, you can apply a character style (such as the Italic character style) to it, or apply direct formatting (such as Shadow formatting).

When you apply direct formatting on top of a style, you create a *style override*. After creating a style override, you can either update the style to incorporate the override or clear the override, restoring the current version of the style by removing the extra formatting.

Creating, updating, renaming, deleting, and importing styles

As covered in Chapter 3, you can update, rename, and delete existing styles, as needed. You can also create your own styles. Here's a quick recap:

- **Update a style.** Click in a paragraph that has the style, change it as needed, and then click Update on the Style pop-up menu in the Format inspector.

- **Rename a style.** In the Format inspector, click the Style pop-up menu, move the mouse pointer over the style's name, and then click the > button. Click Rename Style, type the new name for the style, and then press Return.

- **Delete a style.** In the Format inspector, click the Style pop-up menu, move the mouse pointer over the style's name, and then click the > button. Click Delete Style, choose the replacement style in the dialog that opens, and then click OK.

- **Create a style.** Apply to a paragraph the style on which you want to base the new style, click the Style pop-up menu in the Format inspector, and then click the + button. Type the name for the new style and press Return. You can then change the style's formatting as needed and update the style.

If you have Microsoft Word documents or templates that contain styles you need, you can import them into Pages. To do so, open the Word document or template in Pages, and then either use the Save command to save the document or template as a Pages document or use the Save as Template command to save it as a template.

Setting the Following Paragraph Style

In Pages, styles include a setting called Following Paragraph Style, which you can set using the Following Paragraph Style pop-up menu in the More pane in the Format inspector (see Figure 6.7).

By setting Following Paragraph Style carefully, you can create sequences of styles that apply themselves automatically as you type one paragraph after another. Here are three examples:

- **Title sequence.** Title style, Subtitle style, Introduction First style, Introduction style.

- **Heading sequence.** Heading style, Body Text First style, Body Text style.

- **Figure sequence.** Figure style, Figure Caption style, Production Directive style, Body Text style.

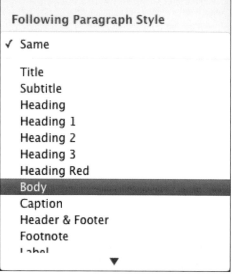

6.7 Open the Following Paragraph Style pop-up menu in the More pane of the Format inspector.

Genius

Your style sequences depend entirely on the styles you create and the templates in which you use them. However, in general, a display style (such as Title or Heading) requires a different style for the following paragraph, whereas a body style (such as, well, Body) requires the same style.

Sharing styles among documents

If you create styles that please you, chances are you want to share them among your documents and templates. At this writing, Pages doesn't provide any formal mechanism for copying or moving styles from one document or template to another, but here are a couple of work-arounds:

- **Paste paragraphs, and then create a new style.** Copy one or more paragraphs containing styles from the source document or template and paste them into the destination document or template. Pages carries across the formatting but not the style names. You can then create a new style based on each different source style.

- **Base one template on another.** If you want to copy the full set of styles in one template to another template you're creating, create a new document based on the source template, and then save the document as the destination template. See the next section for details on templates.

Creating Your Own Templates

As you know by now, a template is a file that forms the basis for a document. Some templates contain only formatting, such as the document size, margins, and styles. Other templates contain an almost-complete document in which you need only fill in some fields before saving it as a finished document.

Pages includes a strong selection of templates to give you a jump-start on creating many different kinds of documents, but you can save even more time by creating your own templates that contain exactly the styles and boilerplate text you need.

Here's how to create a template:

1. **Create a document.** You can either use a blank document as the basis for the template or start the contents of an existing template — whichever approach is quicker and easier for you.

2. **Add to the document all the text, objects, styles, and layout you need for the template.**

3. **Choose File ⇨ Save As Template.** Pages displays the Create a custom Pages template? dialog.

4. **Click Add to Template Chooser (see Figure 6.8) If you want to add the template to the Template Chooser.** This is normally what you want to do because it gives you an easy way to create new documents based on the template. The Template Chooser then appears.

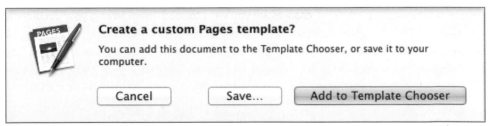

Create a custom Pages template?

You can add this document to the Template Chooser, or save it to your computer.

| Cancel | Save... | Add to Template Chooser |

6.8 Click Add to Template Chooser in the Create a custom Pages template? dialog if you want to add the new template to the Template Chooser for easy access.

Note If you're creating a template for someone else, you probably won't want to add it to the Template Chooser. In the Create a custom Pages template? dialog, click Save, and then choose the folder in which to save the template.

5. **Type the name you want the template to have, and then press Return (see Figure 6.9).**

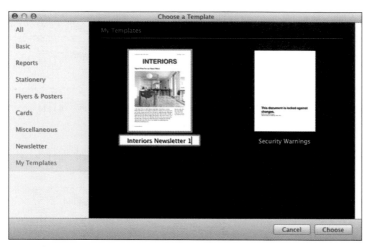

6.9 In the Template Chooser, type the name for the new template, and then press Return.

6. **Click Cancel to close the Template Chooser.**

As covered previously, creating a template is easy. The hard part is deciding what to include in it. Bear these five suggestions in mind when planning your templates:

- **Jot down exactly what your template will do and who will use it.** This will help you to include everything the template needs and make it as useful as possible. At this planning stage, you may realize that you need to create two (or more) related templates rather than just one.

- **Base your templates on Pages' built-in templates wherever feasible.** There's no point in reinventing the wheel, and you can often save time by adapting an existing template rather than starting from scratch. For example, if you're creating a template for a business letter, see if you can use one of Pages' letter templates as the basis.

- **Make your template as close to the final document as possible.** This may seem to be stating the obvious, but you'd be amazed how many people go only partway with templates. For example, say you're creating templates to help reps respond quickly and accurately to customer-service queries. Having a separate template for each major topic helps the reps create the letters faster and more easily than one general-purpose template in which they need to type more text for each letter. (You can also create text-replacement entries to help your colleagues enter essential information in documents quickly and accurately.)

Genius

Normally a template contains *less* material than the final document requires — but you can frequently save time by creating a template that contains *more* material than the final document. For example, you can create a template that contains three paragraphs of boilerplate text, and then delete those the document doesn't need. Deleting extra material is often faster and easier than inserting new material.

- **Create a sequence of related templates.** Say you produce several different newsletters for your company. You could create a single template and then change the masthead and taglines along with the content for each newsletter, but you could probably save time and effort by creating a separate template for each newsletter.

- **Exploit styles to the fullest.** As discussed earlier in this chapter, use the Following Paragraph Style setting to help ensure that the person creating the document needs to apply styles manually as little as possible.

Working with Microsoft Word Documents

At this writing, Microsoft Word is the most widely used word-processing program and runs on both Windows and the Mac. For compatibility, Pages can import Word documents and export its own documents in the Word format.

Note

Pages can open documents in both the .docx file format (the default format for Word 2007 on Windows, Word 2008 on the Mac, and later versions) and the .doc file format (the default format for Word 2003 on Windows, Word 2004 on the Mac, and earlier versions). The .docx file format is technically superior, notably because it is less likely to suffer corruption than the .doc file format, but many people still use the .doc format.

To work with a Word document in Pages, simply open it as you would any other document: Press ⌘+O or choose File ⇨ Open to display the Open dialog, select the document, and then click Open. From the Finder, you can Control+click (or right-click) the document, and then choose Open With ⇨ Pages from the shortcut menu. Pages tries to convert all the document's contents to equivalents in Pages' own formats, which takes a few seconds (depending on how large and complex the document is).

Genius

Just to be clear — you cannot open a Word document in Pages, edit it there, and then save your changes to the original Word document, as you might do using Word itself, OpenOffice.org or LibreOffice, or another word processor. Instead, you have to save the document as a Pages document; if you want a Word version of that document, you can export a version of the document to Word.

Overall, Pages does a solid job of importing Word documents, and imports all of the following items successfully:

- **Text paragraphs.** Pages can import just about any text paragraph from Microsoft Word, including styles, tables, and lists.

- **Footnotes and endnotes.** Pages imports these correctly. You may run into problems with longer documents that contain many notes and those in which you've switched footnotes to endnotes, endnotes to footnotes, or each kind of note to the other.

- **Hyperlinks.** Pages imports these correctly.

- **Tracked changes.** Pages imports the details of deleted text and inserted text, including the time and the user who made the changes. Because Pages itself marks only deleted text and inserted text, Pages marks any moved text in the Word document as a deletion in its old position (before you moved it) and an insertion in its new position. Full details about using tracked changes are in Chapter 5, including exchanging tracked changes with Microsoft Word.

- **Inline objects and floating objects.** Pages imports most text boxes, graphics, charts, and other objects successfully. For example, Pages can handle text boxes that are linked together in Word (so that text flows from one text box, when it's full, to the next).

However, here are some of the things that don't import so well:

- **Bookmarks and cross-references.** Pages removes these from the imported document, but retains their contents. For example, the text of a cross-reference appears, but it will no longer update automatically.

- **Complex tables.** Pages smoothly handles straightforward tables — ones with a regular structure and no nested cells — but nested tables create problems. Pages removes table formulas, retaining only their values. You have to comb through imported tables and make sure everything is where it should be and that all the formulas are working.

- **Charts.** Pages imports Word charts with their underlying data, which is pretty impressive. However, you don't get any links to the data source (for example, a spreadsheet in Excel). It's a good idea to examine each chart closely to make sure that Pages has translated everything successfully.

- **Equations.** Pages removes Word's equations.

These limitations may cause problems if you work with complex Word documents. However, if you mostly work with regular Word documents, such as business letters or reports, Pages' importing capabilities will most likely be good enough.

Usually, the best way to proceed is to open the Word document in Pages and see what you get. The import procedure is nondestructive, leaving the Word document unchanged. So, if you find the Pages document lacks some essential features, you can return to the Word document and figure out another way to transfer them. For example, you might choose to copy and paste an item, and then fix its formatting.

Also, you could change it in Word from an unsupported element to a supported element, and then import the document into Pages again. After a successful import, use the Save command (choose File ⇨ Save or press ⌘+S) to save the Pages document in a new file.

Note

When you need to share a document you've created in Pages with someone who uses Word, choose File ⇨ Export To ⇨ Word.

How Do I Design and Lay Out Spreadsheets in Numbers?

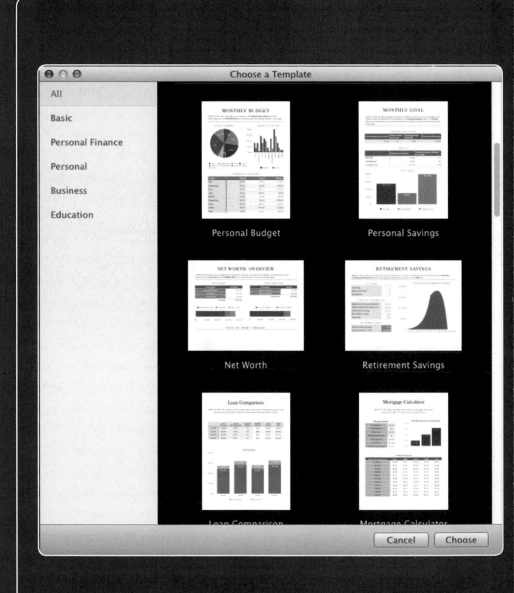

Numbers is a great application for creating powerful, functional, and attractive spreadsheets on your Mac or iOS device, or in iCloud. On each platform, you can quickly create the kind of spreadsheet you need by basing it on a suitable template. You can then input data efficiently by typing it, pasting it, or using the autofill feature to input sequences of data automatically. You can also use sheets and tables to organize the information in your spreadsheet documents logically so that they present data clearly.

Choosing a Suitable Spreadsheet Template

You can build each spreadsheet from scratch if necessary, but usually you can save time and effort by basing each new spreadsheet on a template. This can be one of the templates that Numbers provides, one you create yourself, or one from a third party that you add to Numbers. To choose a template, open the Template Chooser using one of the following techniques you learned in Chapter 2:

- **OS X.** Choose File ⇨ New or press ⌘+N.

Genius

If Numbers on OS X creates a new spreadsheet instead of displaying the Template Chooser when you choose File ⇨ New or press ⌘+N, choose Numbers ⇨ Preferences. In the Preferences window, click the General button to display the General pane, and then click the Show Template Chooser option button in the For New Documents area.

- **iPad.** On the Numbers screen, tap the Create Spreadsheet button.
- **iPhone or iPod touch.** On the Numbers screen, tap the + button in the upper-left corner, and then tap Create Spreadsheet.
- **iCloud.** On the Numbers for iCloud screen, click the Create Spreadsheet button.

You can then select the template in the Template Chooser. Figure 7.1 shows the Choose a Template screen on the iPad. If you want to see the templates in a single category instead of having them all displayed in a single list, tap the Show Categories button and then tap the appropriate category.

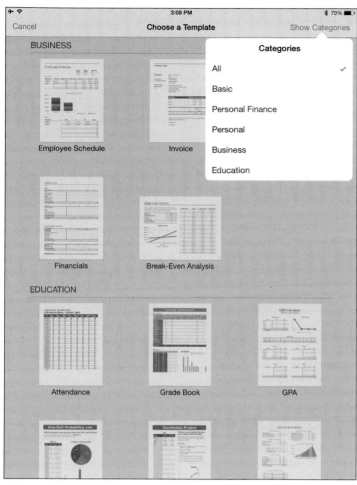

7.1 The Choose a Template screen on iOS.

Inputting Data on a Spreadsheet

You can type or paste data into a table, but Numbers also provides handy features for inputting a series or identical items quickly. Numbers also makes it easy to enter dates and hyperlinks in your tables, and to apply cell formatting to make cell contents appear the way you want them. On the iPad, you can also use a form to add data to a table. The other Numbers platforms don't have this functionality, so make the most of it if you have an iPad.

Inputting data manually

For most spreadsheets, you likely need to input some data manually. Numbers makes data entry as easy as possible, but — as you'd expect — you use different techniques on the different platforms.

Inputting data manually on OS X or in iCloud

Here's how to input data manually on OS X or in iCloud:

1. **Click the cell in which you want to add the data.**

2. **Type the data.**

3. **Press one of the following keys to add the data and select another cell:**

   - **Return.** Numbers selects the next cell down.

   - **Shift+Return.** Numbers selects the next cell up.

   - **Tab.** Numbers selects the cell to the right.

   - **Shift+Tab.** Numbers selects the cell to the left.

   - **Left arrow.** Numbers selects the cell to the left.

   - **Right arrow.** Numbers selects the cell to the right.

   - **Up arrow.** Numbers selects the cell above.

   - **Down arrow.** Numbers selects the cell below.

Here's how to edit the existing data in a cell:

1. **Double-click the cell to open it for editing.**

2. **Position the insertion point in one of the following ways:**

   - **Click to place the insertion point using the mouse.**

   - **Press Left arrow to move the insertion point one character to the left.**

   - **Press Right arrow to move the insertion point one character to the right.**

   - **Press Up arrow to move the insertion point to the beginning of the cell's text.**
     If the text has multiple lines, press Up arrow to move up one line. When the insertion point is in the top line, pressing Up arrow again moves it to the beginning of the text.

   - **Press Down arrow to move the insertion point to the end of the cell's text.** If the text has multiple lines, press Down arrow to move down one line. When the insertion point is in the bottom line, pressing Down arrow again moves it to the end of the text.

3. **Edit the text as needed.**

4. **Press one of the following keys to add the data and select another cell:**

- **Return.** Numbers selects the next cell down.

- **Tab.** Numbers selects the cell to the right.

- **Shift+Tab.** Numbers selects the cell to the left.

Genius

It's often quicker and easier to select a cell and type a new value over the existing value than to open the cell for editing and edit the existing value.

Inputting data manually on iOS

Here's how to add data manually on iOS:

1. **Double-tap the cell in which you want to edit the data.** Numbers displays the keyboard and the Formula Editor.

2. **Tap one of the following buttons to display the keyboard you need:**

- **42.** Tap this button to display the numeric keyboard.

- **Clock.** Tap this button to display the date and time keyboard.

- **T.** Tap this button to display the text keyboard.

- **=.** Tap this button to display the functions keyboard.

3. **Type the data for the cell.**

4. **Tap one of the following buttons to add the data:**

- **Accept (the green circle with the white check mark).** On the iPhone or iPod touch, tap this button to input the data in the cell, stop data entry, and hide the keyboard.

- **Done.** On the iPad, tap this button to input the data in the cell, stop data entry, and hide the keyboard.

- **Next Right.** Tap this button to input the data and select the next cell to the right.

- **Next Down.** Tap this button to input the data and select the next cell down.

To edit the existing data in a cell, double-tap the cell, and then work as explained in the previous list.

Inputting data with autofill

Many tables need predictable sequences of data in adjacent cells. For example, you may need to input a sequence of years in a column or the months of the year in a row, or you may need to input increasing values (such as 5, 10, 15, and so on) in a series of cells.

To help you insert such data quickly, Numbers on OS X and iOS provides a feature called autofill. You select one, two, or more cells that contain the information required to start the series, and then click and drag the autofill handle to tell Numbers which cells you want to fill with the data.

Here's how to use autofill on OS X:

1. **Select the cell or cells that contain the data on which you want to base the autofill.** For example, Figure 7.2 shows three cells selected, with the values 2, 4, and 6.

2. **Move the mouse pointer over the border of the cell in the direction you want to autofill.** Numbers displays a yellow circle on the cell border. You can see this yellow circle in Figure 7.2 on the bottom border of the selection, ready to autofill downward.

3. **Click the yellow circle and drag it in the appropriate direction.** Numbers automatically fills in the sequence. For example, Figure 7.3 shows the selection extended downward. Release the mouse button when you fill all the cells you want to fill.

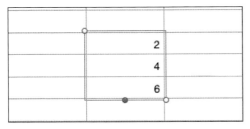

7.2 Select the cells on which you want to base the autofill.

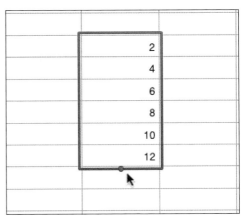

7.3 Drag the yellow circle to autofill the cells.

Here's how to use autofill on iOS:

1. **Select the cell or cells that contain the data you want to use for autofill.** For example, tap a cell to select it. Numbers displays the pop-up control bar (see Figure 7.4).

2. **Tap Fill to display the fill handles around the selection.** At this point, neither the keyboard nor the control bar appears on-screen.

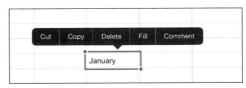

7.4 The pop-up control bar on iOS.

3. **Drag the fill handle (the two parallel lines shown in Figure 7.5) in the direction you want to fill the cells.** Numbers fills in the data. For example, Figure 7.6 shows Numbers filling in the names of the months because the starting cell contained January.

4. **Lift your finger when you reach the cell at which you want to stop filling.**

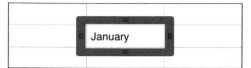

7.5 Drag the fill handle in the direction in which you want to fill the cells.

Here's how to use autofill in iCloud:

1. **Select the cell or cells that contain the data to start the autofill.**

2. **Move the mouse pointer over the lower-right corner of the selection so that the pointer changes to a heavy black cross.**

7.6 Numbers fills in the data as you drag.

3. **Drag through the cells you want to fill.**

4. **Release the mouse button to stop filling the cells.**

Inputting data using forms on the iPad

On the iPad, you can input data by using a form. A *form* in this sense is simply a specialized sheet that contains the fields in a particular table, but it can make data entry much faster and more convenient. Here's how to input data using a form:

1. **Create a table that contains the fields you want to fill in.** For example, Figure 7.7 shows the first fields in a table for collecting data about the participants in a survey, using fields such as First Name, Last Name, State, City, and Age.

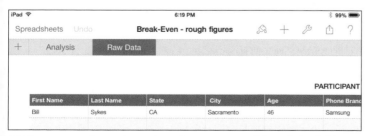

7.7 To prepare to input data using a form, set up a table with the fields you need.

2. **Tap the + button at the left end of the sheets bar to display the New dialog.**

3. **Tap New Form, shown in Figure 7.8.**
Numbers adds a new form called Empty
Form and displays the Choose a Table
screen (see Figure 7.9).

7.8 Tap New Form in the New dialog to create a form.

Note If the document doesn't contain a table, tapping the + button at the left end of the sheets bar causes Numbers to insert a new sheet after the existing ones instead of displaying the New dialog.

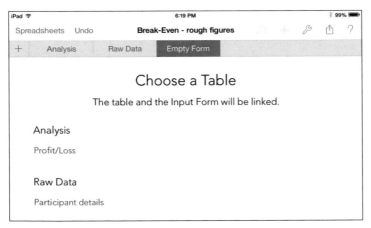

7.9 The Choose a Table screen.

4. **Tap the table to which you want to link the form.** Numbers connects the form to the table, renames the form with the table's name, and then displays the form's fields (see Figure 7.10).

5. **Tap the following buttons at the bottom of the form to navigate the records in the table:**

   - **<.** Tap this button to display the previous record. You can then edit the data as needed.

   - **+.** Tap this button to create a new record. You can then type the data for the record.

   - **Trash.** Tap this button to delete the current record.

   - **>.** Tap this button to display the next record.

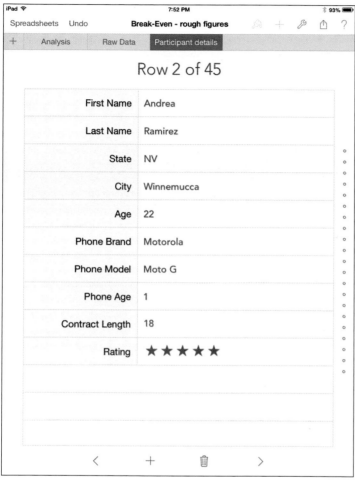

7.10 After connecting the form to the table, you can use the form's fields to input new data or edit existing data.

Inputting dates

Dates can be a real headache for humans to calculate, but Numbers makes them as painless as possible. On iOS, Numbers also provides a special keyboard to help you insert dates easily.

Inputting dates on OS X and in iCloud

You can type a date in a wide variety of formats and have Numbers recognize it. Here are some examples of formats Numbers recognizes:

- 12/13, 12-13, Dec 13, or 13 Dec

Note

If you omit the year when you input a date, Numbers assumes you mean the current year, and adds that year to complete the date.

- 12/13/14, 12-13-14, 13 December 14, 13 Dec 14

- Dec 13, 2014 (with the comma)

- 12/13/2014, 12-13-2014, 13 December 2014

When you input a date in a cell formatted with the Automatic cell format, Numbers automatically displays the date in a standard date format. For example, Numbers typically displays the example date (shown here as December 13, 2014). You can customize the way that Numbers displays dates, as discussed later in this chapter.

Note

If you're used to Excel, you may find Numbers' way of calculating times tricky. Unless you adjust the cell formatting, Numbers assumes you're inputting times in a week-day-hour-minute-second format (for example, 1 week 2 days 3 hours 4 minutes and 5 seconds). When you need to make Numbers calculate only the time, format the cell as hour-minute-second format.

Inputting dates on iOS

To save typing and mistakes, iOS provides a dates keyboard. Here's how to use it:

1. **Double-tap the cell in which you want to input the date.** Numbers displays the keyboard and the Formula Editor.

2. **Tap the clock button to display the date keyboard.**

3. **On the left of the keyboard, you can tap the following buttons:**

   - **Date & Time.** Tap this button to input a date, a time, or both. On the iPad, this button's name appears in full. On the iPhone and iPod touch, the Date & Time button is the one with the 21 icon.

   - **Duration.** Tap this button to input a duration, such as 2 weeks or 3 hours. On the iPad, this button's name appears in full. On the iPhone and iPod touch, the Duration button is the one with the hourglass icon.

4. **Use the controls to input the date, time, or duration.** For example, here's how to input a date:

   a. **Tap the month button in the Formula Editor if it's not already selected.**

   b. **Tap the month for the date.** For example, tap the Jan button for January.

   c. **Tap the day button in the Formula Editor to select it.**

   d. **Type the number for the day.** For example, type 15 for the 15th.

   e. **Tap the year button in the Formula Editor to select it.**

   f. **Type the number for the year.** For example, type 2014.

5. **Tap the Accept button (the green circle containing the white check mark) on the iPhone or iPod touch, or tap the Done button on the iPad, if you're ready to stop inputting data.** Alternatively, move to another cell and continue inputting data.

Adding hyperlinks

For reference, it's often useful to insert hyperlinks in your tables. Numbers lets you create either a hyperlink that opens a browser to a Web address (URL) or a hyperlink that starts a new e-mail message to an e-mail address.

Note At this writing, you cannot add hyperlinks in Numbers for iCloud.

Inputting hyperlinks on Mac OS X

Here's how to enter a hyperlink on OS X and edit it to display text other than the hyperlink's address:

1. **Double-click the cell in which you want to insert the hyperlink.**

Genius If you're going to type the URL into the cell, you can either click the cell or double-click it. If you want to paste in the URL, you must double-click the cell in order to make Numbers change it into a hyperlink when you move to another cell.

2. **Type or paste the URL for the hyperlink.**

3. **Move to another cell.** For example, press Return or Tab. Numbers changes the text to a hyperlink and underlines the hyperlink.

4. **Click the hyperlink to display a pop-up dialog.** This dialog shows the hyperlink's destination, an Edit button, and an Open button.

5. **Click the Edit button to expand the dialog with controls for editing the hyperlink (see Figure 7.11).**

6. **To change the link type from Webpage (the default) to e-mail, click the Link to pop-up menu, and then click Email.**

7. **To change the text displayed in the spreadsheet for the link, select the contents of the Display box, and then type the text you want.** For example, you might want the link to display "Click here to visit our website" instead of displaying the URL.

7.11 You can edit a hyperlink to make it display text other than its URL.

8. **Click in the spreadsheet to close the pop-up dialog.**

Note

Click Open in the pop-up dialog to open the hyperlink in your web browser. This is useful for checking if the address is correct and the website is still there. To remove the hyperlink, click Remove in the pop-up dialog.

Adding hyperlinks on iOS

Here's how to add a hyperlink on iOS and edit it to display text other than the URL:

1. **Double-tap the cell in which you want to add the hyperlink.** Numbers displays the keyboard and the Formula Editor.

2. **Input the URL in the Formula Editor.** Simply type the URL, or tap in the Formula Editor, and then tap Paste on the pop-up control bar.

Genius

You can tap a cell and then tap the Paste button on the pop-up control bar to paste a URL into the cell, but Numbers doesn't convert the URL to a hyperlink when you move to another cell. To create a hyperlink, you must open the cell for editing and paste the URL into the Formula Editor.

3. **Move to another cell, or tap the Accept button (on the iPhone or iPod touch) or the Done button (on the iPad).** Numbers converts the URL to a hyperlink.

4. **Tap the hyperlink to display a dialog for working with the link.**

5. **Open the link for editing in one of the following ways:**

   - **iPad.** Tap Link Settings, shown in Figure 7.12, to display the Link Settings dialog shown in Figure 7.13.

   - **iPhone or iPod touch.** Tap Edit Link Settings to display the Link Settings screen.

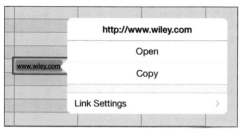

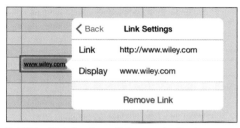

7.12 Tap Link Settings on the iPad to open the link for editing.

7.13 The Link Settings dialog on the iPad.

6. **Tap the Display field and type the text you want to display for the link.**

7. **On the iPad, tap in the spreadsheet to close the Link Settings dialog.** On the iPhone or iPod touch, tap the Done button to close the Link Settings screen.

Using data formats to control how data appears

To make your tables look right, you need to format the cells to suit their contents. For example, you may need to change the number of decimal places shown for numbers, change the currency symbol shown for money, or choose a different date format.

Note By setting up your tables with the appropriate formats in your templates, you can save a large amount of time and effort when creating your spreadsheets.

Applying data formats on OS X

On OS X, you use the Data Format pop-up menu in the Cell pane of the Format inspector to apply data formats to cells. Follow these steps:

1. **Select the cell or cells that need the data format.**

2. **If the Format inspector isn't displayed, click the Format button on the toolbar to display it.**

3. **Click the Cell button to display the Cell pane.**

4. **Click the Data Format pop-up menu, and then click the format to apply (see Figure 7.14).**

223

5. **Use the controls that appear below the Data Format pop-up menu to specify the details of the format.** These controls vary depending on the format you choose. For example, the Currency format (see Figure 7.15) gives you the following options:

- **Decimals.** Set the number of decimal places to use for the currency.

- **Negative Numbers format.** Choose how to represent negative numbers: with a minus sign, in red, in parentheses, or in red and in parentheses.

- **Thousands Separator.** Select this check box to use the thousands separator, a comma (so that 1000 appears as 1,000, and so on).

- **Accounting Style.** Select this check box to align the currency symbol on the left of the cell and the number on the right (instead of putting the currency symbol immediately before the number).

- **Currency.** Click this pop-up menu and choose the currency to use, such as US Dollar or Polish Zloty.

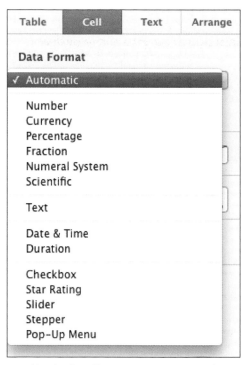

7.14 Use the Data Format pop-up menu in the Cell pane to apply a data format to the selected cell or cells.

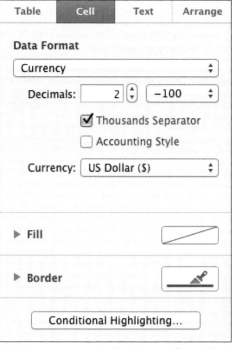

7.15 You can customize the Currency format by choosing the number of decimals and the type of currency.

Applying data formats on iOS

To apply data formats on iOS, you use the Format pane in the Format panel like this:

1. **Select the cell or cells that need the data format.**

2. **Tap the Format button on the toolbar to display the Format panel (see Figure 7.16).**

3. **Tap the button for the data format you want to use.**

4. **To set the details of the data format, tap the Info (i) button on the right of the data format's button.** The Options pane for that data format appears. Figure 7.17 shows the Number Options pane, which gives you access to the options for the Number format. This pane has three subpanes: Number, Scientific, and Fraction.

5. **Set the options for the data format.** For example, for the Number format, you can set these options in the Number pane:

   ● **Decimals.** Set the number of decimal places to use for the currency. Choose Auto if you want Numbers to use automatic settings, which hide decimals for zero values (making 15.00 appear as 15).

   ● **Separator.** Set this switch to On to use the thousands separator, a comma (so that 9999999 appears as 9,999,999, and so on).

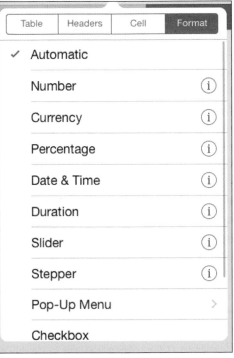

7.16 The Format pane on iOS.

7.17 The Number Options pane.

● **Negative Numbers format.** Choose how to represent negative numbers: with a minus sign, in red, in parentheses, or in red and in parentheses.

6. **If the Options pane contains sub-panes, tap the button for each sub-pane in turn, and then choose settings.** For example, the Number Options pane contains the Scientific subpane (see Figure 7.18) and the Fraction subpane (see Figure 7.19), as well as the Number pane.

7. **Tap in the spreadsheet to close the Format panel.**

Applying data formats in iCloud

To apply data formats in iCloud, use the Data pane in the Format panel like this:

1. **Select the cell or cells that need the data format.**

2. **If the Format panel isn't displayed, click the Tools button on the toolbar and choose Settings ⇨ Show Format Panel to display it.**

3. **Click the Data button to display the Data pane.**

4. **Click the Data Format pop-up menu shown in Figure 7.20, and then click the format to apply.**

5. **Use the controls that appear below the Data Format pop-up menu to specify the details of the format.** These controls vary depending on the format you choose. For example, the Date and Time format gives you these two options:

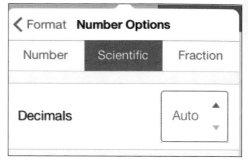

7.18 Choose further options in the subpanes, such as Scientific for the Number format.

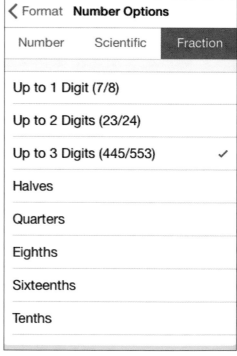

7.19 The Fraction subpane enables you to specify how to represent fractions in your spreadsheets.

- **Date Format.** Click this pop-up menu and choose the date format, such as 01/05/2015 or January 2015.

- **Time Format.** Click this pop-up menu and choose the time format, such as 7:08:09 PM or 19:08.

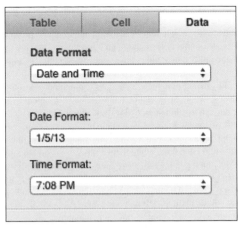

7.20 In iCloud, use the Data Format pop-up menu in the Data pane to apply a data format to the selected cell(s).

Organizing Information with Sheets and Tables

Each Numbers document consists of one or more worksheets, or simply sheets, on which you can place tables and other objects as needed. You can add and delete sheets, move and copy them, and rename them.

Adding and deleting sheets

In many Numbers documents, it is helpful to divide your data among multiple sheets rather than putting it all on one sheet. For example, if your data falls into several categories, you might put each category on a separate sheet. You can quickly add sheets to a Numbers document and delete any sheets you no longer need.

On OS X, you can quickly add a sheet by clicking the + button at the left end of the Sheets bar. Alternatively, choose Insert ⇨ Sheet from the menu bar. To rename the sheet you've just added, double-click its default name (such as Sheet 2), type the new name, and press Return. To delete a sheet, Control+click its tab, and then click Delete on the contextual menu. You can also hold the mouse pointer over the tab, click the pop-up button that appears, and then click Delete on the pop-up menu.

Genius

Numbers doesn't confirm sheet deletions, but you can use Undo immediately to restore the sheet if you make a mistake. If you don't notice the mistake until later, choose File ⇨ Revert To ⇨ Browse All Versions to go back to a version of the Numbers document that still contains the sheet.

Here's how to add a sheet to a Numbers document on iOS:

1. **Tap the + button at the left end of the Sheets bar.**

2. **On the iPad, if the New dialog opens (see Figure 7.21), tap New Sheet.**

227

3. **To rename the sheet, double-tap its default name, type the new name, and then tap elsewhere.**

To delete a sheet, tap its sheet tab outside the name, and then tap Delete on the pop-up control bar (see Figure 7.22).

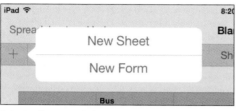

7.21 In the New dialog, tap New Sheet to add a new sheet on the iPad.

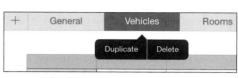

7.22 Tap the sheet tab anywhere except the name to display the pop-up control bar, and then tap Delete.

To add a sheet to a Numbers document in iCloud, click the + button after the last tab on the Sheets bar. Numbers adds a new sheet after the last one. You can then double-click the sheet's name, type the name you want to assign, and then press Return.

To delete a sheet in iCloud, Control+click the sheet's tab, and then click Delete Sheet on the contextual menu (see Figure 7.23).

7.23 In iCloud, you can delete a sheet by clicking Delete Sheet on the contextual menu for the sheet's tab.

Rearranging, Duplicating, or Renaming sheets

You can quickly rearrange the sheets in a Numbers document by dragging a sheet's tab along the Sheets bar. Figure 7.24 illustrates dragging a sheet's tab on OS X, but this move works on all the iWork platforms.

7.24 Drag the sheet tabs to rearrange the sheets in a Numbers document.

Often, it's useful to base a new sheet on an existing one. Numbers enables you to do this on OS X and iOS by duplicating a worksheet in the following ways:

- **OS X.** Control+click the sheet tab, and then click Duplicate on the contextual menu.
- **iOS.** Tap the sheet tab anywhere outside the sheet name, and then tap Duplicate on the pop-up control bar.

Note At this writing, Numbers for iCloud doesn't provide a duplicate command. Instead, select all the contents of the sheet you want to duplicate and copy them. Add a sheet as described in the previous section, and then paste the copied material onto the sheet.

You can rename a sheet at any point by selecting its name, and then typing a new name. Here's how to select the name:

- **OS X.** Double-click the existing name or Control+click the sheet's tab, and then click Rename on the contextual menu.

- **iOS.** Double-tap the existing name.

- **iCloud.** Double-click the existing name or Control+click the sheet's tab and then click Rename Sheet on the contextual menu.

Adding rows or columns in a table

When working with tables, you often need to add rows or columns. Here's how to do that:

- **Add rows or columns to the table.** Select the table, and then use the control at the right end of the column headings or the bottom of the row headings. On OS X and iOS, this control is a spin button that you use to increase or decrease the number of columns. On iCloud, you simply drag the handle to the left or right (to decrease or increase the number of columns), or up or down (to decrease or increase the number of rows).

- **Add rows or columns within the table in one of the following ways:**

  - **iOS.** Tap the column heading or row heading, and then tap Insert on the pop-up control bar (see Figure 7.25).

  - **OS X or iCloud.** Control+click the row heading or column heading, and then click Add Column Before, Add Column After, Add Row Before, or Add Row After on the contextual menu (see Figure 7.26).

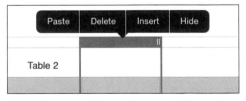

7.25 To insert or delete columns on iOS, tap the column heading, and then tap Delete or Insert on the pop-up control bar.

On OS X and iCloud, you can also move the mouse pointer over the column heading to display the pop-up menu button, click the button to open the pop-up menu, and then choose the command (see Figure 7.27).

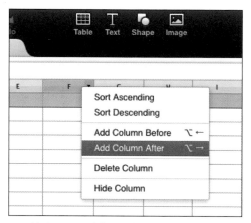

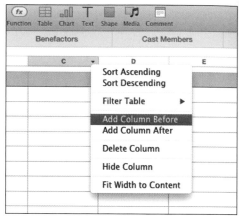

7.26 To insert or delete columns on OS X or iCloud, Control+click the column heading, and then choose the appropriate command from the contextual menu.

7.27 On OS X, you can use the pop-up menu on a column or row heading to add or delete columns or rows.

Deleting, rearranging, or hiding rows or columns from a table

You can also easily delete rows or columns you no longer need from a table in the following ways:

- **OS X.** Control+click the row heading or column heading, and then click Delete on the contextual menu.

- **iOS.** Tap the column heading or row heading, and then tap Delete on the pop-up control bar.

- **iCloud.** Control+click the row heading or column heading, and then click Delete Row or Delete Column on the contextual menu.

You can easily rearrange the rows and columns in a table by clicking or tapping a row heading or column heading and then dragging the row or column to where you want it to appear. Figure 7.28 illustrates moving a column on iOS, but the process is just as easy on OS X and in iCloud.

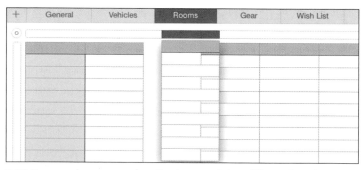

7.28 Drag a column or row heading to move it to a different location.

When you don't need to see a particular row or column, or you would prefer others not to see it, you can hide it in the following ways:

- **OS X or iCloud.** Control+click the row heading or column heading, and then click Hide Row or Hide Column on the contextual menu. You can also choose these commands from the pop-up menu that appears when you hold the mouse pointer over a row heading or column heading.

- **iOS.** Tap the row heading or column heading, and then tap Hide on the pop-up control bar.

When you want to display the hidden rows or columns again, you can unhide them in the following ways:

- **OS X or iCloud.** Control+click any displayed row heading or column heading, and then click the Unhide command for the row or column (for example, Unhide Row 12) or click Unhide All Rows. You can also give these commands from the pop-up menu.

- **iOS.** Tap any displayed row heading or column heading, and then tap Unhide Rows or Unhide Columns on the pop-up control bar.

Adding table header or footer rows, or header columns

To make a table clear to read, you usually need to give it one or more header or footer rows, or a header column. Numbers lets you add up to five of each of these. Normally, one or two is enough, but it's useful to be able to add more when you need them.

Genius

Numbers enables you to freeze the header rows or header columns so that they always remain on-screen even when you scroll the table. Freezing the header rows or header columns is often helpful because it keeps the column label visible, making your data easier to interpret.

Adding header rows or columns, or footer rows on OS X or iCloud

Here's how to add header rows or columns, or footer rows on OS X or in iCloud:

1. **Click anywhere in the table to select it.**

2. **Open the Format inspector or Format panel in one of the following ways:**

   - **OS X.** If the Format inspector isn't displayed, click the Format button on the toolbar to display it.

   - **iCloud.** If the Format panel isn't displayed, click the Tools button on the toolbar and then choose Settings ⇨ Show Format Panel to display it.

231

3. **Click the Table button to display the Table pane.**

4. **In the Headers & Footer area (shown in Figure 7.29 on OS X), click the Header Columns pop-up menu on the left, and then click the number of header columns you want.**

5. **If you want to freeze the header columns, click the Header Columns pop-up menu again and click Freeze Header Columns, placing a check mark next to this menu item.**

6. **Click the Header Rows pop-up menu (the middle pop-up menu), and then click the number of header rows to use.**

7. **If you want to freeze the header rows, click the Header Rows pop-up menu again and click Freeze Header Rows, placing a check mark next to this menu item.**

8. **Click the Footer Rows pop-up menu (the right pop-up menu), and then click the number of footer rows you want.**

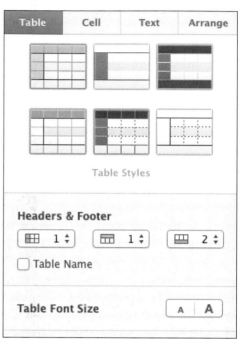

7.29 Use the pop-up menus in the Headers & Footer part of the Table pane to specify the number of headers or columns, or footer rows for the selected table.

Adding header rows or columns, or footer rows on iOS

Here's how to add header rows or columns, or footer rows on iOS:

1. **Tap the table to select it.**

2. **Tap the Format button on the toolbar to display the Format panel.**

3. **Tap the Headers button to display the Headers pane (see Figure 7.30).**

4. **On the Header Rows row, tap the + button or the – button to set the number of header rows.**

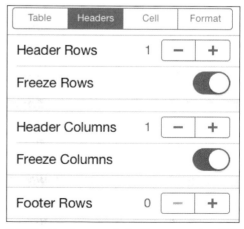

7.30 The Headers pane in the Format panel on iOS.

5. **Set the Freeze Rows switch to On if you want to freeze the rows so that they remain on-screen even when you scroll down the table.**

6. **On the Header Columns row, tap the + button or the – button to set the number of header columns.**

7. **Set the Freeze Columns switch to On if you want to freeze the columns in place.**

8. **On the Footer Rows row, tap the + button or the – button to set the number of footer rows.**

9. **Tap in the spreadsheet to close the Format panel.**

Formatting Tables

To make your tables look attractive and ensure their contents are readable, you may need to format them. Numbers gives you close control over the formatting, providing table styles, text styles (on OS X only), and direct formatting.

Genius You can cut down on the amount of formatting you need to perform by basing each Numbers document on a suitable template and by creating custom table styles for reuse.

Applying a table style

The quick way to format a table is by applying a table style to it. A table style is a set of formatting designed for the table as a whole. You can apply a table style either when you insert a table, or afterward whenever you find it convenient.

When inserting a new table on OS X or iOS, move to the appropriate set of tables in the Add Table pane so that you can create the table with the layout and color scheme you need. In iCloud, insert the table by clicking the Table button on the toolbar and then apply the table style from the Table pane in the Format panel or Format inspector. To change the style applied to an existing table, select the table, open the Table pane in the Format panel, and then tap the style you want.

Formatting with styles on OS X

On OS X, you can apply paragraph styles to any cell within a table like this:

1. **Select the cell or cells you want to format.**

2. **If the Format inspector isn't displayed, click the Format button on the toolbar to display it.**

3. **Click the Text button to display the Text pane (see Figure 7.31).**

4. **Click the Style pop-up menu and then click the style you want to apply.**

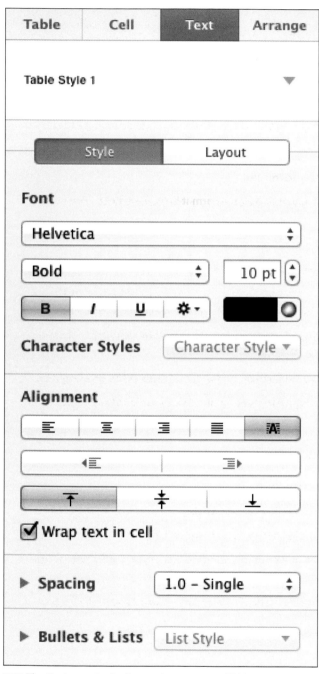

7.31 The Text pane in the Format inspector on OS X.

Note You can also apply character styles. To do so, select the part of the cell's contents you want to format, click the Character Styles pop-up menu in the Text pane, and then click the style you want to apply.

Using direct formatting

On any of the platforms, you can apply direct formatting to enhance a table or make the important parts of it stand out. Here's how to apply direct formatting to a table on OS X:

1. **Select the cell or cells you want to format.**

2. **If the Format inspector isn't displayed, click the Format button on the toolbar to display it.**

3. **Click the Text button to display the Text pane.**

4. **In the Font area, choose the font formatting for the cell or cells.**

5. **If necessary, click the appropriate button or buttons in the Alignment area to change the text's horizontal alignment, indentation, and vertical alignment.**

6. **Select the Wrap text in cell check box if you want Numbers to wrap the text to multiple lines if it's too wide to fit in the cell.**

7. **If you need to change the text's line spacing, use the controls in the Spacing area.**

8. **If you need to apply list formatting to the text, use the controls in the Bullets & Lists area.**

Here's how to apply direct formatting to a table on iOS:

1. **Select the cell or cells you want to format.**

2. **Tap the Format button to display the Format panel.**

3. **Tap the Cell button to display the Cell pane (see Figure 7.32).**

4. **Tap the Bold button, the Italic button, the Underline button, or the Strikethrough button as needed.**

5. **Use the horizontal alignment and vertical alignment buttons to set the alignment for the text.**

6. **Set the Wrap Text in Cell switch to On if you want Numbers to wrap the text to multiple lines if it's too wide to fit in the cell.**

7. **Tap Text Options to display the Text Options pane (see Figure 7.33).**

8. **Use the Size control to change the text size as needed.**

9. **To change the text color, tap the Color swatch, and then choose the color in the Color pane.**

10. **To change the font, tap Font, and then use the Font pane to select the font.** Tap the Info (i) button to choose among the font weights available.

11. **Tap in the spreadsheet to close the Format panel.**

Here's how to apply direct formatting to a table in iCloud:

1. **Select the cell or cells you want to format.**

2. **If the Format panel isn't displayed, click the Tools button on the toolbar, and then choose Settings ⇨ Show Format Panel to display it.**

3. **Click the Cell button to display the Cell pane (see Figure 7.34).**

4. **Use the controls in the Font area to adjust the font formatting as needed.** For example, use the Font pop-up menu to choose the font and then click the color swatch and choose the font color.

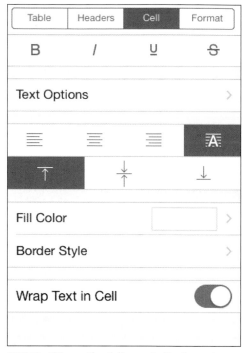

7.32 On iOS, use the Cell pane in the Format panel to control font formatting, alignment, and text wrapping.

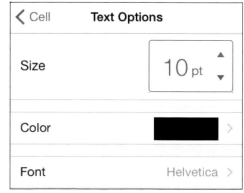

7.33 In the Text Options pane, you can change the font used, its size, and its color.

5. **Use the buttons in the Alignment area to set the horizontal alignment and vertical alignment for the cells.**

6. **Select the Wrap text in cell check box if you want Numbers to wrap the text to multiple lines if it's too wide to fit in the cell.**

7. **If you want to apply a fill to the cell, select the Fill check box, click the color swatch that appears, and then click the color for the fill.**

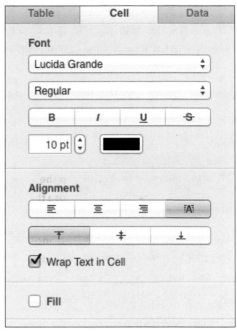

7.34 The Cell pane of the Format panel in iCloud.

How Do I Perform Calculations in Numbers Spreadsheets?

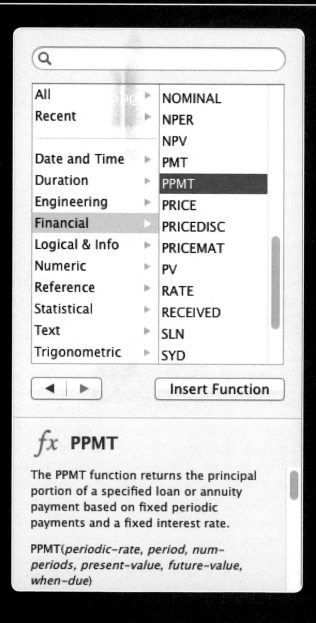

Performing calculations is a vital part of most spreadsheets, and Numbers puts phenomenal power at your fingertips with built-in functions you can insert in moments. Numbers provides a full range of functions, enabling you to perform all types of calculations from dates and durations, to financial, mathematical, and statistical ones. To insert functions, you use the Function Browser, which helps you provide the data each function needs. When you need to go beyond the built-in functions, you can build your own formulas that perform custom calculations, and adjust them by telling Numbers the order in which to evaluate their operators.

Understanding Formulas

To perform a calculation in Numbers, you input a formula in a cell. The *formula* gives the instructions for the calculation you want to perform. The cell containing the formula is called the *formula cell*.

Instead of displaying the text of the formula in the formula cell, Numbers displays the formula's *result*, which is the number or other value it produces. For example, if you input the formula =SUM(B3:B5) in cell B6, telling Numbers to add the values in the range B3:B5, Numbers displays the result in cell B6.

If you then change any of the values in the range B3:B5, Numbers updates the formula result in cell B6 to show the new total. And if cell B6 appears in any other formulas, Numbers updates those too — and any formulas that use the results of those formulas, and so on until the whole spreadsheet is up to date with the latest figures.

Numbers formulas use three components: values, operators, and functions. Here's what these terms mean in Numbers:

- **Values.** A *value* can be text or a number that you type into a formula, but normally it's text or a number that you input in a table cell, and then refer to in the formula by using a cell reference. When you input the data in a table cell, you can change it without having to edit the formula.

Note A value that you type directly in a formula is called a *constant* because it remains the same unless you change the formula.

- **Operators.** An *operator* is a symbol you use to tell Numbers which operation to perform on the value or values in a formula. For example, in the formula =B3/B2, the forward slash (/) is the division operator and tells Numbers to divide the value in cell B3 by the value in cell B2. The equal sign at the beginning tells Numbers that you're creating a formula rather than typing text.

- **Functions.** A *function* is a predefined formula that you can use in your tables. Most functions need one or more *arguments*, pieces of data on which to operate; a few, such as the NOW() function (which inserts the date and time) and the RAND() function (which inserts a random number), need no arguments. For example, when you use the SUM() function, you need to tell it which numbers or cell references to add. To do so, you input the numbers, cells, or range as the argument — for example, =SUM(1,2,3) or =SUM(B3:B5).

Genius

A Numbers function is like a black box: You cannot dig inside the function and change what it does. If Numbers doesn't provide a function for the calculation you want to perform, you can write your own formula instead.

Inserting Functions

With Numbers, you can insert functions in your tables quickly and easily. Numbers provides different tools for inserting functions on its different platforms because of the differences in the user interfaces.

Inserting functions in Numbers for OS X

On OS X, you can insert functions from the toolbar or by using the Function Browser. You can also type a formula into a cell if you prefer. In Numbers for OS X, you can quickly insert the following six widely used functions from the toolbar:

- **Sum.** The SUM() function adds the specified values.

- **Average.** The AVERAGE() function displays the average (mean) value of the specified values.

- **Minimum.** The MIN() function displays the minimum value among the values selected.

- **Maximum.** The MAX() function displays the maximum value among the values selected.

- **Count.** The COUNT() function shows the number of values.

- **Product.** The PRODUCT() function shows the product of the values.

Here's how to insert these functions:

1. **Click the cell in which you want to insert the function.**

2. **Click the Function button on the toolbar to display the Function pop-up menu.**

3. **Click the function you want to insert (see Figure 8.1).** Numbers inserts the function in the cell, using the most appropriate range as values. For example, if you insert the SUM() formula, Numbers uses the cells above the function cell as the values.

4. **To change the cells used as the values, double-click the function to open it for editing (see Figure 8.2).** You can then select the cells you want to use, and then click the green check mark button to input the function in the cell.

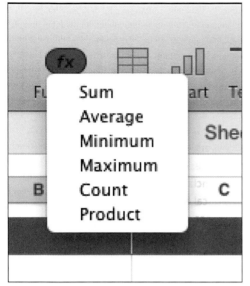

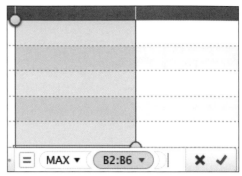

8.2 Double-click the function cell to open it for editing if you need to use different values.

8.1 You can quickly insert the Sum, Average, Minimum, Maximum, Count, and Product functions from the Function pop-up menu on the toolbar.

Note You can also insert these six functions by choosing Insert ➪ Function and then clicking the appropriate function on the Function submenu. Usually, though, the Function button on the toolbar is easier unless you've hidden the toolbar.

Inserting common functions from the toolbar is handy, but often you need to use some of Numbers' other 250-odd functions. Your main tool for doing so is the Function Browser. Here's how to insert a function with the Function Browser:

1. **Click the cell in which you want to place the function.**

2. **Type = (an equals sign) in the cell.** Numbers displays the Function Browser on the right side of the window (see Figure 8.3).

Note You can also display the Function Browser by choosing Insert ➪ Function ➪ Create Formula. However, it's usually easier to type = to open the Function Browser.

3. **In the upper part of the Function Browser, click the category of functions you want.** For example, click Date and Time if you want to see the following functions for calculating dates or times:

   - **All.** This category shows you all the functions. It's a bit unwieldy, but it's handy if you're not sure in which category the function belongs.

   - **Recent.** This category shows you functions you've recently used. If you use the same functions frequently, looking here can save you time.

   - **Search.** To search for a function, type the name or keyword in the search box at the top of the Function Browser. The Function Browser displays a list of all functions that have that term in their name or explanations.

4. **When you find the function you want, click it, and then click Insert Function.** Numbers inserts the function in the formula cell and displays the Formula Editor.

5. **Input the cell references for the function in the Formula Editor (see Figure 8.4).** Click an argument, and then click the cell you want to use. You can input a constant by clicking an argument in the Formula Editor, and then typing the value over it.

6. **When you've entered all the arguments, click the Accept button (the green check mark) or simply press Return to close the Formula Editor.** Numbers displays the result of the function in the cell.

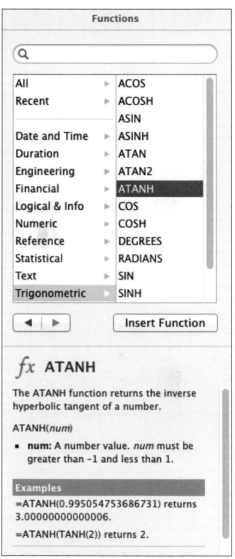

8.3 The Function Browser enables you to insert any of Numbers' many functions.

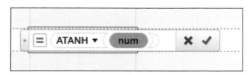

8.4 In the Formula Editor, input the cell references for the function.

243

Note If you've finished with the Function Browser for the time being, click its Close button to close it. Otherwise, Numbers keeps the Function Browser open in case you need it.

Instead of using the Function pop-up menu or the Function Browser, you can simply type a function into a cell, as shown in Figure 8.5. As soon as you start typing, Numbers opens the Formula Editor and Function Browser for you. As you type, the Formula Editor suggests matching functions. Click the function you want, and then add the arguments to it. When you know the name of the function you need, typing it is usually quicker than picking the function from the Function Browser.

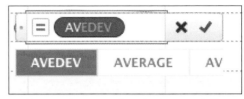

8.5 You can also type a function into a cell. If Numbers suggests the correct function on the blue bar, click it to enter it.

Note You can display the Formula Editor and Function Browser at any time by double-clicking a cell that contains a formula, or by clicking the cell to select it and then clicking it again (slower than a double-click). Alternatively, use the arrow keys to select the formula cell and press Option+Enter to display the Formula Editor and Function Browser.

Inserting functions in Numbers for the iPad

Here's how to insert functions in Numbers for the iPad:

1. **Double-tap the cell in which you want to insert the function.** Numbers opens the cell for editing and displays the keyboard.

2. **Tap the = button to switch to the functions keyboard (see Figure 8.6).**

8.6 Double-tap the cell to display the keyboard, and then tap the = button to display the functions keyboard.

3. **Tap the functions button to display the Function Browser.** The Function Browser has two panes: Recent, which shows the functions you've used recently, and Categories, which enables you to browse the functions by categories.

4. **If the function you need appears in the Recent pane (see Figure 8.7), tap the function to insert it in the cell, and go to step 9.** Otherwise, tap Categories to display the Categories pane.

5. **Tap the category of functions you want to browse (see Figure 8.8).** The screen for that category appears.

6. **Scroll down as needed to find the function you want.**

7. **If you want to see information about a function, tap the Info (i) button to its right (see Figure 8.9).** After determining whether this is the function you want, tap the category name (for example, Numeric, as shown in Figure 8.10) to return to the category screen.

8.7 If the function you need doesn't appear in the Recent pane, tap Categories to display the Categories pane.

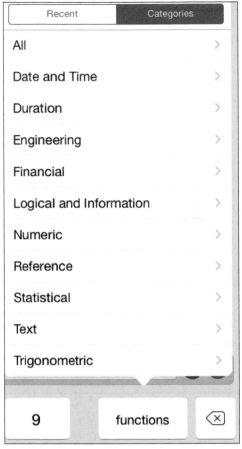

8.8 In the Categories pane, tap the category of functions you want to browse.

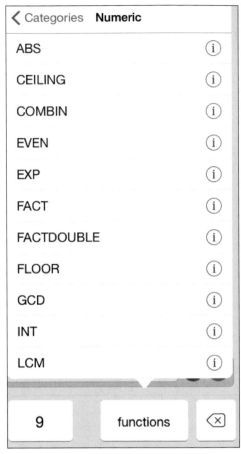

8.9 Tap the Info (i) button to the right of a function to display its details in the Info panel.

8. **On the category screen, tap the function you want to use.** Numbers inserts it in the cell (see Figure 8.11).

9. **Add any values needed to complete the function.** For example, tap a cell to use its contents as a value, or type the value to use.

10. **Tap the green button with the check mark to enter the function in the cell.**

Inserting functions in Numbers for the iPhone and iPod touch

Here's how to insert functions in Numbers for the iPhone and iPod touch:

1. **Double-tap the cell in which you want to insert the function.** Numbers opens the cell for editing and displays the keyboard.

2. **Tap the = button to switch to the functions keyboard (see Figure 8.12).**

3. **Tap the fx button to display the Function Browser (see Figure 8.13).** The Function Browser has two panes: Recent, which shows the functions you've used recently, and Categories, which enables you to browse the functions by categories. Tap Recent or Categories at the bottom of the Function Browser to switch between the panes.

4. **If the function you need appears in the Recent pane, tap the function to insert it in the cell, and go to step 9.** Otherwise, tap Categories to display the Categories pane.

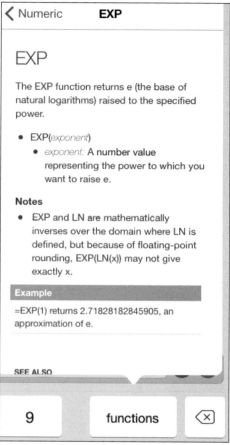

8.10 Tap the category name (here, Numeric) to return to the category screen after browsing the function's details.

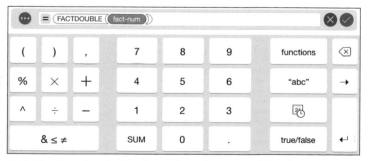

8.11 After inserting the function in the cell, tap the table cells to input the values the function needs.

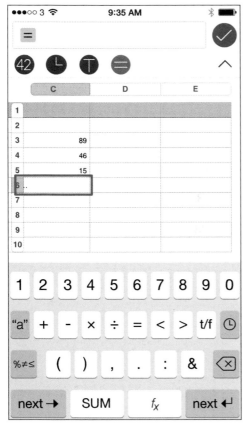

8.12 Double-tap the cell to display the keyboard, and then tap the = button to display the functions keyboard.

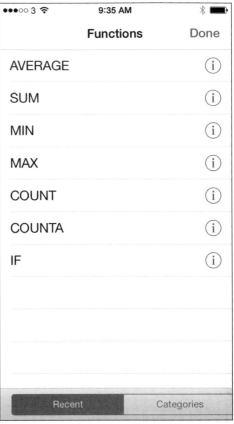

8.13 If the function you need doesn't appear in the Recent pane, tap Categories to display the Categories pane.

5. **Tap the category of functions you want to browse (see Figure 8.14).** The screen for that category appears.

6. **Scroll down as needed to find the function you want.**

7. **If you want to see information about a function, tap the Info (i) button to its right (see Figure 8.15).** After determining whether this is the function you want, tap the category name (for example, Statistical, as shown in Figure 8.16) to return to the category screen.

8. **On the category screen, tap the function you want to use.** Numbers inserts it in the cell (see Figure 8.17).

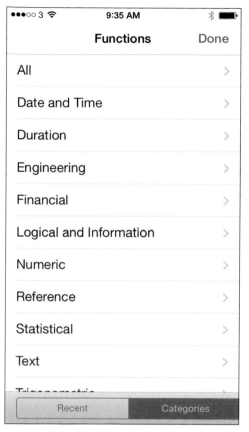

••••○ 3 🛜	9:35 AM	🔋
Functions		Done

All	>
Date and Time	>
Duration	>
Engineering	>
Financial	>
Logical and Information	>
Numeric	>
Reference	>
Statistical	>
Text	>

Recent | Categories

8.14 In the Categories pane, tap the category of functions you want to browse.

••••○ 3 🛜	9:36 AM	🔋
‹ Categories **Statistical**		Done

AVEDEV	ⓘ
AVERAGE	ⓘ
AVERAGEA	ⓘ
AVERAGEIF	ⓘ
AVERAGEIFS	ⓘ
BETADIST	ⓘ
BETAINV	ⓘ
BINOMDIST	ⓘ
CHIDIST	ⓘ
CHIINV	ⓘ
CHITEST	ⓘ

8.15 You can tap the Info (i) button to the right of a function to display its details in the Info panel.

9. **Input any values needed to complete the function.** For example, tap the value in the Function Editor, and then tap the cell that contains the value to use.

10. **Tap the green button with the check mark to enter the function in the cell.**

Inserting functions in Numbers for iCloud

At this writing, the only way to insert functions in Numbers for iCloud is by using the Function Browser. Follow these steps:

1. **Click the cell in which you want to input the function.**

2. **Type = to display the Function Browser on the right side of the window (see Figure 8.18).**

3. **Select the function and assign its values and operators as explained earlier in this chapter.**

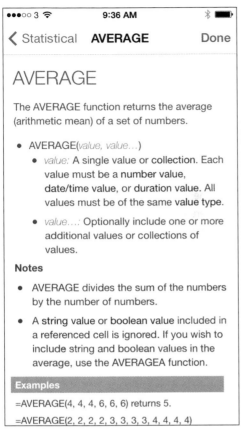

8.16 Tap the category name (here, Statistical) to return to the category screen after browsing the function's details.

8.17 After inserting the function in the cell, tap the table cells to input the values the function needs.

Dealing with Errors in Functions

If Numbers displays a red triangle with a white exclamation point in a cell in which you've inserted a function, there's a problem with the function — for example, you haven't told the function which arguments to use, or you've asked it to do something impossible, such as dividing by zero.

Here's how to deal with errors in functions on OS X or iCloud:

1. **Click the cell to display a pop-up balloon showing brief details of the problem (see Figure 8.19).**

2. **Double-click the cell to open it for editing (see Figure 8.20).**

3. **Correct the problem.** For example, add a missing argument, remove a surplus argument, or provide the correct type of input for an argument.

Here's how to deal with errors in functions on iOS:

1. **Double-tap the cell containing the error (see Figure 8.21).**

2. **View the error message that appears above the keyboard (see Figure 8.22).**

3. **Correct the problem.** For example, add a missing argument, remove a surplus argument, or provide the correct type of input for an argument.

Working with Formulas

Numbers' built-in functions are great for performing the wide variety of tasks for which they're designed. However, unless you create unusually simple spreadsheets, you may also need to create formulas of your own that perform exactly the calculations you need. To create a formula, you use the Formula Editor, the same tool that you use for editing functions.

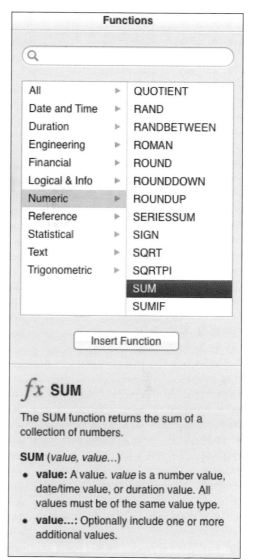

Functions

All	▶	QUOTIENT
Date and Time	▶	RAND
Duration	▶	RANDBETWEEN
Engineering	▶	ROMAN
Financial	▶	ROUND
Logical & Info	▶	ROUNDDOWN
Numeric	▶	ROUNDUP
Reference	▶	SERIESSUM
Statistical	▶	SIGN
Text	▶	SQRT
Trigonometric	▶	SQRTPI
		SUM
		SUMIF

Insert Function

fx **SUM**

The SUM function returns the sum of a collection of numbers.

SUM (*value, value...*)

- **value:** A value. *value* is a number value, date/time value, or duration value. All values must be of the same value type.
- **value...:** Optionally include one or more additional values.

8.18 In iCloud, type = in a cell to display the Function Browser.

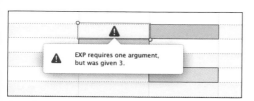

8.19 On OS X, click an error symbol to see a pop-up balloon telling you what's wrong with the function.

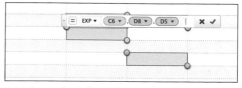

8.20 Open the cell to edit the function and fix the error.

Creating a formula on OS X or in iCloud

Crop 1	645.32	⚠
Crop 2	599.73	

Here's how to create a formula on OS X or in iCloud:

8.21 On iOS, double-tap an error cell to see what is wrong.

1. **Click the cell in which you want to input the formula.** The cell becomes active.

2. **Type = (an equals sign) to start creating the formula.** Numbers displays the Formula Editor and the Function Browser.

3. **Build your formula by doing the following in whichever combination you need:**

    ● **Add a cell reference.** Click the cell you want to add. Numbers adds it to the Formula Editor as a rounded rectangle that shows the cell reference.

Note

If the table has header columns and header rows, the cell reference normally appears as a combination of the names. For example, if the column has the header Arizona and the row has the header 2014, the cell reference appears as Arizona 2014. If the table has no headers, the cell reference appears as the combination of the column letter and row number — for example, C3.

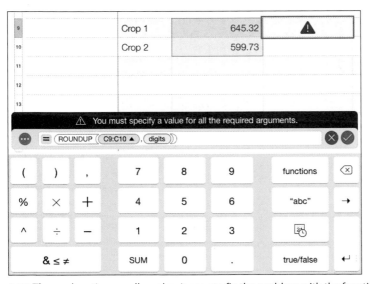

8.22 The explanation usually makes it easy to fix the problem with the function.

Finding Information about Numbers' Functions

You can find out what a function in Numbers does in three ways:

- **Use the Function Browser information.** Open the Function Browser, select the function, and look at the information provided.

- **Read the *iWork Formulas and Functions User Guide*.** You can download this PDF file from the Apple website (manuals.info.apple.com/ MANUALS/0/MA665/en_US/Formulas_and_Functions_User_Guide.pdf). It's a hefty read, but there's no plot, so you can go straight to the parts you need. This guide is a great way to get an overview of all the functions Numbers offers, plus a fair amount of detail on what they do.

- **Read the Help files on OS X.** From Numbers, choose Help ➪ Formulas and Functions Help. You can then view the Formulas and functions overview topic or dive into the area you need to know about.

- **Insert an operator.** Click where you want to place the operator, and then type it. You can skip typing the addition operator (+) because Numbers automatically inserts the addition operator when you click a series of cells in succession. Numbers uses a different color for each cell reference so that you can instantly see which reference in the Formula Editor maps to which cell. Figure 8.23 shows an example.

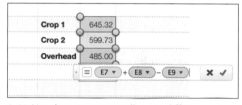

8.23 Numbers automatically uses different colors for cell references in the Formula Editor and the Formula bar so that you can easily tell which cell references go where.

- **Insert a function.** In the Formula Editor, click where you want the function to appear, then go to the Function Browser on the right side of the window. Choose the function, as described earlier in this chapter, and then click Insert Function to insert it. Add any arguments the function needs.

- **Delete an element from the formula.** Click the element, and then press Delete.

- **Rearrange the elements in the formula.** Click and drag the element to its new position.

4. **When you finish creating the formula, click Accept (the green circle with the white check mark) in the Formula bar or press Return to enter it.** If you decide you don't want to keep the formula, click Cancel (the red circle with the white X) or press Esc instead.

Creating a formula on iOS

Here's how to create a formula on iOS:

1. **Double-tap the cell in which you want to input the formula.** The cell becomes active, and the keyboard appears.

2. **Tap the = button to display the functions keyboard.**

3. **Build your formula by doing the following in whichever combination you need:**

   - **Add a cell reference.** Tap the cell you want to add. Numbers adds it to the Formula Editor as a rounded rectangle that shows the cell reference.

   - **Insert an operator.** Tap the point in the formula where you want to place the operator, and then type it. You can skip typing the addition operator (+) because Numbers automatically inserts the addition operator when you tap a series of cells in succession. Numbers uses a different color for each cell reference so that you can instantly see which reference in the Formula Editor maps to which cell. Figure 8.24 shows an example.

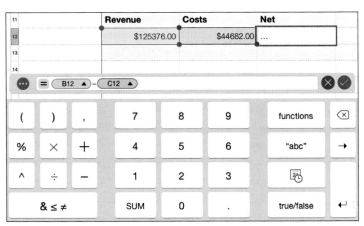

8.24 On iOS, create your formula by typing operators and tapping the cells for which you want to input references.

   - **Insert a function.** In the Formula Editor, tap where you want the function to appear, then tap the functions button or the fx button. Choose the function as described earlier in this chapter, and then add any arguments the function needs.

   - **Delete an element from the formula.** Tap to place the insertion point after the element, tap Delete to select the element, and then tap Delete again to delete it.

   - **Rearrange the elements in the formula.** Drag the element to its new position.

4. **When you finish creating the formula, tap Accept (the green circle with the white check mark) in the Formula bar or press Return to enter it.** If you decide you don't want to keep the formula, tap Cancel (the red circle with the white X).

Referring to cells

To make your formulas work correctly, you need to tell Numbers which cells to use. You do this by using cell references that identify the cells uniquely in the spreadsheet document. You can refer to cells in the following two ways:

- **Using A1-style references.** As in most spreadsheet applications, you can use the letter of the column reference tab and the number of the row reference tab that intersect at the cell. For example, the cell at the intersection of column A and row 1 is cell A1.

- **Using header names.** You can use the name of the column header and the name of the row header. For example, to refer to the cell at the intersection of the column with the header Nevada and the row with the header 2015, you can use Nevada 2015 (with a space between the names).

Note
On OS X, if you prefer A1-style cell references, such as A1, B2, and C3, rather than references that use header names, open General Preferences (choose Numbers ⇨ Preferences), and then deselect the Use header cell names as labels check box. You can then click the cells you want to use in your formulas, and Numbers will use A1-style naming for the references.

As you'd expect, you can use header names only when you've added header columns and header rows to a table. Until then, you must use A1-style references.

Genius
When creating a formula using the keyboard on OS X, use Option to input references quickly. To input a single cell reference, hold down Option, and then use the arrow keys to select the cell. For a range, hold down Option, select the first cell, and then hold down Shift+Option while you select the rest of the range. To move to the next table, press Option+⌘+PageDown; to move to the previous table, press Option+⌘+PageUp.

Referring to another table on the same sheet

To refer to a cell in another table on the same sheet, you need to include the table's name in the reference if there is any ambiguity as to which table you're referring. Numbers automatically adds the table name if it's needed. While creating the formula, simply navigate to the other table and click or tap the cell you want to use.

If the cell reference derived from the column tab (or header) and row tab (or header) of the cell you click is unique in the spreadsheet document, Numbers creates the reference the same way as for a reference within the table. For example, if only one table in the spreadsheet document has a cell named Ohio 2013 (from a column headed Ohio and a row headed 2013), Numbers inputs the reference Ohio 2013.

However, if any other table on the sheet, or elsewhere in the spreadsheet, contains a cell with the same name, Numbers creates the reference with the table's name first, a space, then two colons, another space, and then the cell reference. For example, if the Ohio 2013 cell is in the States table, the reference is States :: Ohio 2013.

Caution

Using the cell reference without the table name (or the sheet name, as discussed next) can lead to mistakes if you subsequently create another table that reuses header names already used by other tables. To avoid ambiguity, add the table name (and if necessary the sheet name) even if Numbers doesn't. Double-click or double-tap the cell reference to open it for editing, type in the extra information, and then click or tap the Accept button.

Referring to a table on another sheet

Referring to a cell in a table on another sheet works the same way referring to another table on the same sheet does, except that you may need to add the sheet's name as well as the table's.

To insert the reference, click or tap the sheet's button, navigate to the table, and then click or tap the cell. When you click or tap the Accept button, Numbers inserts the reference for you. Again, the cell reference Numbers inserts varies depending on the column, row, and table names. Here are the references that Numbers inserts:

- **If the cell reference is unique in the spreadsheet, Numbers inserts the reference without the table name or sheet name.**

- **If the cell reference is not unique but the table name is, Numbers inserts the reference with the table name but without the sheet name.**

- **If neither the cell reference nor the table name is unique, Numbers inserts the sheet name as well, again using a space, two colons, and another space as separator characters.**

For example, if the Ohio 2013 cell is in the States table on the Delegates sheet, the full reference, including the sheet name and the table name, is Delegates :: States :: Ohio 2013. If Numbers doesn't insert the full reference, you may want to do so yourself to prevent confusion if you add sheets or tables.

Choosing between absolute and relative references

Like most other spreadsheet applications, Numbers lets you use the following references:

- **Absolute reference.** This reference always refers to the same cell, even if you move the formula to a different formula cell. For example, say you type 2 in cell B2 and 4 in cell B3. If you enter the formula =$B$2+$B$3 in cell B4, it always adds the values in cell B2 and cell B3, even if you move the formula from cell B4.

Note

Numbers uses the dollar sign ($) to indicate that part of a reference is absolute. For example, the reference $A$1 always refers to cell A1, and the reference $Arizona $2014 always refers to the cell in the column with the header Arizona and the row with the header 2014.

- **Relative reference.** This reference is relative to the formula cell's position in the table. For example, if you enter the formula =B2+B3 in cell B4, it adds the values in cell B2 and cell B3, but the underlying meaning of the formula is *add the cell two cells above the formula cell to the cell directly above the formula cell.* So, if you move the formula to cell C4, the formula adds the values in cell C2 and cell C3 instead. This behavior is handy when you need to copy formulas or rearrange tables.

- **Mixed reference.** This reference is absolute for either the column or row, but not both. For example, if you enter the formula =B$2+B$3 in cell B4, it tells Numbers to add the second cell and third cell (the row reference is absolute) in the same column as the formula cell (the column reference is relative). If you move the formula to cell C5, the formula still operates on rows 2 and 3, because that part of the formula is absolute, but on column C instead of column B.

When you click or tap a cell in a table to add it to a formula, Numbers automatically creates a relative reference. You can then change it to an absolute or mixed reference. Here's how to change the reference type on OS X:

1. **Highlight the reference in the Formula Editor.**

2. **Click the disclosure triangle to display the pop-up panel (see Figure 8.25).**

3. **Select the Preserve Row check box if you want to make the row reference absolute.**

8.25 On OS X, you can quickly change the reference type using the pop-up panel in the Formula Editor.

4. **Select the Preserve Column check box if you want to make the column reference absolute.**

5. **Click outside the pop-up panel to hide the panel again.**

Genius

You can also type an absolute reference or mixed reference using the keyboard. Simply place a dollar sign before each part of the reference you want to make absolute.

Here's how to change the reference type on iOS:

1. **Highlight the reference in the Formula Editor.**

2. **Tap the disclosure triangle to display the pop-up panel.**

3. **In the Start section, set the Preserve Row switch to On (see Figure 8.26) if you want to make the starting row reference absolute.**

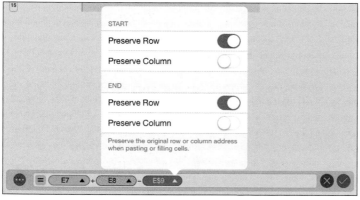

8.26 On OS X, set the Preserve Row and Preserve Column switches to On or Off to change the reference type.

4. **Also in the Start section, set the Preserve Column switch to On if you want to make the starting column reference absolute.**

5. **In the End section, set the Preserve Row switch to On if you want to make the ending row reference absolute.** If the reference has no ending row, there's no need to set this switch.

6. **In the End section, set the Preserve Column switch to On if you want to make the ending column reference absolute.** As with the ending row reference, if the reference has no ending column, there's no need to set this switch.

7. **Tap the reference button in the Formula Editor to hide the pop-up panel.**

Here's how to change the reference type in iCloud:

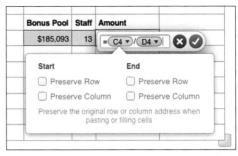

1. **Highlight the reference in the Formula Editor.**

2. **Click the disclosure triangle to display the pop-up panel.**

3. **On the Start side, select the Preserve Row check box (see Figure 8.27) if you want to make the row reference absolute.**

8.27 In iCloud, use the pop-up panel to specify whether to preserve the references to the start row, start column, end row, and end column.

4. **Also on the Start side, select the Preserve Column check box if you want to make the column reference absolute.**

5. **On the End side, select the Preserve Row check box if you want to make the row reference absolute.**

6. **Also on the End side, select the Preserve Column check box if you want to make the column reference absolute.**

7. **Click outside the pop-up panel to hide the panel again.**

Genius

On OS X and in iCloud, you can click a cell reference in the Formula Editor, and then press ⌘+K to cycle through the four reference types. The first press produces the absolute row and column (for example, $B$3). The second press produces the absolute row and relative column (for example, B$3). The third press produces the relative row and absolute column (for example, $B3). The fourth press produces the relative row and relative column (for example, B3).

Copying, moving, or deleting a formula

You can copy or move a formula cell just as you can copy or move the content of any other cell. For example, on OS X, select a formula cell, press ⌘+C to copy its contents or ⌘+X to cut its contents, move to the destination cell, and then press ⌘+V to paste in the formula.

When you paste a formula with a relative component, Numbers changes the cells the formula refers to so that they match the formula cell's new location. For example, if you have a formula in cell B4 that refers to cell B3, moving the formula to cell C4 makes it refer to cell B3 instead.

By contrast, any absolute reference still refers to the same cell no matter where you place it. A mixed reference still refers to its absolute column or absolute row, but its relative component changes to reflect its new location.

When you no longer need a formula, you can quickly delete it in one of the following ways:

- **OS X or iCloud.** Click the formula cell, and then press Delete.

- **iOS.** Tap the cell, and then tap Delete on the pop-up control bar.

Understanding Operators

To perform arithmetic or comparisons in your formulas, you use operators. For example, to add values, you use the addition operator, the plus sign (+); to see if one value is larger than another, you use the greater-than operator (>). To join text items, you use the string operator.

Arithmetic operators

Table 8.1 shows the six arithmetic operators that Numbers uses. They're all straightforward, but there are two things to watch for:

- **Text.** If you try to perform arithmetic on text, you get an error. Numbers alerts you that you've given it a *string* rather than a number. (A *string* is nonnumeric text — for example, your name.)

- **Division by zero.** Dividing by zero is mathematically impossible, so Numbers gives an error when a formula tries to do so. If the cell in question doesn't contain zero or a calculation that produces zero, it may be blank (which Numbers treats as zero).

Table 8.1 Numbers' Arithmetic Operators

Arithmetic Operation	Operator
Addition	+
Subtraction	−
Multiplication	*
Division	/
Exponentiation	^
Percentage	%

Comparison operators

Numbers has six comparison operators you can use to compare values. Table 8.2 shows them. There are four main things to note here:

- **Return values.** Each comparison operator returns TRUE if the condition is true and FALSE if it is not true.

- **Strings are greater than numbers.** Numbers considers any string to be greater than any number. So, for example, the formula =*"cat">10000000* returns TRUE. You probably won't use nonsensical comparisons like this in your spreadsheets, but if you're getting an unexpected TRUE or FALSE value, look to see if a string is causing it.

- **Numeric values of TRUE and FALSE.** Numbers assigns the value 1 to TRUE and the value 0 to FALSE. That means TRUE > FALSE. (Most social scientists think otherwise.)

- **TRUE and FALSE compare only with each other.** Despite TRUE and FALSE having the values 1 and 0, you can't compare them with numbers. For example, using TRUE = 1 returns FALSE even if whatever you're checking is true. You also can't compare TRUE or FALSE with strings of text; doing so always returns FALSE.

Table 8.2 Numbers' Comparison Operators

Comparison Operation	Operator
Equal	=
Not equal	<>
Greater than	>
Smaller than	<
Greater than or equal to	>=
Smaller than or equal to	<=

The string operator and wildcards

Apart from the arithmetic operators and comparison operators, Numbers uses one string operator and three wildcard characters. Table 8.3 shows these operators.

Table 8.3 Numbers' String Operator and Wildcards

Operation	Operator or Wildcard	Explanation
Join strings or cell contents	&	Joins the strings of text or the values of cells, treating them as text even if they're numbers.
Match one character	?	Use this to match any one character. For example, "mi?" matches any three-character string beginning with "mi."
Match multiple characters	*	Use this to match any number of characters. For example, "dr*" matches "dry," "drive," and many other strings.
Match a wildcard	~	Use "~?" to match a real question mark instead of using the question mark as a wildcard.

Note

The string operator can give you surprise results in your calculations. For example, the formula "=50&100" returns 50100 rather than 150. While you're not likely to type the string operator directly in a formula like that, it can creep in when you're creating a formula with cell references.

Overriding the Numbers order for operators

When you put together a formula that contains two or more operators, you sometimes need to know the order in which Numbers will evaluate them. For example, if someone offers to give you the result of 2000–200*5 dollars, will you get $9,000 (2000 – 200 =1800; 1800 × 5 = 9000) or only $1,000 (200 × 5 = 1000; 2000 – 1000 = 1000)?

Sadly, you would get only $1,000, because Numbers performs the multiplication before the subtraction. Table 8.4 shows the order in which Numbers evaluates operators, from first to last.

Table 8.4 Operator Precedence in Numbers

Operator (Descending Order)	Explanation
%	Percentage
^	Exponentiation
* and /	Multiplication and division
+ and –	Addition and subtraction
&	Concatenation
=, <>, <, <=, >, >=	Comparison operators

You can override this order by putting parentheses around the item you want to evaluate first in the formula. For example, (2000 − 200)*5 makes Numbers evaluate 2000–200 first, and then multiply the result of that by 5, giving 9000.

Genius

You can put one item in parentheses inside another item in parentheses if necessary. This is called *nesting* items, and Numbers performs the deepest nested calculation first. For example, in (2000 − (200 − 100))*5, Numbers calculates 200–100 first, so the formula gives a result of 9500. As you enter each closing parenthesis, Numbers highlights its matching opening parenthesis to help you keep track of which calculation you're closing.

How Can I Create Dynamic Spreadsheets?

After you input all the data the spreadsheet needs, it's time to make it look good. You can start by using Numbers' table styles to format each table, and add direct formatting as needed to customize the table. You can then sort the table to make it display the data in your preferred order. You can create powerful charts that draw data from either a single or multiple tables. For extra visual impact, you can add images to a sheet, cell, table, or other object; and for convenience, you can add dynamic controls that let the user manipulate values accurately and easily.

Making a Table Look the Way You Want

This section shows you how to make each table look exactly the way you want by applying table styles, using conditional formatting to automatically monitor cells for unexpected values, and filtering a table so that it shows only the data in which you're interested.

Formatting a table with a style

A quick way to make a table look good is to apply a table style. A *table style* is the complete set of formatting for a table. This includes everything from text formatting for body cells, to the border formatting for header and footer cells, plus any background image or color for the entire table.

On OS X, you can quickly apply a table style like this:

1. **Click anywhere in the table.** You don't need to select the whole table.

2. **If the Format inspector isn't displayed, click the Format button on the toolbar to display it.**

3. **Click the Table button to display the Table pane.**

4. **In the Table Styles area, click the style you want to apply (see Figure 9.1).**

If you've applied any formatting to the table, Numbers keeps that formatting when you apply the new style. For example, if you've applied bold or italics to a cell, that formatting will still be there after you change the style.

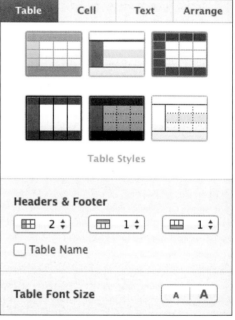

9.1 Use the Table pane in the Format inspector to apply a table style to the selected table on OS X.

Genius

While you cannot apply a style to only part of a table, you can create different tables, apply different styles, and place the tables next to each other to give the appearance of using different styles in different parts of the table. If you remove the header columns and rows, and the footer rows where the tables meet, the tables appear to be a single table.

Here's how to apply a table style on iOS:

1. **Tap the table to select it.**

2. **Tap the Format button on the toolbar to display the Format panel.**

3. **Tap the Table button to display the Table pane (see Figure 9.2).**

4. **Tap the table style to apply.**

Here's how to apply a table style in iCloud:

1. **Click the table to select it.**

2. **If the Format panel isn't displayed, click the Tools button on the toolbar, and then choose Settings⇨Show Format Panel to display it.**

3. **Click the Table button to display the Table pane.**

4. **Click the style you want to apply.**

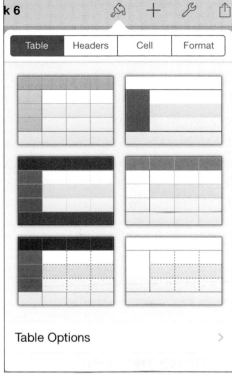

9.2 Use the Table pane in the Format panel to apply a table style on iOS.

Formatting table cells and borders manually

The table style gives you the broad strokes of the table's formatting, but you often need to format some table cells manually to make them stand out.

Genius Use the Alternating Row Color option to make complex tables easier to read. Having a different color for alternating rows helps the eye to follow along the data in a row without straying to the row above or below.

On OS X, you can quickly change the border formatting or fill color of one or more selected cells. You do this using the controls in the Border and Fill areas of the Cell pane in the Format inspector. For example, choose the border style, weight, and color, and then click the thumbnail for the borders on which to apply it.

Note After you apply the formatting you want to one cell, you can apply it to other cells in moments. Click the formatted cell and press Option+⌘+C or choose Format⇨Copy Style. Then click the target cell and press Option+⌘+V or choose Format⇨Paste Style.

To format table cells and borders manually on iOS, follow these steps:

1. **Tap the table to select it.**

2. **Tap the Format button on the toolbar to display the Format panel.**

3. **Tap the Table button to display the Table pane.**

4. **Tap the Table Options button to display the Table Options pane (see Figure 9.3).**

5. **Set the Table Border switch to On.** You can also set the Alternating Rows switch to On if you want to use alternate-row shading.

6. **Tap the Table button to go back to the Table pane.**

7. **Tap the Cell button to display the Cell pane.**

8. **To add a fill, tap the Fill Color button and then choose the fill in the Fill Color pane.** Tap Cell to return to the Cell pane.

9. **Tap Border Style to display the Border Style pane and then tap the borders to use.**

10. **Tap in the spreadsheet to close the Format panel.**

At this writing, in Numbers for iCloud, you can apply a color fill but not border formatting. Follow these steps to do so:

1. **Click the table to select it.**

2. **If the Format panel isn't displayed, click the Tools button on the toolbar and choose Settings ⇨ Show Format Panel to display it.**

3. **Click the Cell button to display the Cell pane.**

4. **Select the Fill check box (see Figure 9.4).**

5. **Click the color swatch, and then click the color for the fill.**

9.3 The Table Options pane on iOS.

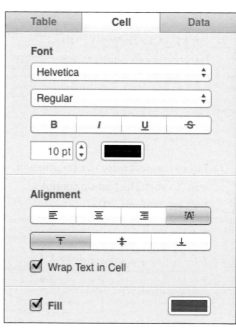

9.4 Use the Cell pane in the Format panel to apply a fill in Numbers for iCloud.

Sorting a Table

One of the great things about tables is that you can easily sort their rows quickly by any of the columns they contain. On OS X, you can also filter a table to make it display only the rows containing the data you want to view. See Chapter 10 for details on filtering.

Note Numbers enables you to sort by only one column at a time. You can perform either an ascending sort or a descending sort. Ascending sorts numbers from small to large, letters from A to Z, and so on. Descending sorts in reverse order: numbers from large to small, letters from Z to A, and so on.

Here's how to sort a table on OS X:

1. **Click the table to select it.**

2. **Move the mouse pointer over the column heading, and then click the pop-up button to display the pop-up menu.**

3. **Click Sort Ascending or Sort Descending, as needed (see Figure 9.5).**

Here's how to sort a table on iOS:

1. **Tap the table to select it.**

2. **Tap the table bar for the column you want to sort.** The pop-up control appears (see Figure 9.6).

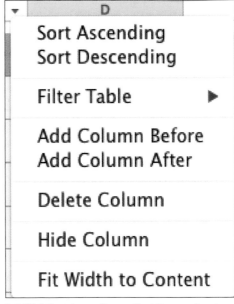

9.5 Click Sort Ascending or Sort Descending to sort by a column.

Note You can also Control+click the column heading, and then click Sort Ascending or Sort Descending on the context menu.

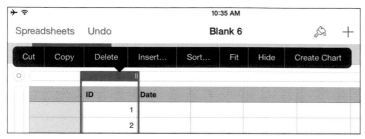

9.6 The pop-up control bar for sorting on iOS.

3. **Tap Sort to display the sorting commands on the pop-up control bar.**

4. **Tap Sort Ascending or Sort Descending (see Figure 9.7), as needed.**

Here's how to sort a table in iCloud:

1. **Click the table to select it.**

2. **Move the mouse pointer over the column heading, and then click the pop-up button to display the pop-up menu.**

3. **Click Sort Ascending or Sort Descending, as needed (see Figure 9.8).**

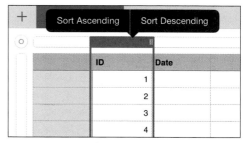

9.7 Tap Sort Ascending or Sort Descending.

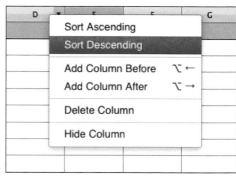

9.8 The pop-up menu for sorting in iCloud.

Note

You can also Control+click the column heading, and then click Sort Ascending or Sort Descending on the context menu.

Creating Charts from Table Data

In Numbers, you can insert charts in your documents using the same techniques as for Pages and for Keynote, as discussed in Chapter 4. However, you may also want to take advantage of the extra charting features that Numbers offers, as discussed here.

Note

At this writing, you cannot create or edit charts in Numbers in iCloud.

Inserting a chart

The standard way of inserting a chart in Numbers is to select the range of adjacent cells that contains the data, and then choose the command for inserting the chart. This works well when your data is neatly arranged and you want to use all of it. However, Numbers enables you to use data from an entire table, from nonadjacent cells, or from two or more tables, as described next.

Creating a chart from nonadjacent cells on OS X

In many spreadsheets, you need to create a chart that uses only some of the data from a table rather than all of it. For example, you may want to omit data that detracts from the point you're trying to convey in your chart, or you may simply find that including all the data may make the chart too complex for easy reading.

You could pull out the data you want into another table, or create a copy of this table and then cut it down to only the data you want, but Numbers has a better way — just select the cells you want within the table.

To create a chart from nonadjacent cells, either click the first cell, or click and drag through the first range of cells. Next, hold down ⌘ while you click each cell you need, or while you click and drag through each additional range of cells. Figure 9.9 shows an example of selecting nonadjacent columns in a table.

	Background Data		Sheet 1		Staffing Levels	
	A	B	C	D	E	
1	State	Ohio	Arizona	Idaho	Colorado	
2	2011	49	12	6	16	
3	2012	45	12	5	16	
4	2013	44	10	5	18	
5	2014	30	8	1	18	
6	2015	30	1	1	24	

9.9 You can create a chart from nonadjacent cells or ranges of cells.

Figure 9.10 shows the chart that results from this selection of data.

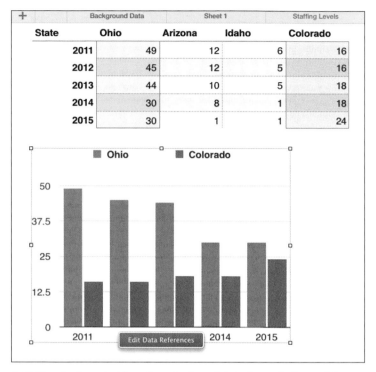

State	Ohio	Arizona	Idaho	Colorado
2011	49	12	6	16
2012	45	12	5	16
2013	44	10	5	18
2014	30	8	1	18
2015	30	1	1	24

9.10 The chart created from the selection of data shown in Figure 9.9.

You can quickly reposition a chart on its current sheet by clicking it, and then dragging it to the new position. To move a chart from one sheet to another, cut it from the current sheet and paste it on the other sheet.

Creating a chart from two or more tables

One handy trick is to create a chart that draws data from two or more tables. By doing this, you can avoid having to consolidate all the data into a single table.

Genius

Drawing data from different tables also lets you contrast different data sets in the same chart. For example, you could create a line chart that shows a competitors' sales declining, and then add data from a different table that shows your company's sales soaring during the same period.

To use data from two or more tables, follow these steps:

1. **Create the chart from the data in the first table as usual.**

2. **Click the chart to select it.**

3. **Click Edit Data References.**

4. **Hold down the ⌘ key while you click the cells or drag through the ranges in another table to add that data.**

5. **Click Done to finish editing the data references.**

Extending a chart with more data

Another move you may need to use with charts is extending a chart so that it displays more data than you originally used to create it. For example, you may need to add the latest sales figures to freshen up a chart. The old-fashioned approach would be to delete the chart and create it again from scratch, but Numbers is smart enough to enable you to sidestep wasting time like this.

You can extend a chart with more data in the following two ways:

- **Insert a new row or column in the table.** If the chart uses data from a single table, you can simply insert a new row or column between the existing rows or columns. Input the data in that row or column, and Numbers updates the chart to show it.

- **Select more cells from the same table.** Examples of this are shown in the following sections.

Extending a chart with more data on OS X

Here's an example of extending a chart with more data on OS X:

1. **Click the chart to select it.** Figure 9.11 shows a simple chart and the table from which it is drawn. The chart uses the Ohio, Arizona, and Idaho columns in the table, but not the Colorado column.

2. **Click Edit Data References.** Numbers selects the cells that supply the data (see Figure 9.12).

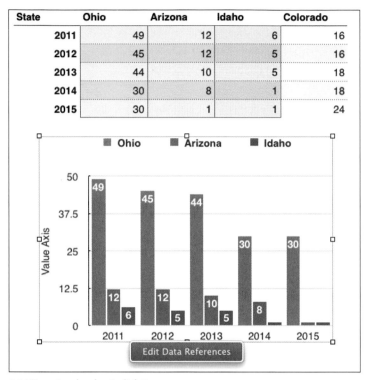

9.11 To extend a chart, click it.

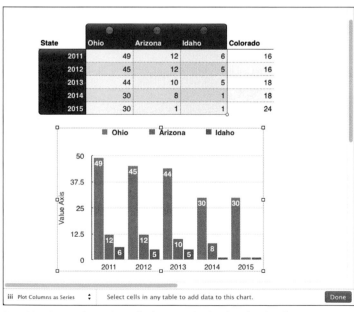

9.12 Numbers selects the cells that supply the data for the chart.

3. **Drag the round handle at the lower-right corner of the selected cells to extend the chart.** In the example shown in Figure 9.13, the handle was dragged to the right to add the Colorado column to the selection. Numbers then added Colorado to the chart.

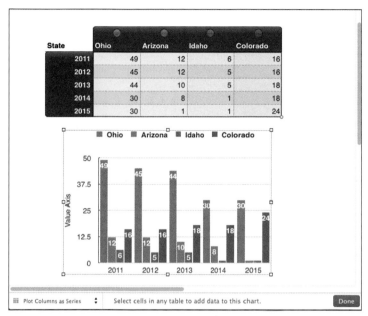

9.13 Drag the round handle at the lower-right corner of the selected cells to extend the chart, and then click Done.

4. **Click Done to stop editing the chart's data.**

Note

You can also reduce the amount of data in the chart.

Extending a chart with more data on iOS

Here's an example of extending a chart with more data on iOS:

1. **Tap the chart to select it.** The pop-up control bar appears (see Figure 9.14).

2. **Tap Edit References on the pop-up control bar.** Numbers selects the cells that provide the data for the chart (see Figure 9.15).

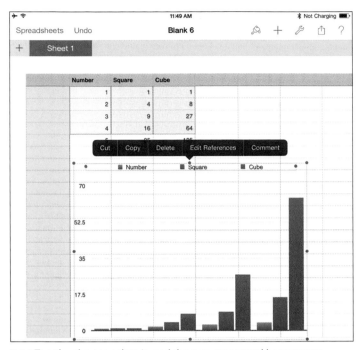

9.14 Tap the chart to select it, and the pop-up control bar appears.

9.15 Numbers selects the cells that contain the source data for the chart.

3. **Drag the round blue handle at the lower-right corner of the selected cells to extend the chart.** In the example shown in Figure 9.16, the handle was dragged down to add an extra row to the selection. Numbers then updated the chart to include the new data.

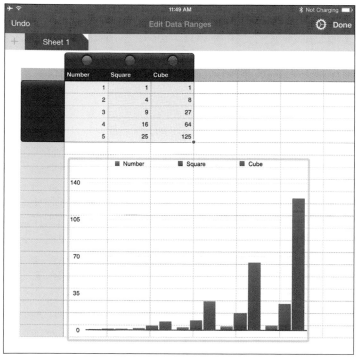

9.16 Drag the round blue handle at the lower-right corner of the selected cells to extend the chart, and then tap Done.

4. **Tap Done to stop editing the chart's data.**

Changing the plotting and axes

To get your charts looking the way you need them, you may need to change the plotting or customize the axes.

Changing the plotting and axes on OS X

Here's how to change the plotting and axes of a chart on OS X:

1. **Click the chart to make it active.**

2. **If the Format inspector isn't displayed, click the Format button on the toolbar to display it.**

3. **Click the Axis button to display the Axis pane.**

4. **Click the button for the axis you want to format.** For example, click the Value (Y) button to display the Value (Y) pane (see Figure 9.17), which contains controls for formatting the value axis.

5. **In the Axis Options area, select the Axis Name check box if you want to display the axis name.** Select the Axis Line check box if you want to display the axis line. Both of these are often helpful, but it depends on the chart and what you need it to show.

6. **Use the following controls in the Axis Scale area to configure the scale of the axis:**

   ● **Axis Scale.** Click this pop-up menu, and then select the scale type: Linear or Logarithmic.

   ● **Scale boxes.** Type the maximum value in the Max box and the minimum value in the Min box.

   ● **Steps boxes.** Use the controls to set the number for major steps in the Major box and the number for minor steps in the Minor box.

7. **In the Value Labels area, you can click the pop-up menu and choose how to format the value labels.** The default is Same as Source Data, which often works well, but you can choose another data format, such as Number or Currency, if you want. Alternatively, choose None to suppress the value labels.

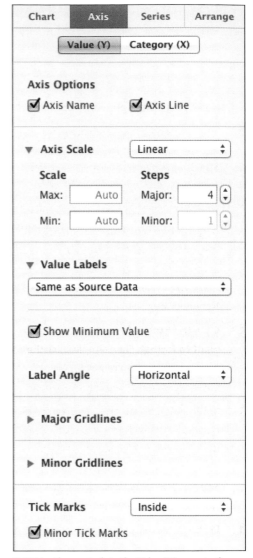

9.17 Use the controls in the Value (Y) pane in the Axis pane to format the value axis of the chart.

8. **Still in the Value Labels area, select the Show Minimum Value check box if you want to show the minimum value for the labels.** Showing the minimum value is usually helpful.

9. **Also in the Value Labels area, you can click the Label Angle pop-up menu and choose the angle at which to show the labels.** For example, if the labels are too wide

to work well with the Horizontal setting, choose Left Vertical or Right Vertical to run the labels vertically instead.

10. **Use the controls in the Major Gridlines section and the Minor Gridlines section to set up the gridlines for the axis.**

11. **To control whether the tick marks appear on the axis, click the Tick Marks pop-up menu and click Inside, Centered, or Outside, as needed.** If you want to hide the tick marks, click None.

12. **If you choose to display tick marks, select the Minor Tick Marks check box if you want to display minor tick marks on the axis.** Otherwise, deselect this check box.

13. **Click the button for the next axis you want to format.** For example, click the Category (X) button to dIsplay the Category (X) pane (see Figure 9.18).

14. **In the Axis Options area, select the Axis Name check box if you want to display the axis name.** Select the Axis Line check box if you want to display the axis line. Select the Series Names check box if you want to display the series names.

9.18 Use the controls in the Category (X) pane to format the category axis.

15. **In the Category Labels pop-up menu, choose one of the following options:**

- **None.** Choose this setting to hide the category labels.

- **Auto-Fit Category Labels.** Choose this setting (the default) to have Numbers make the category labels fit. This tends to be the best choice unless the labels are much too long to fit in the space available.

- **Show All Category Labels.** Choose this setting if you need to show all the labels.

- **Custom Category Intervals.** Choose this setting to customize the intervals as needed.

- **Show Last Category.** Click this item, placing or removing its check mark, to control whether the last category appears. Unlike the other items on the Category Labels pop-up menu, which are a set of choices (selecting one deselects the item that was previously selected), this is an independent item.

16. **If the Label References box shows the wrong cells, edit it to select the right ones.**

17. **If you need to change the angle of the labels, click the Label Angle pop-up menu and choose a suitable angle.**

18. **Use the controls in the Gridlines area to set up any gridlines needed.**

19. **To control whether the tick marks appear on the axis, click the Tick Marks pop-up menu and click Inside, Centered, or Outside, as needed.** If you want to hide the tick marks, click None.

20. **If you choose to display tick marks, select the Minor Tick Marks check box if you want to display minor tick marks on the axis.** Otherwise, deselect this check box.

21. **Click the Series button to display the Series pane.**

22. **If you need to add a data series, click the Value box (see Figure 9.19), and then select the table cells to use as the source.** You can then type the name for the series in the Name box.

| Chart | Axis | Series | Arrange |

▼ **Data**

Value: [   ]

Name: [   ]

▼ **Value Labels**

[Same as Source Data ⬍]

Location: [Top ⬍]

▼ **Trendlines**

[Linear ⬍]

☐ Name: [   ]

☐ Show Equation

☐ Show R² Value

▼ **Error Bars**

[Positive and Negative ⬍]

Use: [Fixed Value ⬍]

Range: [10]

9.19 In the Series pane, you can set several options, including value labels.

23. **Use the controls in the Value Labels area to choose one of the following formats for the value labels for the data series:**

   ● You can choose Same as Source Data to keep the labels as they are in the source, apply a format (such as Number, Currency, or Fraction), or choose None to show no labels.

   ● To specify where the labels are, open the Location pop-up menu, and then click Top, Middle, Bottom, or Outside.

24. **If you want to add trendlines to the chart, choose the type of trendlines in the Trendlines pop-up menu: Linear, Logarithmic, Polynomial, Power, Exponential, or Moving Average.** Use the controls that appear below the Trendlines pop-up menu to choose options for the trendlines, such as displaying a name for them or showing the equation used. (The set of controls that appears below the Trendlines pop-up menu varies depending on the type of trendlines you choose.)

25. **To add error bars to the chart, click the Error Bars pop-up menu, and then choose the type of error bars: Positive and Negative, Positive only, Negative only, or None.** If you choose any type except None, open the Use pop-up menu, and then click the type of error bar to use: Fixed Value, Percentage, Standard Deviation, Standard Error, or Custom Values. If the Range box appears, use it to set the range.

Changing the plotting and axes on iOS

Here's how to change the plotting and axes of a chart on iOS:

1. **Tap the chart to select it.** Numbers displays the pop-up control bar.

2. **Tap Edit References to display the Edit Data Ranges screen.**

3. **Tap the Settings icon (the cogwheel) to display the Series Options pane on the iPad (see Figure 9.20), or the Series Options screen on the iPhone or iPod touch.**

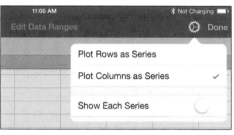

9.20 The Series Options pane on the iPad.

4. **Choose the series by tapping Plot Rows as Series or Plot Columns as Series, placing a check mark to the right of the option you tap.**

5. **Set the Show Each Series switch to On if you want the chart to show each series, or Off if you do not.**

6. **Tap Done to return to your chart.**

Displaying hidden rows or columns in a chart

As covered in the previous chapters, you often need to hide rows or columns in your tables to make them appear the way you want. When you create a chart based on a table with hidden data, you need to decide whether to show that hidden data in the chart or keep it hidden.

Genius

Decide whether to include data that's hidden in the table depending on what the data shows, why it's hidden, and whether showing it will make the chart more or less persuasive. Also, consider whether the audience will be able to tell that the data was hidden in the source table (for example, from a handout); if so, using the data in the chart may be embarrassing rather than helpful.

Here's how to make a chart display the data in any hidden rows or columns in its data range:

- **OS X.** Select the Hidden Data check box in the Chart Options area in the Chart pane of the Format inspector. Deselect this check box to exclude the hidden data from the chart.

- **iOS.** Set the Show Hidden Data switch in the Chart Options pane to On if you want to display the hidden data. Otherwise, set this switch to Off.

Adding Pictures and Shapes to Charts

You can add images, audio files, and movies to your spreadsheets by using the Media Browser, as discussed in Chapter 4. All-singing, all-dancing spreadsheet documents tend to be less useful than multimedia presentations, so you may not need to add audio files or movie files. However, images can greatly enhance a spreadsheet.

The simplest way to add an image is to place it on the sheet canvas. Click the sheet canvas, then insert the image as usual using the Media Browser (on OS X or iOS) or the Image button (in iCloud). You can then format the image as needed. For example, you can mask the image or add a frame.

On OS X, you can add an image as the background to a cell, an entire table, or a chart. This can be a good way to add visual interest or provide context for the data.

Here's how to add a background image to a chart.

1. **Click the chart to select it.**
2. **If the Format inspector isn't displayed, click the Format button on the toolbar to display it.**
3. **Click the Chart button to display the Chart pane.**

4. **Expand the Background & Border Style area if it's collapsed.**

5. **Click the Fill pop-up menu, and then click Image Fill.**

6. **Click the Choose button, select the image file in the dialog, and then click Open.**

7. **Click the pop-up menu above the Choose button, and then click the way to arrange the image: Original Size, Stretch, Tile, Scale to Fill, or Scale to Fit.**

8. **If necessary, drag the Scale slider to resize the image.**

If you want to place an image behind two or more objects, you need to proceed differently. Here's what to do:

1. **Place the image on the sheet canvas.** Use the Photos pane of the Media Browser as usual, or drag the image in from IPhoto or a Finder window.

2. **Resize and mask the image as needed.**

3. **Send the image behind or to the back.** Click the Arrange button to display the Arrange pane in the Format inspector, and then click the Back or Backward button, as needed. Using the Back button is easiest if you're just using one image. If you need to layer one image on top of another, use the Backward button.

4. **Position the tables or other objects over the object.**

5. **Adjust the opacity of the objects.** Click the Style button to display the Style pane and then drag the Opacity slider until the image shows through the object to the degree you want.

Adding Controls to Cells

Normally, people who use your spreadsheet interact with it by using the keyboard or mouse (on OS X and iCloud), or their fingers (on iOS) to type or change values in cells. However, you can also insert the following controls in cells to let users perform particular actions:

- **Check boxes**
- **Star ratlngs**
- **Sliders**
- **Steppers**
- **Pop-up menus**

To add controls to cells, use the following tools:

- **OS X.** Use the Cell pane in the Format inspector (see Figure 9.21).
- **iOS.** Use the Format pane in the Format panel.
- **iCloud.** Use the Data pane in the Format panel.

Adding a check box to a cell

Add a check box to a cell when the user needs to make a simple yes/no or true/false choice in a table. Unlike when a check box appears in a dialog box, a check box in a cell doesn't directly change any settings, but you can reference it in formulas. A selected check box returns TRUE, whereas an unselected check box returns FALSE.

9.21 The Cell pane in the Format inspector on OS X.

Here's how to add a check box to a cell on OS X:

1. **Click the cell in which you want to place the check box.**

2. **If the Format inspector isn't displayed, click the Format button on the toolbar to display it.**

3. **Click the Cell button to display the Cell pane.**

4. **Click the Data Format pop-up menu, and then click Checkbox.** The check box appears in the cell (see Figure 9.22).

Here's how to add a check box to a cell on iOS:

1. **Tap the cell in which you want to place the check box.**

2. **Tap the Format button on the toolbar to display the Format panel.**

3. **Tap the Format button to display the Format pane.**

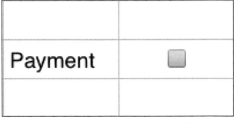

9.22 Add a check box to a spreadsheet for a simple way of marking options.

4. **Tap Checkbox (see Figure 9.23), placing a check mark next to it.** The check box appears in the cell.

Here's how to add a check box to a cell in iCloud:

1. **Click the cell in which you want to place the check box.**

2. **If the Format panel isn't displayed, click the Tools button on the toolbar, and then choose Settings⇨Show Format Panel to display it.**

3. **Click the Data button to display the Data pane.**

4. **Click the Data Format pop-up menu, and then click Checkbox.** The check box appears in the cell (see Figure 9.24).

Adding a star rating to a cell

Add a star rating to a cell when you want to provide an easy way to rate an item on a scale of one to five. Star ratings have an informal feel but can work well in many types of spreadsheets.

Here's how to add a star rating to a cell on OS X:

1. **Click the cell in which you want to place the star rating.**

2. **If the Format inspector isn't displayed, click the Format button on the toolbar to display it.**

3. **Click the Cell button to display the Cell pane.**

4. **Click the Data Format pop-up menu, and then click Star Rating.** The dot placeholders for the stars appear in the cell, and you can click a dot to apply that number of stars (see Figure 9.25).

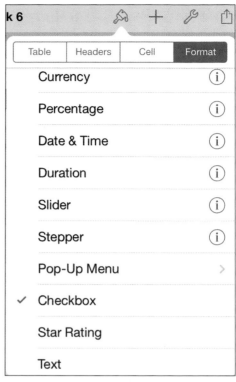

9.23 On iOS, tap Checkbox in the Format pane to add a check box to a cell.

9.24 Choose Checkbox in the Data Format pop-up menu in the Data pane in Numbers for iCloud to add a check box to a cell.

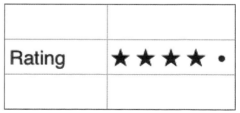

9.25 A star rating can be a quick and easy way to get feedback.

285

Here's how to add a star rating to a cell on iOS:

1. **Tap the cell in which you want to place the star rating.**

2. **Tap the Format button on the toolbar to display the Format panel.**

3. **Tap the Format button to display the Format pane.**

4. **Tap Star Rating, placing a check mark next to it.** The dots for the stars appear in the cell.

Here's how to add a star rating to a cell in iCloud:

1. **Click the cell in which you want to place the star rating.**

2. **If the Format panel isn't displayed, click the Tools button on the toolbar, and then choose Settings⊏⟩Show Format Panel to display it.**

3. **Click the Data button to display the Data pane.**

4. **Click the Data Format pop-up menu, and then click Star Rating.** The dots for the stars appear in the cell.

Note

At this writing, the dots for the star rating appear in iCloud, but they don't work correctly: You cannot click a dot to choose the number of stars.

Adding a slider to a cell

Add a slider to a cell when you want to let the user make large changes to a value within the range you choose. For example, you can add a pricing slider that lets the user change a product's price from $5 to $500 in $5 increments.

Adding a slider to a cell on OS X

Here's how to add a slider to a cell on OS X:

1. **Click the cell in which you want to place the slider.**

2. **If the Format inspector isn't displayed, click the Format button on the toolbar to display it.**

3. **Click the Cell button to display the Cell pane.**

4. **Click the Data Format pop-up menu, and then click Slider.** The Cell pane displays the controls for configuring the slider (see Figure 9.26).

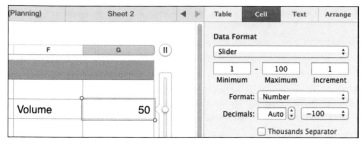

9.26 Use the controls in the Cell pane to configure a slider.

5. **Type the lowest value allowed in the Minimum box.**

6. **Type the highest value allowed in the Maximum box.**

7. **Type the slze of the steps in the Increment box.**

8. **Click the Format pop-up menu and choose how to display the slider.** Your choices are Number, Currency, Percentage, Fraction, Scientific, or Numeral System. For example, if the user is choosing standard pricing in dollars, choose Currency. You can then choose whether to use accounting style (with the currency symbol aligned at the left of the cell) or regular style (with the currency symbol appearing just before the numeric value).

Adding a slider to a cell on iOS

Here's how to add a slider to a cell on iOS:

1. **Tap the cell in which you want to place the slider.**

2. **Tap the Format button on the toolbar to display the Format panel.**

3. **Tap the Format button to display the Format pane.**

4. **Tap Slider, placing a check mark next to it.**

5. **Tap the Info (i) button on the right side of the Slider button to display the Slider Options pane (see Figure 9.27).**

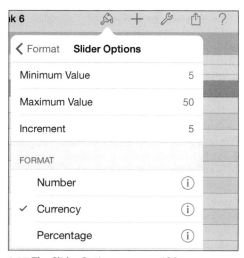

9.27 The Slider Options pane on iOS.

287

6. **Tap the Minimum Value field and type the lowest value allowed.**

7. **Tap the Maximum Value field and type the highest value allowed.**

8. **Tap the Increment field and type the size of the steps.**

9. **In the Format area, tap the data format to use for the slider, placing a check mark next to it.** Your choices are Number, Currency, and Percentage.

10. **Tap the Info (i) button on the right side of the data format's button to display the Options pane for that format.** Figure 9.28 shows the Currency Options pane.

11. **Choose options for the data format.**

12. **Tap in the spreadsheet to close the Options pane.**

The slider appears when you select the cell in the spreadsheet. You can then drag it to adjust the value. Figure 9.29 shows a Currency slider on the iPad.

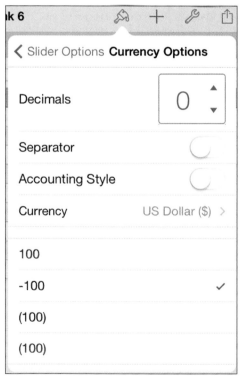

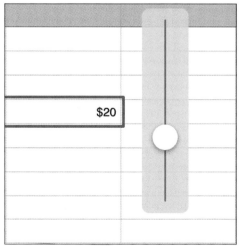

9.28 Choose options for the slider's data format on the Options screen.

9.29 Tap the cell in the spreadsheet to display the slider on the iPad.

Note

On the iPhone and iPod touch, the slider appears horizontally at the bottom of the screen, not next to the cell as on the iPad.

Adding a slider to a cell in iCloud

Here's how to add a slider to a cell in iCloud:

1. **Click the cell in which you want to place the slider.**

2. **If the Format panel isn't displayed, click the Tools button on the toolbar and choose Settings ⇨ Show Format Panel to display it.**

3. **Click the Data button to display the Data pane.**

4. **Click the Data Format pop-up menu, and then click Slider.** The Data pane displays the controls for configuring the slider.

5. **Type the lowest value allowed in the Minimum box.**

6. **Type the highest value allowed in the Maximum box.**

7. **Type the size of the steps in the Increment box.**

8. **Click the Format pop-up menu and choose how to display the slider.** Your choices are Number, Currency, Percentage, Fraction, or Scientific. For example, to show a percentage, click the Percentage format. You can then choose the number of decimals (or leave it set to Auto) and how to represent negative numbers.

Adding a stepper to a cell

Add a stepper to a cell when you want to let the user choose values in predefined increments — for example, 5, 10, 15, 20, and so on.

Adding a stepper to a cell on OS X

Here's how to add a stepper to a cell on OS X:

1. **Click the cell in which you want to place the stepper.**

2. **If the Format inspector isn't displayed, click the Format button on the toolbar to display it.**

3. **Click the Cell button to display the Cell pane.**

4. **Click the Data Format pop-up menu, and then click Stepper.** The Cell pane displays the controls for configuring the stepper (see Figure 9.30).

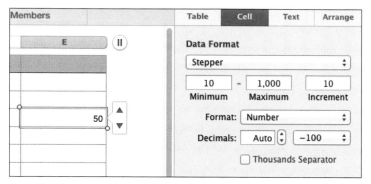

9.30 Click Stepper in the Data Format pop-up menu to insert a stepper.

5. **Type the lowest value allowed in the Minimum box.**

6. **Type the highest value allowed in the Maximum box.**

7. **Type the size of the steps in the Increment box.**

8. **Click the Format pop-up menu and choose how to display the stepper.** Your choices are Number, Currency, Percentage, Fraction, Scientific, or Numeral System. For example, choose Fraction in the Format pop-up menu, then open the Accuracy pop-up menu and choose the accuracy (such as Up to 3 digits or Hundredths).

Adding a stepper to a cell in iOS

Here's how to add a stepper to a cell on iOS:

1. **Tap the cell in which you want to place the stepper.**

2. **Tap the Format button on the toolbar to display the Format panel.**

3. **Tap the Format button to display the Format pane.**

4. **Tap Stepper, placing a check mark next to it.**

5. **Tap the Info (i) button on the right side of the Stepper button to display the Stepper Options pane (see Figure 9.31).**

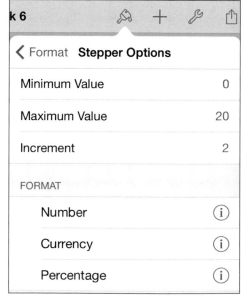

9.31 The Stepper Options pane on iOS.

6. **Tap the Minimum Value field and type the lowest value allowed.**

7. **Tap the Maximum Value field and type the highest value allowed.**

8. **Tap the Increment field and type the size of the steps.**

9. **In the Format area, tap the data format to use for the stepper, placing a check mark next to it.** Your choices are Number, Currency, and Percentage.

10. **Tap the Info (i) button on the right side of the data format's button to display the Options pane for that format.** Figure 9.32 shows the Fraction subpane in the Number Options pane.

11. **Choose options for the data format.**

12. **Tap in the spreadsheet to close the Options pane.**

9.32 The Fraction subpane.

Adding a stepper to a cell in iCloud

Here's how to add a stepper to a cell in iCloud:

1. **Click the cell in which you want to place the stepper.**

2. **If the Format panel isn't displayed, click the Tools button on the toolbar and choose Settings⇨Show Format Panel to display it.**

3. **Click the Data button to display the Data pane.**

4. **Click the Data Format pop-up menu, and then click Stepper.** The Data pane displays the controls for configuring the stepper.

5. **Type the lowest value allowed in the Minimum box.**

6. **Type the highest value allowed in the Maximum box.**

7. **Type the size of the steps in the Increment box.**

8. **Click the Format pop-up menu and choose how to display the stepper.** Your choices are Number, Currency, Percentage, Fraction, or Scientific. For example, to use scientific format, click Scientific, and then choose the number of decimal places to show.

Adding a pop-up menu to a cell

On OS X and iOS, you can also add a pop-up menu to a cell. Add a pop-up menu when you want to provide the user with a limited range of values from which to choose. For example, in an expense report, you may need to include a pop-up menu that lets users choose the office or department for which they work.

Note At this writing, Numbers for iCloud doesn't offer pop-up menu controls. If you open a Numbers document that contains a pop-up menu, you see only the current value set for the pop-up menu.

Adding a pop-up menu to a cell on OS X

Here's how to add a pop-up menu to a cell on OS X:

1. **Click the cell in which you want to place the pop-up menu.**

2. **If the Format inspector isn't displayed, click the Format button on the toolbar to display it.**

3. **Click the Cell button to display the Cell pane.**

4. **Click the Data Format pop-up menu, and then click Pop-Up Menu.** The Cell pane displays the controls for configuring the pop-up menu. Three default menu items — Item 1, Item 2, and Item 3 — appear in the list box.

5. **Double-click the Item 1 item to select it, type the menu item you want, and then press Return.** Replace the Item 2 item and Item 3 item as well. Figure 9.33 shows a pop-up menu under construction.

6. **To add another menu item, click the + button, and then type the menu item over the New Item placeholder text.** If you need to remove a menu item, click it and then click the – button.

7. **If necessary, drag the menu items into the order you want.**

8. **Click the Initial Cell pop-up menu, and then choose Start with First Item or Start with Blank, as needed.**

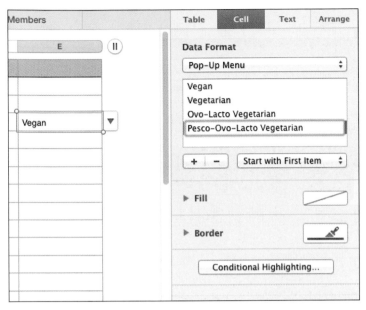

9.33 Type the values for the pop-up menu in the text box in the Cell pane.

When you finish creating the pop-up menu, click the cell in the spreadsheet, and then click the pop-up button to display the menu. Verify that the menu's items appear the way you want them (see Figure 9.34).

Adding a pop-up menu to a cell on iOS

Here's how to add a pop-up menu to a cell on iOS:

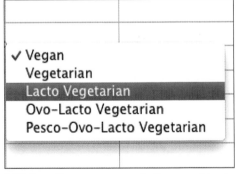

9.34 Open the pop-up menu in the spreadsheet to make sure it's complete.

1. **Tap the cell in which you want to place the pop-up menu.**

2. **Tap the Format button on the toolbar to display the Format panel.**

3. **Tap the Format button to display the Format pane.**

4. **Tap Pop-Up Menu to display the Pop-Up Options pane.** Three default menu items — Item 1, Item 2, and Item 3 — appear in the area at the top, together with an add new item button.

5. **Tap Item 1 to select it, tap the X button to delete the default name, and then type the menu item.** Replace Items 2 and 3, as well (see Figure 9.35).

6. **To add another menu item, tap the add new item button, and then type the name for the item.**

7. **If necessary, use the drag handles (the three horizontal lines on the right side of each menu item's button) to drag the menu items into the order you need.**

8. **In the Initial Value area, tap First Item or Blank to choose the starting value for the pop-up menu.**

9. **Tap in the spreadsheet to close the Pop-Up Options pane.**

The pop-up menu then appears in the spreadsheet. You can tap the cell to open the pop-up menu, and then tap the value you want to insert (see Figure 9.36).

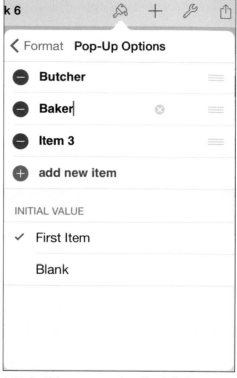

9.35 On iOS, you can replace the default menu items with the menu items you need.

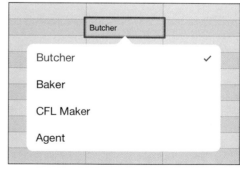

9.36 Tap the cell to display the pop-up menu and choose a value.

How Do I Use the Extra Features in Numbers for OS X?

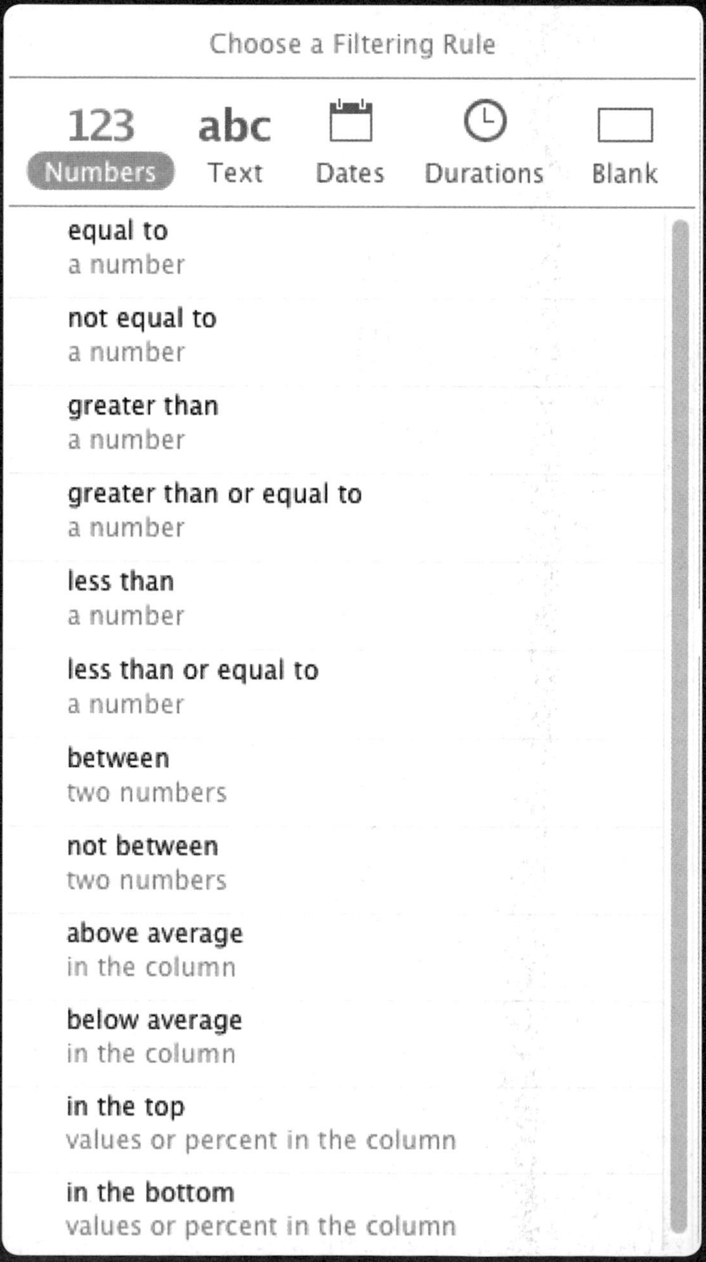

Choose a Filtering Rule

123	abc	📅	🕐	☐
Numbers	Text	Dates	Durations	Blank

equal to
a number

not equal to
a number

greater than
a number

greater than or equal to
a number

less than
a number

less than or equal to
a number

between
two numbers

not between
two numbers

above average
in the column

below average
in the column

in the top
values or percent in the column

in the bottom
values or percent in the column

On a Mac, you can exploit some features that Numbers offers for OS X that are not available on iOS or iCloud. These features include monitoring cells for unexpected values, importing data from Microsoft Excel, and applying filters to a table to make it display only the rows that match the criteria you specify. You can also create a spreadsheet template to enable yourself or your colleagues to build standardized spreadsheets faster and with less effort. You can also export your Numbers spreadsheets to different formats, such as Microsoft Excel or Comma-Separated Values.

Monitoring Cells for Unexpected Values

You can set Numbers to monitor particular cells for particular values and apply certain formatting to any that match the criteria. *Conditional highlighting* enables you to use formatting to alert you to a cell that contains an unexpected — and perhaps incorrect — format.

Genius

You can use the conditional formatting feature in Pages and Keynote as well, but it is usually most useful in Numbers.

To use conditional formatting, follow these steps:

1. **Select the cell or cells you want to affect.** You may want to select an entire row or column if its cells contain the same type of data. Numbers applies the conditional formatting when any of the cells contain a matching value — they don't all have to match.

2. **If the Format inspector isn't displayed, click the Format button on the toolbar to display it.**

3. **Click the Cell button to display the Cell pane (see Figure 10.1).**

4. **Click Conditional Highlighting to display the Conditional Highlighting pane.**

5. **Click Add a Rule to display the Choose a Highlighting Rule pop-up panel (see Figure 10.2).**

10.1 Click Conditional Highlighting in the Cell pane of the Format inspector to start applying conditional highlighting.

Choose a Highlighting Rule				
123	abc			
Numbers	Text	Dates	Durations	Blank

equal to
a number

not equal to
a number

greater than
a number

greater than or equal to
a number

less than
a number

less than or equal to
a number

between
two numbers

not between
two numbers

10.2 In the Choose a Highlighting Rule pop-up panel, click the rule category, and then click the rule.

Choose a Highlighting Rule				
123	abc			
Numbers	Text	Dates	Durations	Blank

yesterday

today

tomorrow

in this

in the next
week, month or year...

in the last
week, month or year...

exactly...

before...

after...

between...

the date...

before the date...

10.3 The Choose a Highlighting Rule pop-up panel enables you to create a wide variety of date-based rules.

6. **At the top of the Choose a Highlighting Rule pop-up panel (see Figure 10.3), click the category of rules you want to use: Numbers, Text, Dates Durations, or Blank (see Table 10.1).** These rules are the same as those for filtering, which you learn about later in this chapter.

7. **Click the rule you want to use.** Numbers enters the rule in the Conditional Highlighting pane (see Figure 10.4).

8. **Input any values needed to complete the rule.**

9. **Click the formatting button for the rule to display its pop-up menu, and then click one of the following formatting options to apply when this rule is triggered:**

- Your choices include Italic, Bold, different text colors (such as Red Text), and different fill colors (such as Yellow Fill).

- To use custom formatting, click Custom Style at the bottom of the pop-up menu and then use the controls that appear to set up the formatting. The most useful extra formatting options here are strikethrough and underline, but you can also choose exactly the text color and fill color — or both — that you prefer.

10. **If you want to add another conditional highlighting rule, click Add a Rule, and then use the controls that appear (see Figure 10.5) to set up the rule and its formatting.**

11. **When you finish adding rules, click Done to close the Conditional Highlighting pane.** The Format inspector appears again in its place.

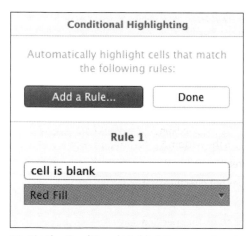

10.4 In the Conditional Highlighting pane, input any values needed to complete the rule and choose the formatting to apply.

10.5 Click Add a Rule if you want to add another formatting rule.

Genius

Test your conditional highlighting rules immediately to make sure they work the way you intend.

Table 10.1 explains the available rules in the five categories. These rules are the same as those for filtering, which are covered later in this chapter.

Table 10.1 Categories and Rules for Conditional Highlighting and Filtering

Category	Rule	Use This Rule To Display
Numbers	equal to	Numeric equivalents to the specified number
Numbers	not equal to	Numbers not equal to the specified number
Numbers	greater than	Numbers greater than the specified number
Numbers	greater than or equal to	Numbers greater than or equal to the specified number
Numbers	less than	Numbers less than the specified number
Numbers	less than or equal to	Numbers less than or equal to the specified number
Numbers	between	Numbers between the two specified numbers
Numbers	not between	Numbers not between the two specified numbers
Numbers	above average	Numbers above the average (mean) for the column
Numbers	below average	Numbers below the average for the column
Numbers	in the top	Numbers in the specified range in the column's values — for example, in the top 10 values in the column
Numbers	in the bottom	Numbers in the specified range in the column's values — for example, in the bottom 5 values in the column
Text	is	Text that directly matches the specified text
Text	is not	Text that does not directly match the specified text
Text	starts with	Text that starts with the specified text
Text	ends with	Text that ends with the specified text
Text	contains	Text that contains the specified text
Text	does not contain	Text that does not contain the specified text
Dates	yesterday	Date values that match the previous day's date
Dates	today	Date values that match today's date
Date	tomorrow	Date values that match tomorrow's date
Date	in this	Date values that fall in the time unit you chose: week, month, quarter, or year

continued

Table 10.1 continued

Category	Rule	Use This Rule To Display
Date	is in the next	Date values that fall in the time unit you chose: week, month, quarter, or year
Date	in the last	Date values that fall in the time unit you chose: week, month, quarter, or year
Date	exactly	Date values that are the specified number of time units (weeks, months, quarters, or years) ago or from now
Date	before	Date values that are before the specified number of time units (weeks, months, quarters, or years) ago or from now
Date	after	Date values that are after the specified number of time units (weeks, months, quarters, or years) ago or from now
Date	between	Date values that are between the two specified numbers of time units (weeks, months, quarters, or years) ago or from now
Date	the date	Date values that match the specified date
Date	before the date	Date values that fall before the specified date
Date	after the date	Date values that fall after the specified date
Date	in the range	Date values that fall between the two specified dates
Durations	equal to	Durations that are equal to the specified duration
Durations	not equal to	Durations that are not equal to the specified duration
Durations	greater than	Durations that are greater than the specified duration
Durations	greater than or equal to	Durations that are greater than or equal to the specified duration
Durations	less than	Durations that are less than the specified duration
Durations	less than or equal to	Durations that are less than or equal to the specified duration
Durations	between	Durations that are between the two specified durations
Durations	not between	Durations that are not between the two specified durations
Durations	above average	Durations that are above average for the values in the column
Durations	below average	Durations that are below average for the values in the column
Durations	in the top	Durations that are in the specified range in the column's values — for example, in the top 10 values in the column
Durations	in the bottom	Durations that are in the specified range in the column's values — for example, in the bottom 100 values in the column
Blank	is blank	Cells containing no entry
Blank	is not blank	Cells containing an entry

Importing Data from Microsoft Excel

Numbers has been around for several years now, but it's one of the newer spreadsheet apps, so it has to get along with Microsoft Excel, the heavyweight champion. Numbers can import Excel workbooks and export its own documents in Excel format. This section covers importing data from Excel; exporting Numbers spreadsheets to Excel format is covered later in this chapter.

Note

Excel can open and export data to workbooks in both the XML-based Excel format and the earlier binary Excel format. The XML-based format uses the .xlsx file extension and is the default file format for Excel 2007 (Windows), Excel 2008 (Mac), and later versions. The binary format uses the .xls file extension and is the default for Excel 2003 (Windows), Excel 2004 (Mac), and earlier versions.

Opening an Excel workbook in Numbers

To work with an Excel workbook in Numbers, simply open it as you would any other spreadsheet: Press ⌘+O or choose File ➪ Open to display the Open dialog, select the Excel workbook, and then click Open. From the Finder, you can Control+click (or right-click) the Excel workbook, and then choose Open With ➪ Numbers from the shortcut menu.

Numbers tries to convert all the Excel workbook's contents to their equivalents in Numbers. This process normally takes a few seconds for a small workbook and can take several minutes for a large and complex one (depending on how powerful your Mac is).

Genius

You cannot open an Excel workbook in Numbers, edit it there, and then save your changes back to the original Excel file. (Some other spreadsheet applications let you do this.) Instead, you must save the file as a Numbers spreadsheet; if you want an Excel version of that spreadsheet, you can export a version of the spreadsheet to Excel format, as explained at the end of this chapter.

Once you open the Excel workbook as a Numbers document, look through it and make sure that everything has converted satisfactorily. You can then save the Numbers document and work with it as normal.

Copying and Pasting Data from Excel

If you need to bring only a small amount of data from Excel into Numbers, try using copy and paste. Provided you need only the data and not any formulas or functions that produce it, copy and paste is normally a fast and satisfactory way of getting data from Excel to Numbers.

If you do need the formulas and functions behind the data, open the Excel workbook in Numbers as described in the main text. If you need only part of a spreadsheet, you can copy it from the new Numbers spreadsheet, paste it into another Numbers spreadsheet, and close the new spreadsheet without saving changes to it.

Understanding problems when importing from Excel

If you open only modest-size Excel workbooks that contain straightforward data and formulas, Numbers can usually open them without any problem. However, if you have larger or more complex Excel workbooks, Numbers may struggle to open them.

Here are things that tend to go wrong when importing Excel workbooks, in descending order of severity:

- **Numbers can import only 255 columns and 65,533 rows.** If you open an Excel workbook that has more rows or columns, Numbers removes the additional rows or columns.

Caution

If Numbers displays the message "Cells outside the boundaries of Numbers were removed" when you open an Excel workbook, treat it as a red flag. This means that the spreadsheet in Numbers is missing data that was in the Excel workbook. Close the spreadsheet, return to the Excel workbook, and rearrange the data to fit within 255 columns and 65,533 rows. You may need to move data to additional worksheets to make this change.

- **Numbers cannot handle huge Excel workbooks.** You cannot miss this problem, because Numbers gives an error when you try to open the Excel workbook. The issue isn't the number of rows or columns, but simply the amount of data in the workbook. There's no specific file size that's too big, as it depends on how much RAM your Mac has, how many other applications it's running when you take on the heavyweight workbook, and how complex the data in the workbook is. Workbooks that Excel for Mac can handle without breaking a virtual sweat can cause Numbers to founder, even on the same Mac.

Note

If you try to open a larger Excel workbook than Numbers can handle, Numbers may simply get stuck. If the progress readout in the Opening dialog stops moving for several minutes, click the X button to the right of the readout to cancel opening the workbook.

- **Numbers strips out Excel worksheet headers and footers.** Excel encourages you to set up worksheet headers and footers that have a left section, a center section, and a right section. At this writing, Numbers does not support headers and footers, so it gets rid of any in Excel worksheets without notifying you.

- **You may need to change some formulas.** For example, if you've used the SUMIF function in Excel, you may need to use the SUMIFS function in Numbers to get the same result. Also, see the next point.

- **Numbers doesn't support all Excel's functions.** Excel has around 500 functions, while Numbers has around 270 functions. The 230-odd functions that Numbers doesn't have are mostly specialized ones, but if you work with statistics, it's a good idea to check that Numbers provides the functions you need. For a full list of Numbers functions, download the iWork Formulas and Functions User Guide from the Support area of the Apple Web site.

Caution

If Numbers displays the message, *Unsupported formulas were removed. The last calculated values were imported*, treat the spreadsheet with extreme caution. You will need to determine which formulas Numbers has removed, and then re-create their calculations using Numbers' own functions before you can trust any calculated values in the spreadsheet.

- **Numbers removes Excel's drop-down lists.** In Excel, you can create a list of predefined values — for example, a list of your company's offices or project codes — and then use a drop-down list to input them in cells. Numbers has a corresponding feature, the Pop-Up Menu item in the Data Format pop-up menu, but doesn't convert Excel's drop-down lists; instead, it removes them. You need to re-create pop-up menus in Numbers after importing an Excel workbook that contains drop-down lists.

- **Some formatting disappears.** For example, Excel lets you rotate text within a cell, so if you need text to run at a 45-degree angle, all you need to do is apply the formatting. Numbers strips out any formatting it cannot handle. To rotate text in Numbers, insert a text box, rotate it, and then type the text.

- **Locking and password protection.** Excel lets you lock cells against editing and protect a worksheet with a password. Numbers doesn't support these features, so it removes the locking and protection when you open an Excel workbook. Numbers warns you about this change in the Some features aren't supported dialog.

- **Numbers removes scenarios.** Numbers doesn't offer scenarios, an Excel feature for trying different sets of data in the same spreadsheet and switching among the sets of data. So, Numbers removes scenarios from workbooks you import.

- **Numbers converts PivotTables to regular tables.** Numbers doesn't offer a PivotTable feature, so it converts PivotTables to regular tables.

Filtering a Table to Show Results

To make a table show data in the most useful way, you may need to perform one of the following actions:

- **Sorting.** Sorting lets you rearrange the rows into a different order. For example, if you have a table of sales by rep, you can sort by the sales total column so that you can see which rep sold the most. To sort a table, use the techniques explained in Chapter 4.

- **Filtering.** Filtering lets you narrow down a table so that it shows only the rows in which you're interested. For example, you can filter a table of customers so that it shows only those with addresses in Buffalo.

You can filter a table quickly by one column, or you can set up multiple filters. To quickly filter a table by one column, Control+click the cell that contains the value by which you want to filter, and then click Filter Table By on the contextual menu. This menu item shows the value of the cell you click — for example, Filter Table by *Nevada*.

If you cannot see the value by which you want to filter, Control+click the column heading of the column by which you want to filter. On the contextual menu, click the Filter Table submenu, and then click the appropriate value in the Show rows containing section.

To filter a table by multiple columns, you use the Filter inspector like this:

1. **Click the table you want to filter.** The table becomes active.

2. **Choose Table ⇨ Filter Table to display the Filter inspector (see Figure 10.6).**

10.6 Click Add a Filter in the Filter inspector to start filtering a table by multiple columns.

Note You can also open the Filter inspector by moving the mouse pointer over the column heading of the column by which you want to sort, clicking the pop-up menu button that appears, and then choosing Filter Table ⇨ Edit Table Filters.

3. **Click Add a Filter to display the Filter by Column list, and then click the heading of the first column by which you want to filter (see Figure 10.7).** The Filter pane displays the add a rule button.

4. **Click add a rule to display the Choose a Filtering Rule pop-up panel (see Figure 10.8).** This panel provides the same rules as the Conditional Highlighting pane, discussed earlier in this chapter. See Table 10.1 for coverage of these rules.

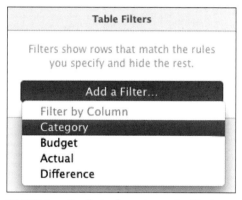

10.7 Choose the first column to use for filtering.

10.8 In the Choose a Filtering Rule pop-up panel, click the rule category, and then click the rule.

5. **At the top of the Choose a Filtering Rule pop-up panel, click the category of filtering rules you want to use: Numbers, Text, Dates, Durations, or Blank.** Table 10.1 explains the available rules in the five categories.

6. **Click the rule you want to use.** Numbers enters the rule in the Filter inspector (see Figure 10.9).

7. **Type any values needed for the rule in the text boxes.**

8. **If you need to add another rule for the column, click or, and then follow steps 5 to 7 to set up the rule.**

9. **If you need to set up filtering on another column, follow steps 3 to 8.**

10. **Select the Filters check box in the Filter inspector to turn filtering on or off.**

11. **If you've created multiple filters, click the Show rows that match pop-up menu, and then click the appropriate filtering option:**

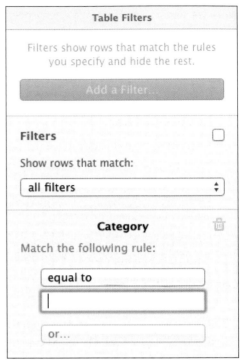

10.9 After choosing the rule, input the value in the Filter inspector.

- **all filters.** Choose all filters to show the rows that match all the filters. For example, you might filter a table of customer data by both state and the product the customer purchased.

- **any filter.** Choose any filter to show the rows that match any of the filters. For example, you might filter a table of meteorological data to show exceptional rainfall or extremes of temperature.

Creating a Spreadsheet Template

When you create a spreadsheet that contains sheets, tables, or charts you want to reuse easily, save the spreadsheet as a template. Doing this enables you to create a new spreadsheet based on the template by choosing File ➪ New and selecting the template in the Template Chooser.

When creating a template from a spreadsheet, set up the template's contents as fully as possible. Perform as many of the following actions as your spreadsheet needs:

- **Remove any unnecessary sheets or tables.** Go through the spreadsheet sheet by sheet, and take out any sheets or tables that don't belong in the final template. For example, you may find rough versions of tables or sheets containing notes about what the template needs.

- **Strip out the variable data from the tables.** If you've created a final spreadsheet, the tables are probably full of the data that this version of the spreadsheet needs — but that other spreadsheets based on your new template will not need. Remove all the variable data to avoid any confusion about whether it belongs there.

Caution When creating a template, be careful not to include sample data that can be mistaken for real data. Instead, insert clear instructions in cells where they're needed, and attach comments to any cells that need additional explanation.

- **Add comments to anything ambiguous.** The spreadsheet may be clear to you because you've created it, but it's likely to be opaque to anyone else. If you've ever puzzled over how someone else's template is supposed to work, or which data goes where, you can appreciate the value of helpful, concise comments.

- **Create any table styles needed.** If you've applied custom formatting to the tables in the spreadsheet, make sure you turn them into styles so that they're easy to apply to new tables that users of the template create.

When you've set up the file as fully as possible, save it as a template like this:

1. **Choose File ⇨ Save as Template.** The Create a custom Numbers template? dialog opens (see Figure 10.10).

Create a custom Numbers template?
You can add this spreadsheet to the Template Chooser, or save it to your computer.

Cancel | Save... | Add to Template Chooser

10.10 Click Add to Template Chooser in the Create a custom Numbers template? dialog to easily create new spreadsheets based on your template.

2. **Click Add to Template Chooser.** The Choose a Template dialog opens, displaying the My Templates category. The new template appears with an edit box around its name.

Note

If you want to save the template to a file without adding it to the Template Chooser on your Mac, click Save in the Create a custom Numbers template? dialog instead of clicking Add to Template Chooser. You would do this if you want to share the custom template with others rather than use it yourself.

3. **Type the name for the template file and press Return to apply it.**

4. **Click the Choose button if you want to create a new presentation based on the template — for example, to make sure the spreadsheet works as intended.** Otherwise, click Cancel to close the Choose a Template dialog.

Protecting a Spreadsheet with a Password

If you need to protect a spreadsheet against unauthorized use, you can protect it with a password. To do so, follow these steps:

1. **Choose File ⇨ Set Password.** Numbers displays the Set a password to open this spreadsheet dialog.

2. **Type the password in the Password and Verify boxes (see Figure 10.11).**

3. **Optionally, type a password hint in the Password Hint box.** Normally, it is best not to provide a password hint, even though Apple recommends doing so. This is because any hint that can help an authorized user remember the password might also enable an attacker to guess the password.

Set a password to open this spreadsheet:	
Password:	••••••••
Verify:	••••••••
Password Hint: (Recommended)	
☐ Remember this password in my keychain	
	Cancel Set Password

10.11 The Set a password to open this spreadsheet dialog.

4. **Select the Remember this password in my keychain check box if you want to store the password in your OS X keychain.** This is a handy way to keep the password safe.

5. **Click Set Password.**

Exporting to Other Formats

After you finish and polish a spreadsheet, you probably want to share it with others, either locally in your office or via the Internet. Numbers lets you easily share a document by sending a link to the document on iCloud or by sending a copy of the document via Mail, Messages, AirDrop, or another sharing tool, as discussed in Chapter 2. You can also export a Numbers spreadsheet to a Microsoft Excel workbook, to a Comma-Separated Values file, or to a Numbers '09 document, as explained in this section.

Exporting to Microsoft Excel

When you need to share a Numbers spreadsheet with someone who uses Microsoft Excel (on either the Mac or the PC), you can save the spreadsheet as an Excel workbook with just a few clicks. However, the conversion between Numbers and Excel isn't perfect; just as some items may move and some data and formatting may disappear when you open an Excel workbook in Excel, so may a Numbers spreadsheet change when you export it to an Excel workbook.

Here's how to export a spreadsheet from Numbers to an Excel workbook:

1. **Choose File ⇨ Export To ⇨ Excel to display the Export Your Spreadsheet dialog with the Excel pane at the front (see Figure 10.12).**

2. **Select the Include a summary worksheet check box if you want to include a summary worksheet in the workbook.** This worksheet is often helpful for spreadsheets that include multiple sheets, but you probably want to see if it works well for your data.

3. **To choose the format for the Excel workbook, click the Advanced Options disclosure triangle to reveal the Advanced Options area (see Figure 10.13).** This area contains the Format pop-up menu.

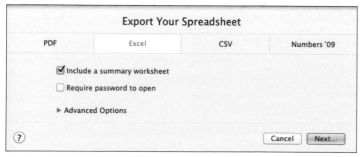

10.12 The Excel pane of the Export dialog box lets you choose whether to include a summary worksheet for spreadsheets that include multiple sheets.

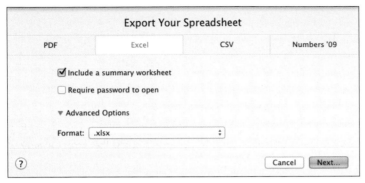

10.13 Use the Format pop-up menu in the Advanced Options area of the Export Your Spreadsheet dialog to choose the .xlsx or .xls format.

Genius

The XML-based .xlsx format is technically superior to the binary .xls format, so it is a better choice unless you need to ensure compatibility with older versions of Excel. The biggest advantages of the .xlsx format are that it supports much larger worksheets and workbooks than the .xls format; it is also more resilient against data corruption.

4. **Click the Format pop-up menu, and then click the format you want:**

   - **.xlsx.** Choose this format to create a workbook in the XML-based Excel format. This format is the default for Excel 2007 for Windows, Excel 2008 for Mac, and later versions of Excel.

   - **.xls (Excel 1997–2003 compatible).** Choose this format to create a workbook in the binary Excel format used by Excel 2003 for Windows, Excel 2004 for Mac, and earlier versions of Excel.

5. **If you want to protect the Excel workbook with a password, select the Require password to open check box.** Otherwise, go to step 8. The Export Your Spreadsheet dialog then expands to reveal the controls for specifying the password and a password hint.

6. **Type the password in both the Password box and the Verify box as shown in Figure 10.14.**

7. **If you want to use a password hint, type it in the Password Hint box.**

8. **Click Next.** Numbers displays the Save As dialog.

9. **Type the filename, and choose the folder in which to store the file.** Numbers automatically assigns the file extension .xlsx or .xls, depending on whether you chose the XML-based format or the binary format.

10. **Click Export.** Numbers exports the file, displaying the Creating an Excel file progress dialog as it does so, and then displays your spreadsheet again.

Checking the Excel Workbooks You Create

When you export a Numbers spreadsheet to Excel, always open it in Excel and check it to make sure that it has translated successfully before you send it to anyone else. Spreadsheets can become extremely complex, and moving them to a different format often introduces errors. While it's no great loss if a text box moves in a Pages document when you export it, if a formula goes wrong when converting from Numbers to Excel, it may take ages to track down the problem — and if you don't catch the error, it may prove expensive for you and your company.

If you have access to a PC but you don't have Microsoft Excel, download the free Excel Viewer from the Microsoft Web site (www.microsoft.com/downloads) to check the workbooks you export to Excel format. The Excel Viewer lets you open Excel workbooks and view them, including the objects they contain. Although you cannot edit a workbook in the Excel viewer, you can examine an exported workbook well enough to catch gross errors that you will need to fix.

10.14 Type the password and password hint for the exported presentation, and then click Next.

Note If Numbers has to make serious changes in your spreadsheet when converting it to Excel format, the same changes were made to your exported spreadsheet dialog opens. This dialog notes the main changes, such as *Interactive charts were converted to regular charts*. Read the conversion notes, and then click OK to close the dialog. If necessary, remove the problematic features from the Numbers worksheet, and then export it again.

Exporting to CSV

When you need to export a spreadsheet in a format that's compatible with as many other applications and operating systems as possible, export it as a Comma-Separated Values (CSV) file. The CSV file retains only the text values from the spreadsheet — there's no formatting, no charts, no graphics, and no other objects.

In a CSV file, the value of each cell is separated from the value of the next cell with a comma. If a cell contains one or more real commas, the cell's contents are enclosed in double quotation marks to show that the comma isn't one of the separators.

Here's how to create a CSV file from a Numbers spreadsheet:

1. **Choose File ➪ Export To ➪ CSV to display the Export Your Spreadsheet dialog with the CSV pane at the front.**

2. **If you want to choose the text encoding, click the Advanced Options disclosure triangle to reveal the Advanced Options area (see Figure 10.15).** This area contains only one control, the Text Encoding pop-up menu.

10.15 Exporting a spreadsheet to a CSV file strips it down to bare data that's compatible with almost every spreadsheet application.

3. **Click the Text Encoding pop-up menu and choose the text encoding to use for the text file.** Here are a few things to keep in mind:

   - Normally, the best choice is Unicode (UTF-8), because almost all computers and operating systems can read it.

   - If you will use the text file only on the Mac, you can choose Western (Mac OS Roman) instead.

   - For Windows, you have the option of using Western (Windows Latin 1).

4. **Click Next.** Numbers displays the Save As dialog.

5. **Type the filename, and choose the folder in which to store the file.** Numbers automatically assigns the file extension .csv (which identifies a CSV file).

6. **Click Export.** Numbers exports the file, displaying the Creating a CSV file progress dialog as it does so, and then displays your spreadsheet again.

Exporting to Numbers '09

You can export a spreadsheet in Numbers '09 format to make sure your colleagues who still use Numbers '09 can open it and work with it. Here's how to export a spreadsheet to Numbers '09:

1. **Choose File ⇨ Export To ⇨ Numbers '09 to display the Export Your Spreadsheet dialog with the Numbers '09 pane displayed.**

2. **If you want to secure the exported file, select the Require password to open check box.** Type the password in the Password box and the Verify box, and then type a password hint in the Password Hint box if you want to include a hint.

3. **Click Next to display the Save As dialog.**

4. **Type the name for the Numbers '09 file in the Save As box.** Use a different name or a different folder unless you want to overwrite the existing file.

5. **Choose the folder in which to store the file.**

6. **Click Export.** Numbers exports the presentation, displaying the Creating a Numbers '09 file progress dialog as it does so.

7. **If Numbers needs to make significant changes to your spreadsheet because of the format change, it displays the Some changes were made to your exported spreadsheet dialog.** Review the changes, and then click OK. Numbers then displays your spreadsheet again, and you can resume work.

with Keynote?

Keynote is a fantastic tool for creating colorful and convincing presentations and delivering them to your audience in person or via the Internet. To create presentations swiftly and efficiently, start by choosing the right theme for the presentation. You can then set up your presentation with the slides it needs, arrange them into your preferred order, and fill them with text, media, and other contents. To enliven your presentation, you can add animation builds to slides and add transitions between them. Additionally, to help the presenter deliver the presentation, you can add detailed presenter notes to the slides.

Choosing the Right Theme for Your Presentation

To make your presentations and slides look great, you need to understand how themes and master slides work, and how you use them. Here's what they are:

- **Master slide.** A *master slide* is a layout of objects for a slide. For example, the master slide for a title slide may include a text box formatted with a large font size for the title of the presentation and a second text box formatted with a smaller size for the subtitle. A master slide for an information slide may contain a title across the top, a box containing bulleted text on the left, and a placeholder for a picture on the right.

- **Theme.** A theme is a set of master slides that are related in design. For example, most themes use similar backgrounds, colors, and fonts to give a "family feel" to the master slides.

To control how a presentation looks overall, you apply a theme to it. Normally, you apply the theme by using the Theme Chooser when you start creating the presentation. The Theme Chooser divides the themes into a Standard set (see Figure 11.1) and a Wide set (see Figure 11.2).

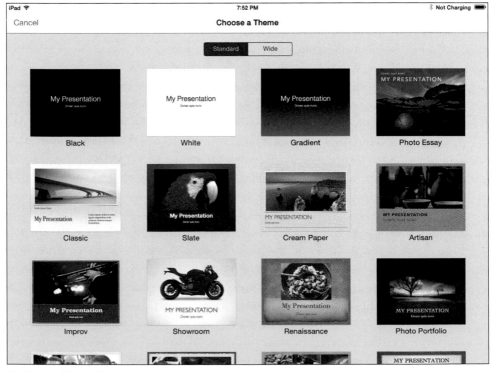

11.1 In the Theme Chooser, select the theme for a new presentation.

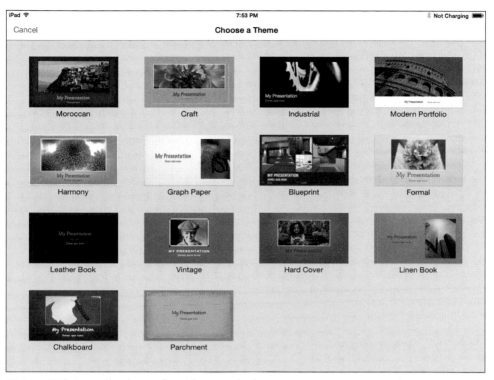

11.2 Tap Wide to see the themes for widescreen displays.

Note On OS X, you can change the theme of an existing presentation by choosing File ⇨ Change Theme and then choosing another theme in the Theme Chooser. After changing the layout of a slide, you can choose Format ⇨ Reapply Master to Slide to reapply the master layout. Keynote for iOS and iCloud do not provide these features.

The Wide themes have similar designs to the Standard themes, but they are designed for widescreen displays. Click or tap Standard or Wide to navigate between the two.

Adding, Deleting, and Rearranging Slides

To create a presentation, you need to add slides and input your material on them. You can delete any slides you find you no longer need, and you can easily rearrange your slides into the best order.

On OS X, Keynote has four views, which I cover later. For now, make sure you're using Navigator view, which displays the Slides pane on the left side of the window, giving you an easy means of navigating among your slides. Click the View button at the left end of the toolbar (see Figure 11.3) and then click Navigator on the pop-up menu.

11.3 On OS X, click the View menu, and then click Navigator to switch to Navigator view.

Genius

On OS X, you can change the width of the Slides pane by dragging the dividing line to the left or right. Increase the width to enlarge the thumbnails and make their contents easier to see; decrease the width to shrink the thumbnails so that you can see more of them at once.

Adding a slide

Adding a slide works in the same way on each of the iWork platforms. Follow these steps:

1. **Click or tap the slide after which you want to insert the new slide.**

2. **Click or tap the + button at the bottom of the Slides pane to display the New Slide panel (on OS X, the iPad, and iCloud) or the New Slide screen (on the iPhone and iPod touch).** Figure 11.4 shows the New Slide panel on OS X.

3. **Click or tap the slide layout you want to insert.**

On OS X and in iCloud, you can quickly add a slide using the same layout as an existing slide. Control+click the existing slide, and then click New Slide on the contextual menu to insert a new slide with the same layout after this slide.

Deleting a slide

When you no longer need a slide, you can delete it quickly in the following ways:

- **OS X or iCloud.** Click the slide in the Slides pane, and then press Delete. Alternatively, Control+click the slide, and then click Delete on the contextual menu.

- **iOS.** Tap the slide in the Slides pane, tap again to display the pop-up control bar, and then tap Delete (see Figure 11.5).

Rearranging slides

Even if you create a presentation from scratch, you often need to rearrange slides in a different order. Keynote makes this easy to do on any of the iWork platforms. When you need to move only a single slide, you can drag it up or down the Navigator or the Outline easily. When you need to move multiple slides, it's much easier to drag them to a new position if you switch to Light Table view.

11.4 In the New Slide panel, click or tap the layout for the new slide.

11.5 On iOS, you can delete a slide by tapping it in the Slides pane, tapping again to open the pop-up control bar, and then tapping Delete.

On OS X, you can rearrange the slides in a presentation easily in any view except Slide Only. Here's how to rearrange slides:

- **Navigator view.** Click the slide's thumbnail, and then drag it up or down the Slides pane. To move multiple slides, select them and then drag.

Genius

In Navigator view, you can drag the right border of the Slides pane to the left to reduce the size of the slides so you can see more of them at once, making it easier to move a slide to its destination. In Light Table view, you can drag the zoom slider to reduce the size of the slides so that you can see more of them at once.

- **Light Table view.** Click the slide's thumbnail, and then drag it to its new location. To move multiple slides, select them and then drag.
- **Outline view.** Click the slide's icon in the Slides pane and then drag it up or down. To move multiple slides, select them and then drag.

Rearranging slides in a presentation could hardly be easier on iOS. Follow these steps:

1. **In the navigator pane on the left, tap and hold the thumbnail for the slide you want to move up or down the order in the presentation.**

2. **When the thumbnail briefly expands, indicating it is ready to move, drag it up or down the navigator pane to its new position.**

3. **Release the thumbnail, and it appears in its new position.**

To rearrange the slides in a presentation in iCloud, click a slide in the Slides pane and drag it up or down, as needed. You cannot move multiple slides simultaneously.

Grouping slides

Keynote also lets you organize slides into groups. You can then handle a group of slides as a single unit or collapse the slides you don't want to see in the Slides pane. The slide that controls the group is called the *parent* slide; the slides it controls are called *child slides* or *children*.

Grouping slides on OS X

Here's how to organize slides into groups in Keynote on OS X:

1. **Switch to Navigator view.** Click on the View pop-up menu on the toolbar and then click Navigator. Alternatively, choose View ➪ Navigator from the menu bar.

2. **In the Slides pane, click the slide you want to make a child slide of the slide before it.** For example, if you want to make Slide 2 a child of Slide 1, click Slide 2.

3. **Press Tab or drag the slide to the right until Keynote shows a blue triangle above it, indicating the level to which it will be indented.** Keynote displays a gray disclosure triangle to the left of the parent slide to indicate that it has one or more children.

4. **Click and drag other slides as needed.** You can indent one child slide under another child slide.

5. **To remove a child slide from a parent, click it and drag it back to the left until Keynote shows a blue triangle at the right indent level.** You can also click the slide and then press Shift+Tab once for each indent you want to remove.

After you group your slides into parents and children, you can click a parent's disclosure triangle to hide its children (if they were displayed) or display them (if they were hidden). By hiding the children you don't want to see, you can collapse the slides in the slide navigator so that you see the key points of a presentation.

Grouping slides on iOS

Here's how to organize slides into groups on iOS:

1. **In the left pane, tap the slide you want to make a child of the slide before it, and then drag the slide to the right (see Figure 11.6).**

2. **Tap and drag other slides as needed.** Figure 11.7 shows Slide 1 as the parent slide for Slides 2 and 3, as you can see from the slide numbers. You can indent one child slide under another child slide.

11.6 Drag a slide to the right to make it a child of the parent slide above it. In this example, Slide 2 becomes a child of Slide 1.

3. **Tap the disclosure triangle next to a parent slide to display or hide its child slides.**
Figure 11.8 shows the child slides under a parent slide.

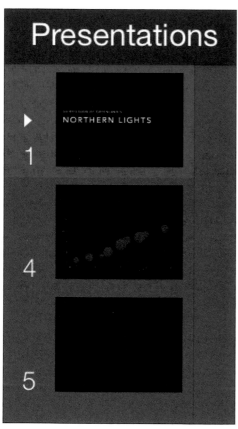

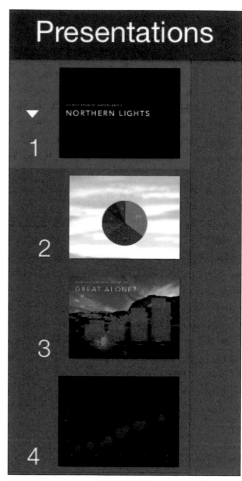

11.7 The slide numbers enable you to work out how many hidden child slides a parent slide has.

11.8 Tap a parent slide's disclosure triangle to display or hide its child slides.

Grouping slides in iCloud

Here's how to organize slides into groups in Keynote in iCloud:

1. **In the Slides pane, click the slide you want to make a child of the slide before it.**
For example, if you want to make Slide 2 a child of Slide 1, click Slide 2.

2. **Drag the slide to the right until Keynote shows a blue triangle above it, indicating the level to which it will be indented.** Keynote displays a gray disclosure triangle to the left of the parent slide to indicate that it has one or more children.

3. **Click and drag other slides as needed.** You can indent one child slide under another child slide.

4. **To remove a child slide from a parent, click it and drag it back to the left until Keynote shows a blue triangle at the right indent level.**

Adding Content to Slides

You can quickly build the slides in your presentation by adding content to them. The content can include the many types of objects that iWork supports, such as text, media files, tables, charts, and shapes.

Adding text

To add text to a slide, double-click or double-tap the placeholder text in a text box and then type the text. You can also copy text from another location and paste it into a text box.

Each text box has default formatting for the text, but you can adjust the formatting by using standard iWork techniques. For example, on OS X, use the Text pane in the Format panel (see Figure 11.9) to change the text formatting of a selected text box.

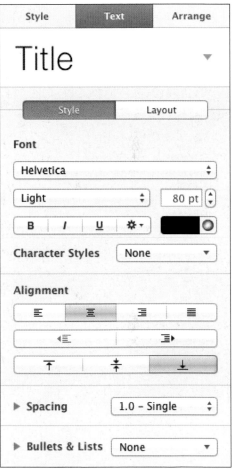

11.9 Use the Text pane in the Format panel to format a text box on OS X.

Adding media files

You can add various kinds of media files to your slides by using the techniques explained in Chapter 4. For example, on OS X you can add photos, audio tracks, and movies, whereas on iOS and in iCloud you can add photos.

After adding a media file, use the controls in the Format panel to adjust its appearance as needed. For example, on OS X, you can use the Style pane to select the picture style and add any border,

325

shadow, reflection, or opacity needed (see Figure 11.10). You can use the Image pane to edit the mask, create an instant alpha effect, adjust the exposure or saturation, or enhance the image.

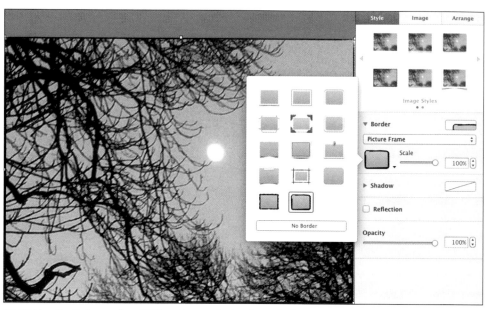

11.10 Use the Style pane on OS X to choose the border style, look, and color for an image.

Adding tables

Tables can be a great way of presenting information on slides, but it's essential to make sure they're easy to read. While you can copy a table from a Numbers spreadsheet or a Pages document and paste it into a Keynote slide, such tables often contain too much data to present effectively on a slide. So, you often get better results from creating a table in Keynote and typing or pasting the appropriate information into it. To insert a table in Keynote, use the Table button on the toolbar on OS X or the Table pane in the Add panel in iOS. After inserting the table, use the controls in the Table pane to format it. For example, use the Table pane in the Format inspector on OS X (see Figure 11.11) to change the style, choose the number of header rows and columns, set the borders, and choose whether to use alternate row shading.

Note At this writing, you cannot create or edit tables in Keynote for iCloud.

Adding charts and shapes

A chart can be a great way to present data in a presentation, especially because the chart can provide a simple and easy-to-grasp view of complex data. You can create charts in Keynote on OS X and iOS, but if you already have the chart in a Numbers spreadsheet, you can simply copy the chart and paste it onto a slide.

When you paste a chart into Keynote from Numbers, the source data comes along with the chart, so you can edit the data by clicking the Edit Chart Data button on OS X or tapping the Edit Data button on the pop-up control bar on iOS. Keynote doesn't link the chart back to its source in Numbers, so if you update the chart in the spreadsheet document, you will need to paste the new version into Keynote.

You can add shapes to slides using the techniques explained in Chapter 4. Shapes can be great for bringing home your points or simply for adding visual appeal.

Adding Animation Builds to Slides

Animation can be a great way to grab and hold your audience's attention. Keynote enables you to animate your slides in the following ways:

11.11 Use the controls in the Table pane in the Format inspector to format a table on OS X.

- **Object build.** An object build lets you make an object (such as an image or a table) automatically appear on a slide or vanish from the slide.

- **Object action.** An object action lets you animate an object on a slide. For example, you can animate a chart so that it grows in size or animate a shape so that it spins around.

- **Transition.** A transition animates the switchover from one slide to the next.

Note

At this writing, Keynote for iCloud doesn't have animation. Any animation in a presentation doesn't appear in iCloud.

Understanding the three types of object builds

Keynote lets you use the following three kinds of object builds:

- **Build In.** These effects make objects move onto a slide or appear on it. You can use Build In effects to reveal the objects on a slide gradually.

- **Build Out.** These effects make objects move off a slide or simply disappear from it.

- **Action (OS X only).** These effects animate the objects on a slide (without moving the objects onto the slide or off it, or making them appear or disappear).

You use the same technique to create each type of object build.

Genius

Use a Build In effect to focus the audience's attention on a single object, and then on each item you reveal in succession. Use an Action effect to draw attention to a particular object on a slide. Use a Build Out effect to remove items you no longer need and leave the audience with only your takeaway point to look at.

Animating objects on OS X

Here's how to animate an object on OS X:

1. **Click the object you want to animate.**

2. **Click the Animate button on the toolbar to display the Animate inspector.** You can also choose View ➪ Inspector ➪ Animate.

3. **Click the Build In button, the Action button, or the Build Out button at the top of the Animate inspector to display the pane for the type of object build you want to use.** This example uses the Action pane.

4. **Click Add an Effect to display the pop-up panel of available actions (see Figure 11.12).**

5. **Highlight the effect you think you want.**

6. **Click Preview to the right of the highlighted effect.** Keynote plays a preview of the effect.

7. **Repeat steps 5 and 6 to preview effects until you identify the effect you want.**

8. **Click the effect you want to add.** The controls for the effect appear in the pane you're using. Figure 11.13 shows the controls for the Bounce effect in the Action pane.

9. **Use the controls to configure the effect.** The controls depend on the effect. For example, the Bounce effect provides these controls:

   - **Duration slider.** Drag this slider to set the duration of the effect. You can also type a value in the text box or click the up button and down button to adjust the time.

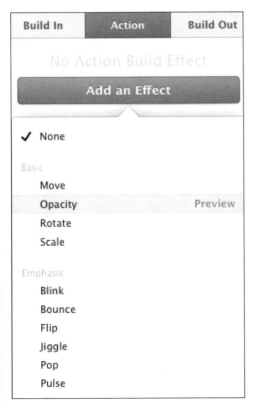

11.12 Click Add an Effect, and then click the effect to add.

11.13 The Animate inspector displays the controls for configuring the effect.

- **Number of Bounces.** Drag this slider (or type a value, or click the up and down buttons) to set the number of bounces for the effect.

- **Decay.** Select this check box to control whether the bounces grow smaller.

- **Order.** Use this pop-up menu to set the order in which the animations occur.

10. **Click Preview to see how the effect looks with its current settings.**

This example showed the Action pane, but the Build In pane and the Build Out pane work in the same way. Figure 11.14 shows the Build Out pane.

Animating objects on iOS

In Keynote for iOS, you can apply Build In effects and Build Out effects but not Action effects. Here's how to animate an object on iOS:

11.14 Use the Build Out pane to remove an object from a slide.

1. **Tap the object you want to animate.** The pop-up control bar appears.

2. **Tap the Animate button on the pop-up control bar.** Keynote displays the animation screen.

3. **Tap the Build In button or Build Out button on the pop-up control bar.** Keynote displays the Build In panel or Build Out panel (on the iPad) or the Build In screen or Build Out screen (on the iPhone or iPod touch). This panel or screen contains four panes: Effects, Options, Delivery, and Order.

4. **In the Effects pane, tap the effect you want to apply.**

5. **Tap the Options button to display the Options pane.**

6. **Set the options for the effect.** For example:

    - **Duration slider.** Drag this slider to set the duration of the effect.

    - **Start Build area.** Tap the On Tap option to set the effect to run when you tap the screen, or tap the After Transition option and drag the Delay slider to specify the delay after a transition.

7. **Tap the Delivery button to display the Delivery pane.**

8. **Tap the button for the delivery means you want the effect to use.** The delivery means available depend on the object you're animating. Here are details on the main objects:

   - **Text or Shape.** You can choose All at Once, By Paragraph, By Paragraph Group, or By Highlighted Paragraph.

   - **Image.** There are no options.

   - **Table.** See the next section.

   - **Chart.** See the next section.

9. **Tap the Order button to display the Order pane.** This pane shows the order in which the slide's effects will occur.

10. **Change the order as needed by dragging the effects up and down the list.**

11. **To animate another object, tap it and then follow steps 4 to 10.**

12. **When you finish setting up effects, tap Done.**

Using builds with tables and charts

On both OS X and iOS, when you present complex data using a table or a chart, you can apply a custom build on the Build In or Build Out panes to make the information easier to read. Table 11.1 explains the delivery options you can use for tables.

Similarly, Keynote lets you reveal a chart either all at once or piece by piece. Table 11.2 explains the delivery options you can use for charts.

Table 11.1   Keynote's Delivery Options for Tables

Delivery Option	What It Does
All at Once	Reveals or removes the table all at once.
By Row	Reveals or removes the table one row at a time.
By Row Reverse	Reveals or removes the table one row at a time in reverse order.
By Row Content	Reveals the whole table's frame, and then displays the content one row at a time; or removes the content one row at a time and then removes the whole table's frame.
By Row Content Reverse	Reveals the whole table's frame, and then displays the content one row at a time in reverse order; or removes the content one row at a time in reverse order, and then removes the whole table's frame.

continued

Table 11.1 continued

Delivery Option	What It Does
By Column	Reveals or removes the table one column at a time.
By Column Reverse	Reveals or removes the table one column at a time in reverse order.
By Column Content	Reveals the whole table's frame, and then displays the content one column at a time; or removes the content one column at a time and then removes the whole table's frame.
By Column Content Reverse	Reveals the whole table's frame, and then displays the content one column at a time in reverse order; or removes the content one column at a time in reverse order, and then removes the whole table's frame.
By Cell	Reveals or removes the table one cell at a time.
By Cell Reverse	Reveals or removes the table one cell at a time in reverse order.
By Cell Content	Reveals the whole table's frame, and then displays the content one cell at a time; or removes the content one cell at a time and then removes the whole table's frame.
By Cell Content Reverse	Reveals the whole table's frame, and then displays the content one cell at a time in reverse order; or removes the content one cell at a time in reverse order and then removes the whole table's frame.

Table 11.2 Keynote's Delivery Options for Charts

Delivery Option	What It Does
All at Once	Reveals or removes the chart all at once.
Background First	Reveals the chart axes, and then reveals the data elements all at once; or removes the data elements all at once and then removes the chart axes.
By Series	Reveals the chart axes, and then reveals the data, series by series; or removes the data, series by series, before removing the chart axes.
By Element in Series	Reveals the chart axes, and then reveals the data, element by element within a series; or removes the data, element by element within a series, and then removes the chart axes.
By Set	Reveals the chart axes, and then reveals the data, set by set; or removes the data, set by set, before removing the chart axes.
By Element in Set	Reveals the chart axes, and then reveals the data, element by element within a set; or removes the data, element by element within a set, and then removes the chart axes.

Note Table 11.2 shows the standard chart options. Some chart types have other options because of their natures. For example, the Pie chart has only the options All at Once and By Wedge.

Applying Transitions Between Slides

A *transition* is a visual effect that Keynote plays to animate the switchover from one slide to another. Keynote provides a wide range of transitions that you can use to add visual appeal to your presentations. The Push transition causes the incoming slide to push the outgoing slide in the direction you choose (for example, from right to left), while the Cube transition uses the same rotating-cube effect as OS X's Fast User Switching feature.

Note Be careful not to overdo transitions. Used carefully, they're fun and can enhance the presentation's message; used wildly, they can waste your time and distract the audience. If your transitions draw more attention than your slides, you probably won't get your point across. For formal presentations, you're usually better off sticking to a single, subtle transition (such as Dissolve) for the whole presentation.

Applying transitions on OS X

Here's how to add a transition between two slides on OS X:

1. **Navigate to the slide after which you want the transition to appear.**

2. **Click the Animate button on the toolbar to display the Transitions pane (see Figure 11.15).**

3. **Click Add an Effect to display the Add an Effect pop-up panel.**

4. **Highlight the effect you think you want (see Figure 11.16).** On OS X, Keynote breaks the transitions down like this:

   - **None.** Select this item to let the slides switch over without any effects. This sounds boring, but it often works well. You don't *have* to use an effect.

11.15 Click Add an Effect in the Transitions pane to start adding a transition on OS X.

   - **Recent Effects.** This category lets you quickly choose one of the effects you've used recently rather than having to plumb the depths of the list.

   - **Magic Move.** This is a special effect you can use for slides that have some of the same objects, but those objects appear in different positions.

   - **Text Effects.** These effects — Shimmer, Sparkle, and Swing — play with the letters in the words. They work best with text-based slides dominated by a few words.

- **Object Effects.** These effects — Object Cube, Object Flip, Object Pop, Object Push, Object Zoom, Perspective — move all the slide's objects off the first slide and then replace them with the objects from the next slide. These effects work best with slides dominated by objects rather than by text.

- **Appear & Move.** These effects — Clothesline, Confetti, Dissolve, Drop, Fade Through Color, Iris, Move In, Push, Reveal, Switch, and Wipe — move one slide off the screen and the next slide onto the screen with two-dimensional visual effects. These are the most subtle effects and work fine on just about any graphics card.

- **Flip, Spin & Scale.** These effects — Blinds, Color Planes, Cube, Doorway, Fall, Flip, Flop, Mosaic, Page Flip, Pivot, Reflection, Revolving Door, Scale, Swap, Swoosh, Twirl, and Twist — move one slide off the screen and the next slide onto the screen with three-dimensional visual effects. These effects may be jerky if your Mac's graphics card is underpowered.

5. **Click Preview to the right of the highlighted effect.** Keynote plays a preview of the effect.

6. **Repeat steps 4 and 5 to preview effects until you identify the effect you want.**

11.16 In the Add an Effect pop-up panel, highlight an effect, and then click Preview to it.

7. **Click the effect to add it to the Transitions pane (see Figure 11.17).**

8. **Use the effect-specific controls in the Transitions pane to customize the effect.** The controls vary depending on the effect you choose, but this example for the Object Push effect gives you an idea of your options:

   - **Duration & Direction slider.** Drag the slider to set the duration of the transition. You can also type a value in the text box or click the up button and down button to adjust the time.

   - **Duration & Direction pop-up menu.** Click this pop-up menu and then click the direction. For the Object Push effect, the directions are Left to Right, Right to Left, Top to Bottom, and Bottom to Top.

9. **Click the Start Transition pop-up menu, and then click one of the following timing options:**

   - **On Click.** Select this option to run the effect when you (or the presenter) click. Use this timing for slides that may need more time depending on the audience.

   - **Automatically.** Select this option to advance automatically after the time you set in the Delay box.

10. **If you need to check the order of the effects and transitions you've applied, click Build Order at the bottom of the Animate inspector.** Keynote displays the Build Order dialog (see Figure 11.18). You can then drag the effects to change their order, and click Preview to see a preview of their effect.

11.17 After adding the effect in the Transitions pane, you can preview, customize, or change it.

11.18 Use the Build Order dialog to preview the effects you've applied or change their order.

335

Applying transitions on iOS

Here's how to add a transition between two slides on iOS:

1. **Tap the slide's thumbnail in the Slides pane to select it.**

2. **Tap the slide's thumbnail again to display the pop-up control bar.**

3. **Tap Transition to display the Transitions panel (on the iPad) or the Transitions screen (on the iPhone and iPod touch).** This panel or screen has two panes: Effects and Options, as shown in Figure 11.19.

4. **In the Effects pane, tap the effect you want to apply.**

5. **Tap Options to display the Options pane (see Figure 11.20).**

6. **Choose options for the effect.** You may need to scroll down the Options pane to reach some options (see Figure 11.21). The options depend on the effect, but many effects have the following settings:

   - **Duration.** Drag this slider to set how long the effect lasts.
   - **Direction.** Drag the arrow to set the direction for the effect.
   - **Start Transition.** In this area, tap On Tap to run the effect when you tap the screen. Otherwise, tap After Previous Transition and then drag the Delay slider to specify how long to wait after the previous transition.

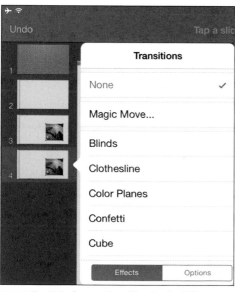

11.19 On iOS, choose the effect in the Effects pane, and then tap Options to display the Options pane.

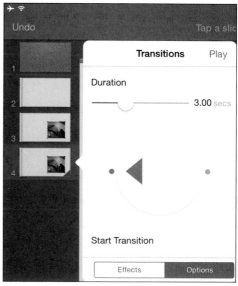

11.20 In the Options pane, choose options to configure the effect.

336

7. Return to your presentation in one of the following ways:

- **iPad.** Tap outside the Transitions panel.

- **iPhone or iPod touch.** Tap Done.

Applying transitions in iCloud

Here's how to add a transition between two slides in iCloud:

1. In the Slides pane, click the slide after which you want the transition to run.

2. If the Format panel isn't displayed, click the Tools button on the toolbar, and then choose Settings ➪ Show Format Panel to display it. The Slide Transition pane appears (see Figure 11.22).

3. Click the Effect pop-up menu, and then click the effect to use.

4. Use the controls that appear below the Effect pop-up menu to choose options for the effect. For example:

- **Direction.** Click this pop-up menu and then click the direction to use, such as Left to Right or Bottom to Top.

- **Duration.** Drag this slider to set how long the effect lasts. You can also type a value in the text box, or click the up or down buttons to adjust the time.

11.21 If necessary, scroll down the Options pane to reach further options.

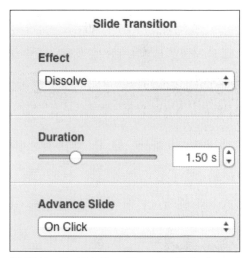

11.22 Use the Slide Transition pane in the Format panel to apply a transition in Keynote for iCloud.

5. **Click the Advance Slide pop-up menu, and then choose one of the following timing settings:**

- **On Click.** Select this option to run the effect when you click.

- **Automatically.** Select this option to advance automatically after the time you set in the Delay box by dragging the slider, typing a value, or clicking the buttons.

Adding Presenter Notes

To help yourself or another presenter to deliver the presentation, you can add presenter notes to any slide. These notes can consist of as much text as you need for the presentation.

Note Presenter notes appear on the presenter display, a secondary display you can use when you connect another display for the presentation. If you deliver the presentation using only the screen of your Mac or iOS device, the presenter notes do not appear.

Note At this writing, Keynote for iCloud does not support presenter notes. Any presenter notes you have added to a presentation using Keynote on another platform do not appear in iCloud.

Here's how to add presenter notes to a presentation on OS X:

1. **Click the View button on the toolbar, and then click Show Presenter Notes.**
   Alternatively, choose View ➪ Show Presenter Notes from the menu bar. Keynote displays the presenter notes pane below the slide pane.

Genius You can display the presenter notes pane in Slide view, Navigator view, and Outline view, but not in Light Table view. If you need to add presenter notes for more than one slide, use the Navigator or Outline view because they enable you to navigate easily from slide to slide without closing the presenter notes pane.

2. **Navigate in one of the following ways to the slide to which you want to add presenter notes:**

- **Slide view.** Choose Slide ➪ Go To and then click the appropriate command on the Go To submenu: Next Slide, Previous Slide, First Slide, or Last Slide.

- **Navigator view or Outline view.** Click the slide's thumbnail in the Slides pane.

3. **Type or paste the material you want to include in the notes (see Figure 11.23).** You can drag the top border of the presenter notes pane up or down to resize the pane as needed.

Welcome to the
Coast Retreat Center

Pastor Farian Leiter
Greeter-in-Chief

Good evening, everyone!

[something about the weather]

I hope you've all settled in comfortably.

11.23 On OS X, type or paste material in the presenter notes pane.

4. **To format the text, click the Format button on the toolbar to display the Format inspector, and then use the controls in the Presenter Notes pane.** You can apply font formatting and list formatting, and change the default note style.

5. **When you finish working with presenter notes, close the Presenter Notes pane in one of these ways:**

   - **Click the View button on the toolbar and then click Hide Presenter Notes.**

   - **Choose View➪Hide Presenter Notes from the menu bar.**

   - **Drag the top edge of the presenter notes pane down to the bottom of the Keynote window.**

Here's how to add presenter notes to a presentation on iOS:

1. **Tap the Tools button on the toolbar and then tap Presenter Notes.** Keynote switches to Presenter Notes view.

2. **In the left pane, tap the slide to which you want to add presenter notes.**

3. **Type the text of the notes (see Figure 11.24).**

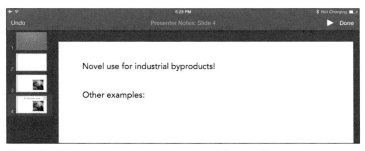

11.24 On iOS, type your presenter notes, and then tap Done.

4. **Tap Done to close Presenter Notes view.**

How Do I Give Presentations Using Keynote?

After creating your presentation using the techniques explained in the previous two chapters, you should be ready to deliver the presentation. This chapter explains how to set up your presentation for delivery by adding interactive hyperlinks, displaying slide numbers, and enabling or disabling remotes. This chapter also covers how to deliver the presentation, either in person or by other means, such as sharing a presentation via e-mail, copying it to iTunes, or printing it, either on paper or to a PDF file. I also discuss how to create a presentation that plays automatically, which can be ideal in certain situations, such as trade shows.

Setting Up a Presentation

To get your presentation ready for delivery, you can add interactive hyperlinks to the slides to provide easy navigation and access to additional content. You can add slide numbers to make identifying slides and navigating to them easier. You can enable remote controls and disable them when you no longer need them. Finally, you can create looping presentations and even presentations that play themselves.

Adding interactive hyperlinks

During a presentation, you often need to jump quickly to another slide in the same presentation or to open your default Web browser (for example, Safari) to a particular web page that contains relevant information. These capabilities can come in handy in presentations you distribute online as well. You may also want to let the viewer quickly create an e-mail message to provide a way to contact your company or organization.

Note At this writing, you can add interactive hyperlinks in Keynote on OS X and iOS but not on iCloud.

Adding interactive hyperlinks on OS X

Here's how to add interactive hyperlinks to a presentation on OS X:

1. **If the text or object you want to use for the link doesn't yet exist, create it on a slide.**

2. **Select the text or object for the link.**

3. **Control+click the selection, and then click Add Link on the contextual menu to display the Add Link dialog (see Figure 12.1).**

4. **Click the Link to pop-up menu, and then choose one of the following targets for the hyperlink:**

   - **Slide.** Select the option button for Next slide, Previous slide, First slide, Last slide, Last slide viewed, or Slide and choose the slide number in the pop-up menu.

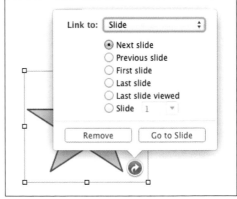

12.1 In the Add Link dialog, choose the slide or other item to which you want to link.

- **Webpage.** Type or paste the page's address into the Link box (see Figure 12.2).

- **Email Message.** Type or paste the e-mail address in the To box. Type the default subject line in the Subject box. (Users will be able to change this in their e-mail applications.) In the Display box, type the descriptive text you want to display on the slide (for example, Contact Us).

12.2 To create a link to a web page, select Webpage in the Link to pop-up menu, and then type or paste the URL in the Link box.

- **Exit Slideshow.** Choose this item to create a link that closes the slide show. There are no options for this type of link.

5. **Click outside the Add Link dialog to close the dialog.**

Adding interactive hyperlinks on iOS

Here's how to add interactive hyperlinks to a presentation on iOS:

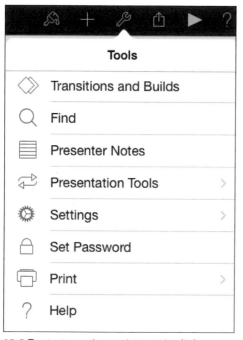

12.3 To start creating an interactive link on iOS, tap the Tools button, and then tap Presentation Tools.

1. **If the text or object you want to use for the link doesn't yet exist, create it on a slide.**

2. **Tap the Tools button to display the Tools pane (see Figure 12.3).**

3. **Tap Presentation Tools to display the Presentation Tools pane (see Figure 12.4).**

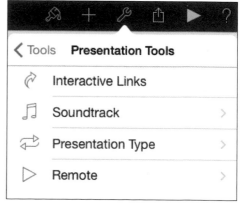

12.4 The Presentation Tools pane.

345

4. **Tap Interactive Links to display the Link pane (see Figure 12.5).**

5. **At the bottom of the Link pane, tap the button for the kind of link you want to create:**

   - **Slide.** To specify a slide by number, tap Link To Slide, and then tap the appropriate slide in the Link pane that appears. Otherwise, tap Next Slide, Previous Slide, First Slide, Last Slide, or Last Slide Viewed.

   - **Webpage.** Type or paste the page's address into the Link box (see Figure 12.6).

   - **Mail.** Tap Mail, and then type or paste the e-mail address in the To box.

6. **Tap Done to finish inputting the link.**

Note At this writing, Keynote for iOS does not give you a way to specify the default subject line for the e-mail message in a link. The link creates a message with a blank subject line, so the user can type any subject line or leave it blank.

12.5 In the Link pane, tap the type of link you want to create.

12.6 To link to a web page, tap Webpage at the bottom of the Link pane, and then type or paste the URL in the Link box.

Adding slide numbers

You can add numbers to your slides to make it easy to identify them and to navigate through your presentations. The iWork platforms have different capabilities for slide numbers:

- **OS X.** You can choose whether any given slide displays a slide number. For example, you can set slide 1 to display its slide number but set slide 2 not to display its number.

- **iOS.** You can choose whether the presentation as a whole displays slide numbers. You cannot choose different settings for different slides.

- **iCloud.** At this writing, you cannot add slide numbers on iCloud.

Here's how to add slide numbers to a slide on OS X:

1. **If the Format inspector isn't displayed, click the Format button on the toolbar to display it.**

2. **Open the Slide Layout pane (see Figure 12.7).** How you do this depends on which of the following views you're using:

   - **Navigator view.** Click the slide's thumbnail in the Slides pane.

   - **Slide Only view.** Click the slide itself, outside all the objects it contains. If the slide is covered by an image or another object, you cannot click the slide itself. Instead, switch to Navigator view and then click the slide's thumbnail in the Slides pane.

   - **Light Table view.** Click the slide's thumbnail.

   - **Outline view.** Switch to Navigator view (or Light Table view) and click the slide's thumbnail.

3. **Select the Slide Number check box in the Appearance section of the Slide Layout pane.**

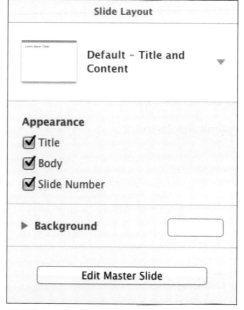

12.7 Select the Slide Number check box in the Appearance section of the Slide Layout pane to add numbers to your slides.

Here's how to add slide numbers to your slides on iOS:

1. **Tap the Tools button to display the Tools panel.**

2. **Tap Settings to display the Settings panel (see Figure 12.8).**

3. **Set the Slide Numbers switch to On to display slide numbers.**

4. **Tap outside the Settings panel to close the panel.**

Enabling and disabling remotes

When giving a presentation from your Mac or iOS device, you can use a remote control to run the presentation. Before using a remote control, you need to enable remotes for Keynote.

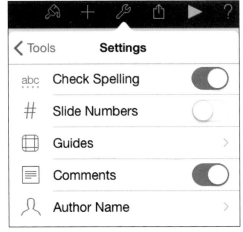

12.8 On iOS, set the Slide Numbers switch in the Settings panel to On if you want to display slide numbers.

Note

Chapter 13 shows you how to link an iPhone or an iPod touch to use as a remote control for Keynote on OS X.

Here's how to enable or disable remotes on OS X:

1. **Choose Keynote ⇨ Preferences to display the Keynote preferences window.** You can also press ⌘+, (⌘ and the comma key).

2. **Click the Remote tab to display the Remote pane (see Figure 12.9).**

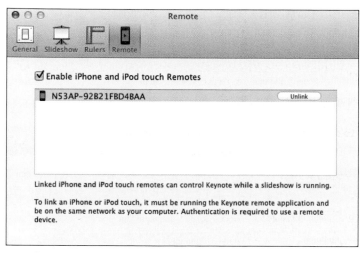

12.9 The Keynote Remote preferences pane.

3. **Select or deselect the Enable iPhone and iPod touch Remotes check box.**

4. **Click the Close button (the red button at the left end of the window's title bar) to close the Remote preferences window.**

Here's how to enable or disable remotes on iOS:

1. **Tap the Tools button on the toolbar to display the Tools panel.**

2. **Tap Presentation Tools to display the Presentation Tools pane.**

3. **Tap Remote to display the Remote Settings pane on the iPad (see Figure 12.10), or the Remote Settings screen on the iPhone or iPod touch.**

4. **Set the Enable Remotes switch to On to enable remotes or to Off to disable them.**

5. **Return to your presentation in one of the following ways:**

   ● **iPad.** Tap outside the Remote Settings pane.

   ● **iPhone or iPod touch.** Tap Done to close the Remote Settings screen.

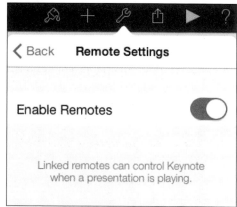

12.10 The Remote Settings pane on the iPad.

349

Creating looping and self-playing presentations

Live and in person is usually the most effective way of giving your presentation, because you can adapt the presentation to the audience's needs, gauge their reactions, and take questions to make sure you've nailed every point. However, when you cannot be there, a presentation that plays automatically is a fair substitute. You can set up this type of presentation on OS X and iOS but not on iCloud.

To create a presentation that plays automatically, build the presentation as usual using the techniques described in Chapters 10 and 11. You probably want to set up most of the builds and transitions to run automatically after a delay you specify, but you can also set a default delay for builds and transitions set to run on a click. If the presentation needs a soundtrack, give it one, or record narration.

Creating an automatic or looping presentation on OS X

Here's how to create a presentation that plays automatically on OS X:

1. **Click the Setup button on the toolbar to display the Presentation Setup inspector (see Figure 12.11).** You can also choose View ⇨ Inspector ⇨ Presentation Setup.

2. **Click the Presentation Type pop-up menu and click Self-Playing.**

3. **In the Delay area, set the delays to use for all transitions and builds set to run on click.** Usually, you want a much shorter interval for builds than transitions.

12.11 On OS X, use the Presentation Setup inspector to create a self-playing presentation.

4. **In the Slideshow Settings area, choose the following settings as needed:**

- **Automatically play upon open.** Select this check box if you want Keynote to launch the presentation as soon as someone opens it.

- **Loop slideshow.** Select this check box to make Keynote play the presentation repeatedly until you stop it by pressing Esc.

- **Restart show if idle for.** If you're letting visitors run the slide show in their own time, select this check box, and then set a low number of minutes (such as 3 m or 5 m). If a visitor abandons the slide show before the end, Keynote waits for the timeout, and then starts the show from the beginning.

- **Require password to open.** If you want to protect a presentation with a password, select this check box, and then specify the password in the Set a password to open this presentation dialog.

5. **Save the presentation, and then test that the delays are suitable for the transitions and builds.** Adjust the delays if necessary.

Creating an automatic or looping presentation on iOS

Here's how to create a presentation that plays automatically on iOS:

1. **Tap the Tools button on the toolbar to display the Tools panel or Tools screen.**

2. **Tap Presentation Tools to display the Presentation Tools pane or Presentation Tools screen.**

3. **Tap Presentation Type to display the Presentation Type pane (see Figure 12.12) or Presentation Type screen.**

4. **Set the Loop Presentation switch to On if you want the presentation to restart playing from the beginning when it reaches the end.**

5. **Set the Restart Show if Idle switch to On if you want the presentation to restart automatically if it is idle for a specified length of time.** Drag the slider that appears below the Restart Show if Idle switch to set the length of idle time.

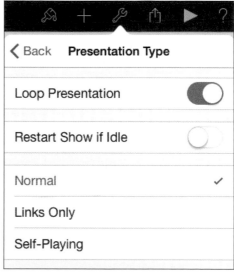

12.12 On iOS, use the Presentation Type pane to create a self-playing presentation.

6. **In the lower part of the Presentation Type pane or Presentation Type screen, tap Self-Playing, placing a checkmark next to it.** The Transition Delay and Build Delay sliders appear at the bottom of the Presentation Type pane. You may need to scroll down to see these sliders.

7. **Drag the Transition Delay slider (see Figure 12.13) to set the number of seconds to wait for transitions.**

8. **Drag the Build Delay slider (see Figure 12.13) to set the number of seconds to wait for builds.**

9. **Return to your presentation in one of the following ways:**

   - **iPad.** Tap outside the Presentation Type pane.

   - **iPhone or iPod touch.** Tap Done to close the Presentation Type screen.

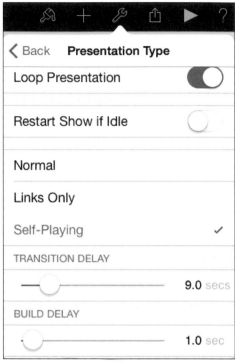

12.13 Use the Transition Delay slider and Build Delay slider to set the timing for the self-playing presentation.

Delivering a Presentation

After you finish setting up your presentation, you're ready to deliver it. In this section, I go through your options for delivering the presentation, cover connecting your Mac or iOS device to an external display, and look at how to set up the presenter display feature on iOS.

Keynote offers the following ways to deliver a presentation to your audience:

- **Live and in person.**
- **Share via e-mail or other means, such as Messages or AirDrop.**
- **Copy it from an iOS device to iTunes and share it with your computer.**
- **Copy it from an iOS device to a WebDAV server to make it available to others.**
- **Print it on paper or to a PDF file.**

The following sections explore these options. First, let's look at how to connect to an external display.

Connecting to an external display

Unless you're using a Mac that already has a huge screen, you probably want to connect to an external display to give your presentation. You can connect a Mac or an iOS device either via cable or wirelessly with AirPlay.

Connecting a Mac to an external display

To connect a Mac to an external display, you need a suitable cable, or adapter and cable. On the Mac end, you normally need a Thunderbolt connector. These are the display ports that Macs have:

- **All current Macs and most recent Macs come with one or more Thunderbolt ports for display output.**

- **Macs from a few years ago used the Mini DisplayPort port, which is the same size and shape as the Thunderbolt port.**

- **Earlier Macs used the Mini DVI port.** For this, you need a Mini DVI connector.

On the display end, you normally need one of these connectors:

- **HDMI.** This standard port is widely used in both TVs and monitors.

- **DVI.** This digital port is widely used for computer monitors.

- **VGA.** This analog port is an older technology that became such a widespread standard that it now refuses to die. Many projectors provide a VGA port; if you're lucky, a projector will also have a better port, such as DVI or HDMI.

Armed with the right cable (or adapter and cable), connect the Mac's output port to the input port on the display device. You can then set up your displays as described in the section after next.

Connecting a Mac to an Apple TV and display

If you have an Apple TV connected to a TV or another display, you can show your presentation on that TV or display via the Apple TV. This can be a great way of showing a presentation on a larger screen, especially because you don't need to fiddle with cables.

To connect a Mac to an Apple TV, connect the Mac to the same network as the Apple TV. This can be a wireless or wired network, or a network that has both wireless and wired parts. Click the AirPlay menu on the right side of the menu bar, and then highlight Connect to AirPlay Display. Click the Apple TV on the Connect to AirPlay Device submenu. The Apple TV's name appears here (such as Office Apple TV or Conference Room Apple TV) so you can easily distinguish one Apple TV from another.

Choosing Displays preferences for an external display

After connecting the external display, use Displays preferences to tell OS X where the display is positioned and which resolution to use for it. Follow these steps:

1. **Control+click System Preferences on the Dock and click Displays to open the System Preferences app and display the Displays pane.** This pane opens on each of the displays connected to your Mac.

2. **In the Displays pane on your main display, click the Arrangement button to display the Arrangement pane.**

3. **Drag the display thumbnails so that they represent the physical placement of the displays.** For example, if the external display is to the left of your Mac's screen, position the external display's thumbnail to the left of the thumbnail for your Mac's screen.

4. **Drag the gray menu bar strip to the thumbnail of the display on which you want the menu bar to appear.**

5. **If necessary, use the Display pane on each display to adjust the display resolution.**

6. **Click the Close button (the red button at the left end of the window's title bar) to close the System Preferences window.** You can also press ⌘+Q or choose System Preferences ⇨ Quit System Preferences.

Connecting an iOS device to an external display

An iPad's screen is just about big enough to give a presentation to one or two other people in an informal setting, but the screen on an iPhone or iPod touch is excessively small. Normally, you want to connect your iOS device to an external display, using either a cable connection or AirPlay.

To connect an iOS device to a display, you need a suitable adapter or cable like the following, which are available from Apple:

- **Lightning Digital AV Adapter.** Use this adapter to connect an iOS device that has a Lightning connector to a TV or monitor that has an HDMI input.

- **Apple 30-pin Digital AV Adapter.** Use this adapter to connect an iOS device that has the older 30-pin Dock Connector port to a TV or monitor that has an HDMI input.

Genius You can find third-party equivalents to the Lightning Digital AV Adapter and Apple 30-pin Digital AV Adapter. You can also find third-party adapters and cables for making a connection between a Lightning port or Dock Connector port and other types of TV or monitor input, such as DVI or VGA. It is a good idea to verify that the Lightning adapter is certified by Apple to guarantee compatibility.

Once you get the adapter or cable, connect the Lightning or Dock Connector end to your iOS device, and the HDMI end to the TV or monitor. Your iOS device then transmits the screen image across the cable, so that the TV or monitor displays it.

Note You may need to change the input port on the TV or monitor manually to get the image from your iOS device to appear. Some TVs and monitors automatically detect input and switch automatically to the correct port, but others don't — especially if they are also receiving valid input on their current port (for example, from a set-top box).

Connecting an iOS device to an Apple TV and display

If you have an iOS device, an Apple TV provides an easy way to give a presentation on a large screen. Here's how to connect an iOS device to an Apple TV:

1. **Make sure the iOS device is connected to the same network as the Apple TV.** If not, go to the Home screen, tap Settings to open the Settings app, tap Wi-Fi, and then connect to the right network.

2. **Swipe up from the bottom of the screen to open Control Center.** You can do this either from the Home screen or from an app (such as Keynote).

3. **Tap the AirPlay icon to display the AirPlay dialog (on the iPad) or the AirPlay screen (on the iPhone and iPod touch).**

4. **Tap the button for the Apple TV, putting a check mark next to it.** When you make the Apple TV active like this, the Mirroring switch appears.

5. **Set the Mirroring switch to On.** Your iOS device's screen appears on the TV or monitor connected to the Apple TV.

6. **On the iPad, tap outside the AirPlay dialog to close the dialog.** On the iPhone or iPod touch, tap Done to close the AirPlay screen.

Note If you don't set the Mirroring switch to On, your iOS device plays audio through the speakers connected to the Apple TV, but the TV or display doesn't show the iOS device's screen.

Setting up your presenter display on an iOS device

Once you've connected your iOS device to an external display (either directly or through an Apple TV), Keynote's presenter display feature becomes available. Presenter display lets you choose what to display on your iOS device's screen while the presentation itself appears on the external display.

355

Here's how to set up the presenter display:

1. **Tap the Play button on the toolbar to start playing the slide show.** It doesn't matter from which slide you start — you're only playing the show in order to choose the presenter display layout.

2. **Tap the Layouts button on the toolbar to display the Layouts pane (on the iPad) or the Layouts screen (on the iPhone or iPod touch).**

3. **Tap the layout you want:**

   - **Current.** This layout shows only the current slide.

   - **Next.** This layout shows only the next slide so you can see what's coming next. (You can see the current slide on the audience's display.)

   - **Current and Next.** This layout shows the current slide and the next slide. Being able to see two slides is handy, but the slides are necessarily smaller, so the text may be harder to read.

   - **Notes.** This layout shows the presenter notes under the current slide.

4. **Return to your presentation in one of the following ways:**

   - **iPad.** Tap outside the Layouts pane.

   - **iPhone or iPod touch.** Tap Done to close the Layouts screen.

Giving a presentation live

After setting up any external display for the presentation and choosing your presenter display, you're ready to give the presentation. Keynote for OS X provides a much wider range of options for giving a presentation than Keynote for iOS or Keynote for iCloud. I dig into these options in depth in Chapter 13.

Giving a presentation from an iOS device

Here's how to give a presentation from an iOS device:

1. **Tap the slide at which you want to start the presentation.**

2. **Tap the Play button on the toolbar (see Figure 12.14) to start the presentation.** If you've connected an external display, the presentation appears on that display, and the presenter display appears using the layout you chose.

12.14 Tap the Play button on the toolbar to start your presentation.

3. **If the Pinch to end slideshow dialog opens (see Figure 12.15), tap OK to close it.**

12.15 Tap OK to close the Pinch to end slideshow dialog.

4. **Navigate through the presentation in the following ways:**

   - **Display the next slide.** Tap the slide.

   - **Display the previous slide or reset the builds on the current slide.** Swipe right on the slide.

   - **Display a different slide.** Tap the left side of the screen to display the slide navigator, and then tap the slide you want to show.

   - **Display the laser pointer.** Tap and hold on the screen until the laser pointer appears (see Figure 12.16), and then move your finger as needed. The pointer disappears when you lift your finger.

12.16 Tap and hold to display the laser pointer.

5. **Place two or more fingers apart on the screen and pinch them together to end the presentation.**

Giving a presentation from iCloud

Here's how to give a presentation from iCloud:

1. **Click the slide at which you want to start the presentation.**

2. **Click the Play button on the toolbar to start the presentation.**

3. **Navigate through the presentation in the following ways:**

- **Display the next slide.** Click anywhere on the current slide.

- **Display a different slide.** Move the mouse pointer to the left side of the screen to display the slide navigator and then click the slide you want to display. Move the mouse pointer off the slide navigator to hide the slide navigator again.

4. **Press Esc if you want to end the presentation before it finishes.**

Sharing or copying a presentation

Instead of delivering the presentation in person, you can share it easily via e-mail. To do so, work as explained in Chapter 2. Here's a brief recap of the essentials:

- **OS X.** Click Share on the menu bar, highlight Send a Copy, and then click Email.

- **iPad.** Tap Share on the toolbar, tap Send a Copy, and then tap Mail.

- **iPhone or iPod touch.** Tap Tools on the toolbar and then tap Share and Print. Tap Send a Copy and then tap Mail.

- **iCloud.** Click Share on the toolbar, click Send a Copy, and then click Keynote in the Send a Copy via iCloud Mail dialog.

From an iOS device, you can copy a presentation either to iTunes to put it on your computer or to a WebDAV server to make it available to others. To copy a presentation to iTunes, use the iTunes File Sharing feature, as explained in Chapter 2. Briefly, you connect your iOS device to your computer, and then use the File Sharing area on the Apps screen in the iOS device's management screens to copy the file from Keynote and save it on your computer.

Printing a presentation

Another way of sharing the presentation is by printing it. On OS X or iOS, Keynote can print a presentation directly to a printer. Keynote for iCloud can create a PDF file of the presentation, which it then downloads to your computer so that you can print it.

Printing a presentation on OS X

On OS X, Numbers provides a wide range of print options. Here's how to use them:

1. **Choose File ⇨ Print to display the Print dialog.**

2. **If the Print dialog is collapsed to its small size, hiding most of the options, expand it by clicking Show Details.** The Hide Details button replaces the Show Details button in the expanded dialog.

3. **Make sure Keynote is selected in the pop-up menu in the middle of the dialog.**

4. **In the box below the pop-up menu, click one of the following options (see Figure 12.17):**

   - **Slide.** Choose this option to print each slide on a separate page. This type of printout is good for reviewing the slides on paper.

   - **Grid.** Choose this option to print multiple slides on each page. This type of printout is useful for getting an overview of the presentation.

   - **Handout.** Choose this option to print handouts for the audience. See Chapter 13 for more details on printing handouts.

   - **Outline.** Choose this option to print a text-only outline of the presentation. This type of printout is best for developing the argument or theme of the presentation.

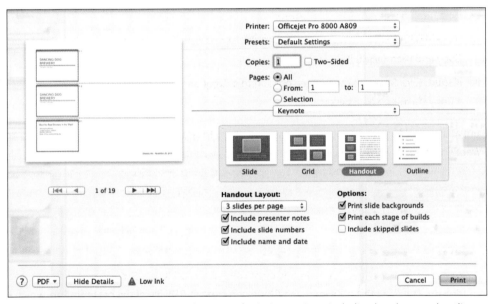

12.17 Numbers on OS X gives you a wide range of printing options, including handouts and outlines.

5. **Use the Layout options to choose what to include in the printout.** The options available differ in the following ways depending on what you're printing:

   - **Slide Layout options.** You can choose whether to use the page margins and whether to include presenter notes, slide numbers, and the filename and the date.

   - **Grid Layout options.** You can choose the number of slides to print per page and whether to include the slide numbers, the filename, and the date.

- **Handout Layout options.** You can choose the number of slides to print per page and whether to include presenter notes, slide numbers, and the filename and the date.

- **Outline Layout options.** You can choose whether to include the filename and the date.

6. **In the Options area, select the check boxes for any of the following options you want to use:**

   - **Print slide backgrounds.** Select this check box to include the slide backgrounds. If you're printing on a monochrome printer, you may want to leave out the slide backgrounds to make the text and other objects easier to see.

   - **Print each stage of builds.** Select this check box if you want to print a separate slide for each stage of a build. This can be helpful when you're creating a handout for the presenter to use when preparing the presentation, but the audience doesn't usually need to see the builds.

   - **Include skipped slides.** Select this check box to include any slides in the presentation (or in the selection) that are marked for skipping. This setting is useful when you need to provide the audience with more information than the presenter can deliver in the allotted time.

7. **Click Print to send the presentation to the printer.**

Genius

Instead of printing your presentation on paper, you can print it to a PDF file. Click PDF in the lower-left corner of the Print dialog, and then click Save a PDF on the pop-up menu.

Printing a presentation on iOS

Here's how to print a presentation on iOS:

1. **Tap the Tools button to display the Tools pane (on the iPad) or the Tools screen (on the iPhone or iPod touch).**

2. **On the iPhone or iPod touch, tap Share and Print to display the Share and Print screen.**

3. **Tap Print to display the Layout Options pane on the iPad (see Figure 12.18), or the Layout Options screen on the iPhone or iPod touch.**

4. **Tap the icon for the layout type you want.** Your choices are as follows:

   - **Slide.** This layout shows a single slide on each page.

   - **Grid.** This layout shows multiple slides on each page.

   - **Notes.** This layout shows a single slide and the presenter notes.

   - **Handout.** This layout shows multiple slides with blank lines next to them for writing notes.

5. **Set the Print Builds switch to On if you want to print each build.** Printing the builds is helpful for presenters and developers but tends to be overkill for audience members.

12.18 The Layout Options pane on the iPad.

6. **Set the Print Backgrounds switch to On if you want to print backgrounds on the slides.** If you're printing on a monochrome printer, you may want to leave out the slide backgrounds to make the text and other objects easier to see.

7. **Tap Next to display the Printer Options pane on the iPad (see Figure 12.19), or the Printer Options screen on the iPhone or iPod touch.**

8. **If the Printer line doesn't show the correct printer, tap it, and then tap the printer on the Printer screen.**

9. **To print only some of the pages, tap Range to display the Page Range pane (on the iPad) or the Page Range screen (on the iPhone or iPod touch), and then select the range.**

12.19 The Printer Options pane on the iPad.

10. **Tap the + or - buttons to set the number of copies to print.**

11. **Tap Print.**

Printing a presentation to a PDF from iCloud

From iCloud, you can only print a presentation to a PDF file. Follow these steps:

1. **Click the Tools button to display the Tools panel.**

2. **Click Print.** Numbers automatically creates a PDF and then displays the Your PDF is ready to print dialog.

3. **Click Open PDF.** Your browser downloads the PDF file to your computer's default downloads folder, such as the Downloads folder in your user account on the Mac, and opens it automatically if a suitable app is available. For example, on a Mac, the PDF normally opens in the Preview app.

4. **Choose the Print command from the app.** For example, choose File ➪ Print.

Note

If the PDF file doesn't open automatically, go to your downloads folder and open it manually.

How Can I Use the Extra Features for Keynote in OS X?

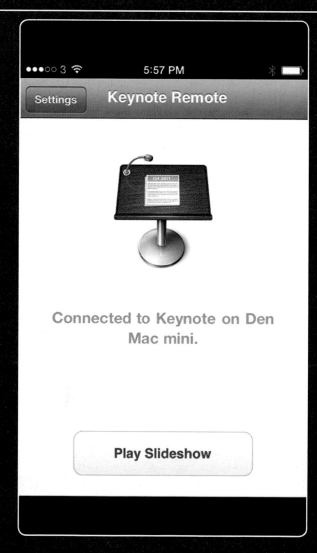

In Keynote for OS X, you can create master slides and presentation themes, choose different views, customize the window to suit the way you work, and use advanced ways of creating slides. In this chapter, I also cover how to deliver a presentation live using Keynote's presenter-friendly features and how to create handouts of your presentations for either the presenters or the audience. I also discuss how to share a presentation in other ways, such as by exporting it to PowerPoint or QuickTime, or by creating image files or web pages of the slides.

Creating and Editing Master Slides and Presentation Themes

Each of Keynote's themes includes various master slides for different needs — title slides, slides with horizontal or vertical photos, slides with charts, slides with tables, and so on. If the masters in the themes you use meet your needs, you're all set. However, if you find you need to customize the slides you create from the masters, you can save time by creating your own masters that contain exactly what you need.

Similarly, Keynote comes with a great selection of presentation themes, but for the ultimate in flexibility, you will probably want to create themes of your own. When you do, you will also likely customize the master slides they contain.

Editing master slides

Here's how to change a master slide:

1. **Open the master slide navigator.** Choose View ➪ Edit Master Slides from the menu bar. Alternatively, click the View button on the toolbar and then click Edit Master Slides.

Genius If another theme or presentation contains a suitable slide or master, you can simply import it into the presentation. Open a presentation that contains the slide or master you want, and arrange the Keynote windows so that you can see both the source window and the destination window. Then drag the slide from the source to the Slides pane in the destination window, or drag the master from the source to the Master Slides pane in the destination window.

Genius Before changing a master slide, it's usually a good idea to duplicate it so that you have an untouched copy to which you can return if necessary. To duplicate a master slide, Control+click (or right-click) it in the master slide browser and choose Duplicate.

2. **Click the master slide you want to change.** Keynote displays its contents, together with the master guides and alignment guides (see Figure 13.1).

Note By default, the master guides use the same color as the alignment guides. If you want to distinguish the master guides from the alignment guides, choose Keynote ➪ Preferences to open the Preferences window, click the Rulers tab to display the Rulers pane, and then click the Master Guides swatch to choose a different color.

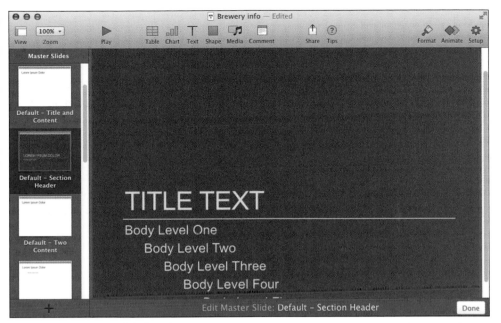

13.1 Opening a master slide for editing.

3. **If the Format inspector isn't displayed, click the Format button on the toolbar to display it.** The Master Slide Layout pane appears in the Format inspector.

4. **In the Appearance area, select the check box for each item you want to include: Title, Body, Slide Number, or Object Placeholder.** Drag each item to where you want to position it, and then resize it as needed. Click the slide in the Master Slides panel when you need to display the Master Slides Layout pane again in the Format inspector. Alternatively, click the master slide background outside any of the objects it contains.

5. **If you want to create a media placeholder on the slide, select the Object Placeholder check box in the Layout area.** Click the placeholder, and then resize and reposition it as needed.

Changes you make to a master slide in a presentation carry through to each of that presentation's slides that are based on the master.

Note

6. **If the master slide needs a fill, gradient fill, image fill, or tinted image fill, use the controls in the Background area of the Master Slide Layout pane to set it up.** For example, choose Gradient Fill in the Background pop-up menu, select the colors, and choose the gradient direction and angle.

7. **Add any text or images needed to the background of the master slide.** For example, drag in a theme graphic or a company logo from the Media Browser, or place a text box, and then type or paste text.

Genius

After you add a background image or text placeholder to a master slide, it's a good idea to lock it in place to prevent anyone from moving it. Click the image or object, click the Arrange pane in the Format inspector, and then click the Lock button. (If necessary, you can unlock the object by clicking it and then clicking the Unlock button in the Arrange pane.)

8. **Click another slide and repeat steps 4 to 7 to customize it.**

9. **Choose View ⇨ Exit Master Slides to close the master slide navigator.** You can also click the View button on the toolbar and then click Exit Master Slides.

After you finish customizing the master slides, save changes to the presentation.

Creating and modifying styles

To make the objects in your slides look the way you want, you should customize the styles in your themes. You can customize both object styles and text styles, and you can either modify an existing style or create a new style. Normally, you want to modify an existing style when you no longer want to use it with its original look, and create a new style when you need to apply different formatting, but want to retain the existing styles for use.

Here's how to create a new object style:

1. **Insert the type of object for which you're going to use the style, and then select it.** If the presentation already has an object of that type available, select it.

2. **If the Format inspector isn't displayed, click the Format button on the toolbar to display it.**

3. **Use the controls in the Format inspector to apply to the object the formatting you want the style to have.**

4. **Choose Format ⇨ Advanced to display the Advanced submenu, and then choose Create Style.** This command shows the type of object you're working with — for example, Create Text Box Style or Create Chart Style.

After creating an object style, you can apply it by selecting it from the Style list at the top of the Style pane in the Format Inspector.

Here's how to modify an object style:

1. **Select the appropriate type of object in your presentation.** If necessary, insert a new object and select it.

2. **If the Format inspector isn't displayed, click the Format button on the toolbar to display it.**

3. **Click the Style button to display the Style pane.**

4. **In the Style list, click the style you want to apply.**

5. **Use the controls in the Format inspector to format the object in the way you want to change the style.**

6. **Control+click the style in the Style list, and then click Redefine Style from Selection on the contextual menu.** Keynote displays a dialog telling you how many objects are using this style.

7. **Select the appropriate option button:**

   - **Update all objects that use the current style.** Select this option if you're customizing a presentation or theme and it's okay to change the formatting of all the other objects of this type.

   - **Don't update objects, and disconnect them from the style.** Select this option if you're working in a live presentation and you don't want to change the formatting of all the other objects of this type.

8. **Click OK.** Keynote updates the style.

Note

To delete an object style, Control+click the style in the Style list and click Delete Style on the contextual menu.

To create a new text style or modify an existing text style, work as explained in Chapter 3. Here's a quick recap:

- **Create a new style.** Click the Style pop-up menu in the Text pane of the Format inspector, click the + button in the Paragraph Styles pane, and then type the name for the new style and press Return.

- **Modify an existing style.** Apply the style to some text, modify the formatting as needed, and then click the Update button to the right of the style's name in the Text pane of the Format inspector.

Creating a custom theme

Creating your own masters and custom styles can save you a great deal of time, but you probably also want to take the next step, which is to create one or more of your own custom themes. This is the best way to keep your custom masters and custom content together in a format you can reuse in moments.

You can create a custom theme in one of these ways:

- ● **Customize an existing theme.** If one of Keynote's themes can provide a suitable starting point, this is usually the quickest way to create a custom theme.

- ● **Create a new theme from scratch.** Create a new presentation by pressing ⌘+N or choosing File ⇨ New. Delete any master slides you don't need. You can then customize the remaining master slides as needed and create new master slides to add to them.

When you've set up the theme to your liking, follow these steps to save it:

1. **Choose File ⇨ Save Theme.** Keynote displays the Create a custom Keynote theme? dialog (see Figure 13.2).

13.2 In the Create a custom Keynote theme? dialog, you can add the presentation to the Theme Chooser or save it to your Mac.

2. **Click Add to Theme Chooser.** The Choose a Theme dialog opens, displaying the My Themes tab. The new theme appears with an edit box around its name.

Note

If you want to save the theme to a file without adding it to the Theme Chooser on your Mac, click Save in the Create a custom Keynote theme? dialog instead of clicking Add to Theme Chooser. You do this if you want to share the custom theme with others rather than use it yourself.

3. **Type the name for the theme file and press Return to apply it.**

4. **Click the Choose button if you want to create a new presentation based on the theme — for example, to test-drive the theme.** Otherwise, click Cancel to close the Choose a Theme dialog.

You can then start a new presentation based on your custom theme by choosing File ➪ New, clicking the My Themes tab, clicking the theme, and then clicking Choose.

Genius

If you download a Keynote theme or receive one from a colleague, you can add it to the Theme Chooser. Open a Finder window to the folder that contains the theme, and then double-click the theme file. In the Do you want to add this custom theme to the Theme Chooser? dialog, click Add to Theme Chooser.

Using Views and Customizing the Keynote Window

To work quickly in Keynote, it's a good idea to make the most of the four views it offers. You may also want to customize the Keynote window so that it shows only the elements you find helpful.

Using Keynote's views effectively

Keynote offers you four ways to view your slides. You can change the view by clicking the View pop-up menu button on the toolbar or the View menu on the menu bar, and then choosing from the following:

- **Navigator view.** Navigator view displays the Slides pane on the left of the window with a thumbnail of each slide. You can change the size of the thumbnails by dragging the right border of the Slides pane to the right (to enlarge the thumbnails) or to the left (to reduce them). This is the view in which Keynote first displays a presentation, and it's the one you will probably use the most when building a presentation, unless you're working on a small screen.

- **Outline view.** Outline view replaces the Slides pane on the left of the window with an outline of the text on each slide. Figure 13.3 shows an example of outline view. Use outline view when you're focusing on the text of the presentation. You can double-click a slide's icon to collapse it to just the title or expand it again. Outline view displays the slide text using the font size you chose in the Outline View Font pop-up menu in the General pane of the Preferences window.

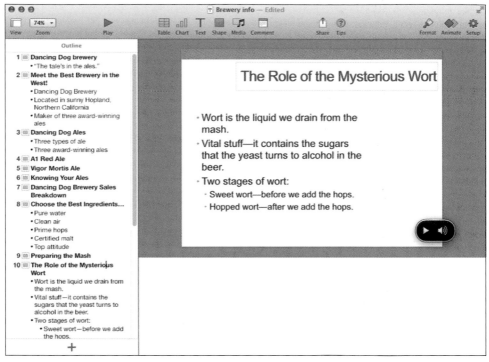

13.3 In Outline view, you can quickly develop the text content of your presentation and rearrange slides.

- **Slide Only view.** Slide Only view hides the Slides or Outline pane to give you more room to view and edit a single slide. Use Slide Only view to work on a single slide rather than on the presentation as a whole or on the outline.

- **Light Table view.** Light Table view, as shown in Figure 13.4, shows thumbnail versions of the slides spread out across a light table (the backlit, translucent glass table that photographers use for viewing photographic slides or negatives). Use Light Table view for rearranging the slides in your presentation or getting an overview of all the slides at once. In Light Table view, you can change the size of the thumbnails by dragging the slider at the bottom of the Keynote window.

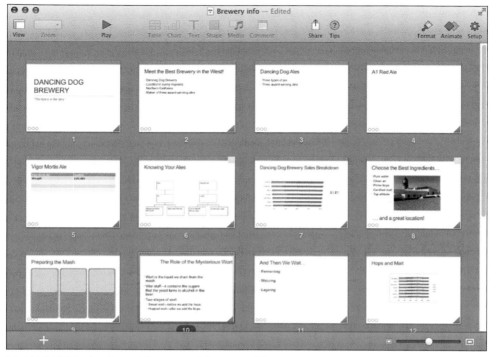

13.4 Light Table view is great for reorganizing your slides.

Customizing the Keynote window

Keynote lets you display or hide various parts of its window to suit the presentation you're working on and the tasks you're performing. These are the elements you can display and hide:

- **Toolbar.** Most people find the toolbar handy for instant access to essential features, but you can also hide the toolbar if you need more screen space. To display or hide the toolbar, use one of these options:

  - **Mouse.** Control+click anywhere on the toolbar or any empty space in the title bar and click Hide Toolbar, placing a check mark next to it, to hide the toolbar. Repeat this move to remove the check mark and display the toolbar again.

  - **Keyboard.** Press ⌘+Option+T.

  - **Menu bar.** Choose View ➪ Hide Toolbar or View ➪ Show Toolbar.

● **Rulers.** When you need to position objects exactly, display the horizontal ruler and vertical rule using one of these options:

   ○ **Mouse.** Click the View pop-up menu on the toolbar and choose Show Rulers or Hide Rulers.

   ○ **Keyboard.** Press ⌘+R.

   ○ **Menu bar.** Choose View ➪ Show Rulers or View ➪ Hide Rulers.

● **Comments.** To view the comments added to a presentation, click the View pop-up menu on the toolbar or the View menu on the menu bar and choose Show Comments. To hide the comments again, click the menu and choose Hide Comments.

● **Presenter Notes area.** To add notes for the presenter to a slide, open the Presenter Notes area at the bottom of the Keynote window by clicking the View pop-up menu on the toolbar or the View menu on the menu bar and choosing Show Presenter Notes. You can then type or paste in text as needed and format it by using the Format inspector. When you no longer need the Presenter Notes area, click on one of these View menus again and choose Hide Presenter Notes.

● **Find & Replace panel.** When you need to use the Find and Replace feature, open the Find & Replace panel in one of these ways:

   ○ **Mouse.** Click the View pop-up menu on the toolbar and choose Show Find & Replace.

   ○ **Keyboard.** Press ⌘+F.

   ○ **Menu bar.** Choose Edit ➪ Find ➪ Find.

Note

You can leave the Find & Replace panel open while you work if you find it doesn't get in the way. When you're ready to close it, click its Close button (the red button at the left end of the panel's title bar), click the View pop-up menu on the toolbar and choose Hide Find & Replace, or choose Edit ➪ Find ➪ Hide Find Panel.

● **Master slide navigator.** When you need to create a new master slide or duplicate an existing one, you can display the master slide navigator by choosing Edit Master Slides from the View pop-up menu on the toolbar or the View menu on the menu bar. When you finish using the master slide navigator, choose Exit Master Slides from the View pop-up menu on the toolbar or the View menu on the menu bar.

Mastering Advanced Ways of Creating Slides

When you need to create a presentation quickly, you can import slides from an existing Keynote presentation, or open a Microsoft PowerPoint presentation in Keynote and work with its slides. In this section, you also learn how to put a sound or movie on a slide, add a soundtrack to a presentation, and reapply a master to a slide.

Importing slides from another presentation

Keynote offers no command for importing slides from another presentation, but you can easily add slides by using Copy and Paste. Follow these steps:

1. **In Keynote, open the presentation that contains the slides you want to copy.**

2. **Select the slides.** You can select them either in the Slides pane or in Light Table view.

3. **Give the Copy command.** For example, Control+click the selection, and then click Copy on the contextual menu or simply press ⌘+C.

Genius

If the slides you want are in a PowerPoint presentation, open that presentation in Keynote (see the next section for more details). You can then copy the slides and paste them into the destination Keynote presentation. Don't try copying a slide in PowerPoint and pasting it into Keynote — doing this creates not the new slide you want but a picture of the PowerPoint slide pasted onto a Keynote slide.

4. **Switch to the destination presentation, and then choose the Paste command in either the Slides pane or Light Table view.** For example, choose Edit ⇨ Paste, or press ⌘+V.

Solving Font Problems When Transferring Presentations Between Macs

When you save a Keynote presentation, you can copy the audio files, movie files, and theme images into the presentation file to make sure that these items are available for the presentation no matter which Mac you open it on.

However, you cannot include the fonts used in the presentation — so some (or all) of the fonts you need for the presentation may not be available on another Mac. There are three main solutions to this problem:

- **Use only fonts you know are installed on the other Mac.** This may sound limiting, but most Macs include such a good variety of fonts that it isn't a hardship for many presentations.

- **Copy the fonts to the other Mac.** If you know which Mac you're going to use for the presentation and there are no licensing issues with copying the fonts, installing them on the other Mac will enable it to display the presentation in its full glory.

- **Substitute the missing fonts with similar ones.** For all but highly specialized fonts, you can usually find a close-enough match among the fonts on the other Mac. Unless your audience is packed with graphic designers, you can be pretty sure they won't notice.

Opening Microsoft PowerPoint presentations

However much you love Keynote, chances are that you also work with people who use PowerPoint, the Microsoft Office presentation program. Keynote is largely compatible with PowerPoint — Keynote can open PowerPoint files and can export presentations as PowerPoint files — but as with Pages and Numbers, the devil is in the details. The more complex the presentation, the more likely you are to run into problems when importing it into Keynote or exporting it in PowerPoint format.

To open a PowerPoint presentation in Keynote, choose File ⇨ Open, click the PowerPoint file in the Open dialog, and click Open. Keynote automatically converts the contents of the file to Keynote's equivalents and then displays the results.

Note Keynote can open presentations in both the XML-based PowerPoint format and the earlier binary PowerPoint format. The XML-based format uses the .pptx file extension and is the default file format for PowerPoint 2007 (Windows) and PowerPoint 2008 (Mac) and later versions. The binary format uses the .ppt file extension and is the default for PowerPoint 2003 (Windows), PowerPoint 2004 (Mac), and earlier versions.

Keynote manages to import most PowerPoint slides pretty well, but the process isn't perfect. This isn't surprising given the differences between the applications, but it means you often need to straighten things out after importing a presentation.

If there are problems, Keynote displays the Some features aren't supported dialog. Read through the list of problems, and then click OK to close the dialog. Depending on the issues Keynote has flagged, decide which (if any) you need to fix — either in Keynote or by going back to PowerPoint (assuming you have PowerPoint).

You're likely to have problems in the following three areas when you bring a PowerPoint presentation into Keynote:

- **Charts.** Charts are staples of business presentations, and Keynote does its best to preserve PowerPoint's charts. On the plus side, Keynote does give you a version of the chart that you can edit with the Chart Data Editor. On the minus side, Keynote sometimes can't get PowerPoint's data series and axes entirely straight. So, whenever you use Keynote to open a PowerPoint presentation that contains one or more charts, check immediately that Keynote's version of each chart is accurate. If it's not, you may need to create the chart again in either Keynote or Numbers.

Genius One of PowerPoint's most useful charting features is linking a chart to its underlying source data in an Excel workbook; when the source data changes, you can update the chart automatically. When you open a PowerPoint presentation in Keynote, you lose any links back to an Excel data source. The only workaround is to open the Excel workbook in Numbers, save it as a Numbers document, and re-create the chart from there.

- **Shockwave and HTML links.** Links to Shockwave files or HTML files may disappear. You simply need to replace these items once you save the presentation in Keynote.

- **Font substitutions.** If the PowerPoint presentation includes fonts that aren't available on your Mac, Keynote substitutes them. Unless any of the fonts in the PowerPoint presentation are so unique that you can't possibly replace them, this substitution has little impact. If the substituted fonts don't work for you, replace them with others from the selection on your Mac.

Adding a soundtrack to a presentation

You can add audio (not to mention movies) to the slides in a presentation by using the standard techniques explained in Chapter 4, but you may also want to use audio in another way: by adding a soundtrack to a presentation.

A soundtrack is audio that starts playing automatically when the presentation begins and continues until you end the presentation. If individual slides contain audio, that plays on top of the soundtrack — it doesn't interrupt the soundtrack.

Here's how to add a soundtrack to a presentation:

1. **Click the Setup button on the toolbar to display the Setup inspector.**

2. **Click the Audio button to display the Audio pane.**

3. **Click the Add Audio File button in the lower-right corner of the Audio pane to display a pop-up panel showing available audio.**

Note   You can also drag an audio file from a Finder window or a track from iTunes to the Audio well in the Audio pane.

4. **Click the audio track you want to use.**

5. **Repeat steps 3 and 4 to add other audio files as needed for the soundtrack.**

6. **Drag the audio files up or down the Audio well to get them into the order you want.**

7. **Click the Soundtrack pop-up menu, and then click the appropriate option:**

   - **Off.** Choose this setting to prevent the soundtrack from playing. This is useful when you need to have the soundtrack available for the presentation but not use it every time.

   - **Play Once.** Choose this setting to play the audio through once (assuming the presentation goes on that long) and then stop.

   - **Loop.** Choose this setting to play the audio repeatedly until the presentation ends.

8. **Drag the Volume slider to set the volume for the soundtrack.**

Genius   To store the soundtrack in the presentation so that it's available when you copy or move the presentation file to another computer, select the Copy audio and movies into document check box in the General pane in Keynote preferences.

Reapplying a master to a slide

If you've changed the layout of a slide and want to restore the standard design, reapply the slide master to it. To do so, Control+click the slide in the Slides pane, and then click Reapply Master to Slide on the contextual menu.

Genius

You can also reapply a master by clicking the slide and choosing Format ⟡ Reapply Master to Slide. If the slide doesn't have a background and isn't completely covered with objects, Control+click an empty part of the slide, and then click Reapply Master to Slide.

Delivering a Presentation Live

As mentioned in Chapter 12, Keynote for OS X gives you far more options for delivering your presentation than Keynote for iOS or Keynote for iCloud. This section first shows you how to set up and use remotes, choose Slideshow preferences, rehearse the presentation, and check your presenter display. It then explains how to run the presentation and (if you need to) use other apps during it.

Setting up and using remotes

In the Remote pane in Keynote's Preferences pane, you can set up an iPhone or iPod touch as a remote control for Keynote, and use the device to run your presentations.

Genius

If you have an iPhone or iPod touch and you use Keynote, the Keynote Remote app is a great use for the device. If you don't have one, it's a strong argument for your company to buy one for you.

Here's how to set up an iPhone or iPod touch as a remote:

1. **Download the Keynote Remote app from the App Store section of the iTunes Store.**
   Usually, it's easiest to download the app using iTunes, and then synchronize it to the device. However, if you prefer, you can download it directly to the iPhone or iPod touch, and then synchronize it back to iTunes.

2. **On the iPhone's or iPod touch's Home screen, touch the Keynote Remote app's icon to display the Keynote Remote screen.** This icon's name is Remote rather than Keynote Remote — but you can find it by searching for *key*.

3. **Touch the Link to Keynote button to display the Settings screen (see Figure 13.5).** You may not even have to touch the button: When you haven't yet linked to Keynote, the Keynote Remote app automatically displays the Settings screen for you after a moment.

4. **Tap the New Keynote Link button to display the New Link screen.** This shows a four-digit passcode and instructions.

5. **On your Mac, select the Enable iPhone and iPod touch Remotes check box in the Remote pane in the Preferences window (see Figure 13.6).**

6. **On your Mac, click the Link button for the iPhone or iPod touch in the list box.** In the Enter Passcode dialog that appears (see Figure 13.7), type the passcode that the iPhone or iPod touch is displaying. When you type the passcode correctly, this dialog closes.

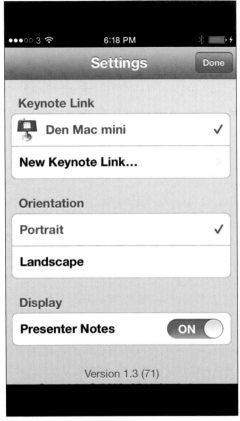

13.5 Tap New Keynote Link on the Settings screen for the Keynote Remote app to start setting up an iPhone or iPod touch as a remote.

Genius

If the iPhone or iPod touch doesn't appear in the Remote pane in Keynote preferences, verify that the iOS device and the Mac are connected to the same network. If they are, but the iOS device still doesn't appear, you may need to ask the network administrator to unblock some networking ports to enable the iOS device and the Mac to communicate.

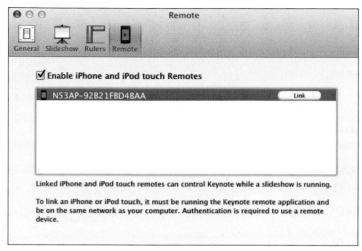

13.6 Use the Remotes pane in Keynote preferences on OS X to set up an iPhone or iPod touch as a remote.

7. **On your Mac, verify that an Unlink button has replaced the Link button for the iPhone or iPod touch.** On the iPhone or iPod touch, when the New Link screen closes, check that your Mac's name appears in the Keynote Link area of the Settings screen.

8. **In the Orientation area, touch Portrait or Landscape to choose the orientation you will use.**

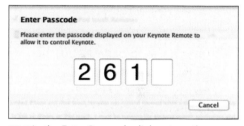

13.7 In the Enter Passcode dialog, type the passcode shown on your iPhone or iPod touch.

9. **If you chose Portrait orientation, choose whether to display presenter notes.** In the Display area, slide the Presenter Notes switch to On if you want to see presenter notes on the iPhone or iPod touch, or to Off if you don't. Presenter notes aren't available in landscape orientation, so iOS makes the Presenter Notes switch unavailable.

You're now all set to control a Keynote presentation from the iPhone or iPod touch.

Note

Portrait orientation lets you see presenter notes on the iPhone or iPod touch, but you can see only the current slide. Landscape orientation lets you see both the current slide and the next slide, but not the presenter notes.

Note

If you need to stop using the iPhone or iPod touch as a remote temporarily, open the Remotes pane in Keynote preferences, and then deselect the Enable iPhone and iPod touch Remotes check box. To stop using an iPhone or iPod touch as a remote permanently, click the device's Unlink button in the Remotes pane.

Choosing Slideshow preferences

When preparing to give your presentation, you will usually want to change — or at least check — the Slideshow preferences in Keynote. First, open the Slideshow pane by choosing Keynote ⇨ Preferences, and then clicking the Slideshow button. You can then choose preferences as discussed in the following sections.

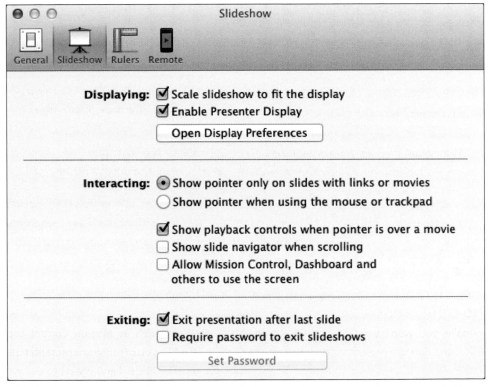

13.8 Use the Slideshow pane in the Preferences window to control how Keynote appears and behaves while you deliver a presentation.

Choosing display preferences

Select the Scale slides up to fit display check box if you're using slides that are lower resolution than the display you're using. For example, if your slides are 800 × 600 resolution and the display is 1024 × 768 resolution, you may want to scale them up so that they fill the entire screen. The disadvantage to scaling the slides up is that video quality usually suffers a bit.

Select the Enable Presenter Display check box to enable the Presenter Display feature, which shows your view of the current slide, your notes for it, the upcoming slide, and so on. You use a separate display for Presenter Display.

Choosing interactive preferences for the mouse pointer

Usually, when giving a slide show, you won't want the mouse to appear on-screen because it can be distracting to the audience. On the other hand, it's likely you will want to use the mouse to control the presentation and move from slide to slide.

To help you, Keynote gives you a choice of options for the mouse:

- **Show pointer only on slides with hyperlinks or movies.** Select this option if you want the mouse pointer to appear on such slides so that you can click the hyperlinks or play the movies.

- **Show pointer when the mouse moves.** Select this option if you want Keynote to keep the pointer hidden until you deliberately move the mouse (clicks don't count).

Whichever option you prefer, you can select or deselect the Show playback controls when pointer is over a movie check box to make Keynote display the playback controls for movies when you move the pointer over them. Similarly, select the Show slide navigator when scrolling check box if you want Keynote to display the slide navigator when you scroll during a presentation.

Choosing whether to enable Mission Control, Dashboard, and other apps

Normally, you won't want to use OS X's navigation features, such as Mission Control and Dashboard, during a presentation, so Keynote turns them off while you're running a presentation. If you do want to use them, select the Allow Mission Control, Dashboard and others to use the screen check box.

Choosing exit preferences

In the Exiting section of the Slideshow pane, you can choose from the following settings:

- **Exit presentation after last slide.** Select this check box if you want Keynote to close the presentation automatically after the last slide finishes. Deselect this check box if you prefer to keep the final slide on-screen as you finish the presentation. (For example, you might display talking points or your company's contact information as the final slide, or just show a blank slide to stimulate discussion.)

- **Require password to exit slideshows.** Select this check box to prevent unauthorized people from exiting the slideshow. This feature can be useful when you leave the slide show running, such as at trade shows or similar kiosk situations. When you select this check box, the Require a password to exit slideshows on this computer dialog opens. Type the password in the Password text box and the Verify text box (see Figure 13.9), and then click Set Password.

13.9 You can set a password to prevent others from exiting the slide show.

Using System Preferences to configure displays

If you need to configure display settings for the presentation, open the Displays preferences pane in System Preferences in one of these ways:

- **From Keynote.** Click the Open Displays Preferences button in the Displaying area of the Slideshow preferences pane in Keynote.

- **From OS X.** Control+click the System Preferences icon on the Dock, and then click Displays on the contextual menu. If you don't have the System Preferences icon on the Dock, choose Apple ➪ System Preferences, and then click Displays.

Once you open Displays preferences, you can choose settings as needed on the three panes it contains:

- **Display pane (see Figure 13.10).** Here, you can choose the following settings:

  - **Resolution.** Choose the Best for display option to have OS X automatically use the best resolution for the display. Otherwise, choose the Scaled option and select the resolution in the list box that appears.

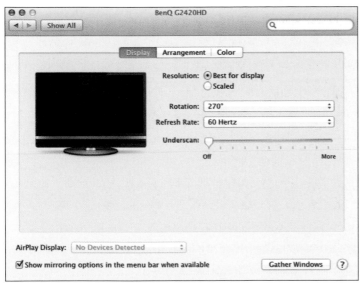

13.10 You can set the resolution, rotation, and refresh rate in the Display pane in Displays preferences.

Genius

Displays preferences contains a Display pane and a Color pane for each display. The Arrangement pane appears only on the primary monitor.

- **Rotation.** If the display is rotated, open this pop-up menu and choose the rotation to use.

- **Refresh rate.** If the display is flickering, open this pop-up menu and choose a higher refresh rate if one is available.

- **Underscan.** If the picture is overlapping the sides of the display, drag this slider to the right to shrink the picture down to size.

- **Arrangement pane.** Here, you can follow these steps to adjust the display placement and contents:

  1. **To see which display is which, click a display thumbnail.** A red line appears around both the thumbnail and the display.

  2. **Drag the display thumbnails so that they correspond to the physical placement of the displays.**

  3. **Drag the gray menu bar to the monitor you want to use as the primary monitor.**

  4. **Select the Mirror displays check box if you want to display the same image on both (or all) displays.**

- **Color pane.** Here, you can choose the color profile to use on the display. Select the Show profiles for this display only check box if you want to limit the Display Profile list to only those designed for the display.

In the main part of the Displays preferences window, below the controls on the three tabs, are the following controls for AirPlay and mirroring:

- **AirPlay Display.** To use an AirPlay device, such as a TV or monitor connected to an Apple TV, open this pop-up menu and click the device. If you can't find the device you're looking for, make sure both the Mac and the AirPlay device are connected to the same network.

- **Show mirroring options in the menu bar when available.** Select this check box to display the Mirroring menu on the right side of the menu bar when a mirroring device is available. This menu gives you an easy way to connect and disconnect AirPlay displays, turn mirroring on and off, and choose between extending your desktop and mirroring the desktop.

Rehearsing a presentation and setting up your display

To help you polish your presentation, Keynote includes a rehearsal view that you can use with a single monitor — a great advantage over having to add an external display in order to practice. The rehearsal view is the same as presenter display except that there's no screen for the audience.

Here's how to rehearse your presentation:

1. **From the menu bar, choose Play ⇨ Rehearse Slideshow.** Keynote switches to rehearsal view and displays the first slide and the slide or build after it (see Figure 13.11).

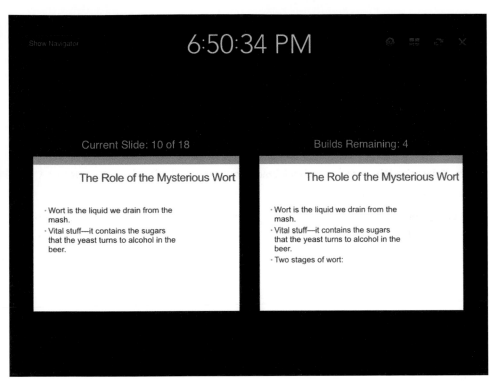

6:50:34 PM

Show Navigator

Current Slide: 10 of 18   Builds Remaining: 4

The Role of the Mysterious Wort

· Wort is the liquid we drain from the
  mash.
· Vital stuff—it contains the sugars
  that the yeast turns to alcohol in the
  beer.

The Role of the Mysterious Wort

· Wort is the liquid we drain from the
  mash.
· Vital stuff—it contains the sugars
  that the yeast turns to alcohol in the
  beer.
· Two stages of wort:

13.11 Rehearsal view lets you run through your presentation and practice your timings using a single screen.

2. **Practice delivering your presentation, referring to your presenter notes as needed.** Use the Time display and Elapsed Time display (if you chose to show them) to track how long you're taking.

Note

If your presenter notes don't appear in rehearsal view, move the mouse pointer up to the top of the screen to display the presentation toolbar, click the Options pop-up menu, and then select Customize Presenter Display. In the Customize Presenter Display dialog, select the Notes check box, and then click Done.

3. **Click to display the next build or slide.** Control+click (or right-click) to move back a step in the presentation.

4. **To move to other slides, use the navigator.** Click the Show Navigator button in the upper-left corner of the screen. In the Navigator that appears on the left of the screen (see Figure 13.12), click the slide you want to display, and then click Go.

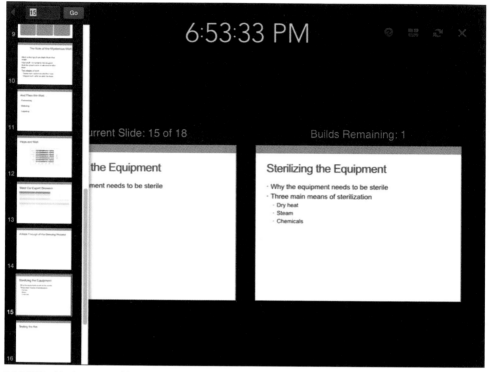

13.12 The Navigator enables you to jump quickly from slide to slide in your presentation.

5. **Click the Presenter Display button (the one with two squares on top of a wide rectangle) to display the Presenter Display pop-up panel.** Here, you can choose which of the following to include in the presenter display:

- **Current Slide.** Select this check box if you want to have the current slide appear in the presenter display. Seeing this is usually handy as long as your screen has enough space to display the slide along with all the other information you need. If the screen is too small, you may choose to forego the slide, especially if you can easily see what the audience is viewing.

- **Next Slide.** Select this check box if you want your display to show the next slide. Usually, seeing the next slide is helpful for monitoring what's coming up and, thus, keeping your presentation firmly on track. If you don't have enough space on-screen, you may prefer to sacrifice the next slide so that you have more space for the current slide. The next slide appears at a smaller size than the current slide.

- **Presenter Notes.** Select this check box to display the presenter notes across the bottom of the presenter display. Usually, these are helpful, as long as you have space for them.

- **Clock.** Select this check box to display the clock with the current time so that you can see how you're doing.

- **Timer.** Select this check box if you want to see a timer on the presenter display. You can then select the Remaining option button and set the number of hours and minutes in the box, giving yourself a countdown, or select the Elapsed option button so that you see a straightforward readout of how long your presentation has been running.

6. **Press Esc when you want to end the rehearsal.**

Running a presentation

To start the presentation running, click the slide you want to start with, and then click the Play button on the toolbar or choose Play ⇨ Play Slideshow.

The first slide appears on the audience's display, and the first two slides appear on the presenter display, along with the presenter display tools you've chosen (for example, presenter notes, the clock, and the timer). You can then run the presentation using the mouse, the keyboard, an Apple Remote, or an iPhone or iPod touch, as discussed in the next sections.

Controlling a presentation with a mouse or keyboard

Here's how to control the presentation with the mouse:

- **Display the next build or slide.** Simply click.

- **Display the previous build or slide.** Control+click (or right-click).

- **Display the navigator.** Click the Show Navigator button in the upper-left corner of the screen.

You can also run the presentation using the keyboard shortcuts shown in Table 13.1.

Table 13.1 Keyboard Shortcuts for Running a Presentation

Action	Keyboard Shortcut
Play the slide show from the current slide	Option+Click the Play button
Play the slide show from the current slide	⌘+Option+P
Show the first slide	Home or Fn+Left Arrow
Show the last slide	End or Fn+Right Arrow
Show the next build	N, Spacebar, Return, Page Down, Right Arrow, or Down Arrow
Show the previous build	Shift+Left Arrow, Shift+Page Up, or [
Show the next slide	Shift+Down Arrow, Shift+Page Down, or]
Show the previous slide	P, Delete, Page Up, Left Arrow, Up Arrow, or Shift+Up Arrow
Show the last slide viewed (not necessarily the previous slide)	Z
Hide Keynote, showing the last application used	H
Freeze the presentation at the current slide	F
Show a black screen (pausing the presentation)	B
Show a white screen (pausing the presentation)	W
Resume the presentation from frozen, black screen, or white screen	Press any key
Show or hide the mouse pointer	C
Display the navigator and select a slide by number	Press the slide's number
Select the next slide in the slide switcher	+ or =
Select the previous slide in the slide switcher	-
Close the slide switcher and show the selected slide	Return
Close the slide switcher without changing slide	Esc
Reset the presenter-display timer to zero	R
Scroll the presenter notes up	U
Scroll the presenter notes down	D
Swap the primary display and secondary display	X
End the presentation	Esc, Q,. (period), or ⌘+. (period)

Controlling a presentation with the Apple or Keynote Remotes

If you have an Apple Remote, you can use it to control the presentation as follows:

- **Start the presentation.** Activate Keynote, and then press the Play button.

- **Move to the next build or slide.** Press the Next/Fast-forward button.

- **Move to the previous build or slide.** Press the Previous/Rewind button.

- **Display the slide switcher.** Press the Menu button. Press the Next/Fast-forward button or the Previous/Rewind button to select the slide you want, and then press the Play button.

When you set up Keynote Remote to make your iPhone or iPod touch a remote control for Keynote on your Mac, you can quickly run a slide show from the device. On the Home screen, touch Remote to launch Keynote Remote. Keynote Remote automatically connects to your Mac and displays the Connected to Keynote screen.

Touch Play Slideshow to start the slide show. You then see the first screen and presenter notes if you're using portrait orientation (see Figure 13.13) or the first two slides if you're using landscape orientation.

Here's how to run the slide show from the iPhone or iPod touch:

- **Display the next slide.** Swipe your finger from right to left across the screen.

- **Display the previous slide.** Swipe your finger from left to right across the screen.

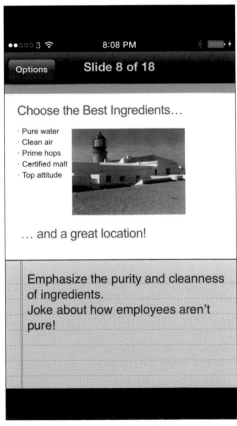

13.13 The Remote app on the iPhone or iPod touch can display one slide and any presenter notes attached to it.

- **Jump to the first slide.** Touch Options to display the Options dialog (see Figure 13.14), and then touch First Slide.

- **End the show.** Touch Options, and then touch End Show.

Using other applications during a presentation

If you need to use other applications while giving the presentation, you can simply press H to hide the presentation screens, revealing your desktop and any applications and windows open on it. You can then use the applications as normal — for example, you can launch Safari from the Dock if you need to view a Web site. When you're ready to return to the presentation, click the Keynote icon in the Dock. OS X activates Keynote, and you can restart the presentation.

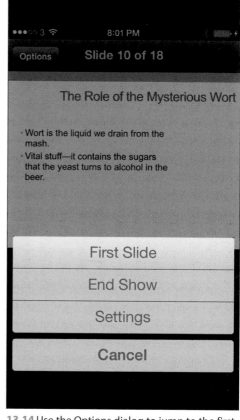

13.14 Use the Options dialog to jump to the first slide, end the slide show, or change the settings.

Genius

If you've selected the Allow Mission Control, Dashboard and others to use the screen check box in Keynote's Slideshow Preferences, you can also use the keyboard shortcuts, mouse shortcuts, or hot corners for these tools to reveal other applications and access them. For example, use your Mission Control All Windows shortcut to display miniatures of all your open windows so that you can click the one you want.

Creating Handouts of a Presentation

Often, you might give your audience handouts of your presentation, either so they can get up to speed on the topic while waiting for you to start or as a takeaway after your presentation to reinforce your message.

Keynote makes creating a handout easy. Follow these steps:

1. **Open the Print dialog.** Choose File ➪ Print or press ⌘+P.

2. **If the Print dialog is collapsed to its small size, hiding most of the options, expand it by clicking the Show Details button.** The Hide Details button replaces the Show Details button in the expanded dialog.

3. **Make sure Keynote is selected in the pop-up menu in the middle of the dialog.**

4. **In the box below the pop-up menu, click Handout to display the options for printing handouts (see Figure 13.15).**

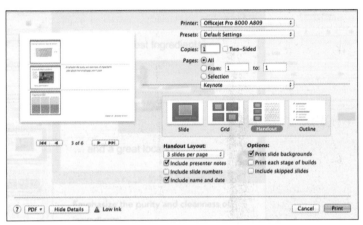

13.15 When printing handouts from your presentation, choose the number of slides per page and decide whether to include presenter notes.

5. **Open the Handout Layout pop-up menu and choose the number of slides per page.** The preview on the left shows how the pages will look, and the page readout shows how many printed pages there will be. You can click the arrow buttons to move from page to page in the preview.

6. **Choose options for the handout by selecting and deselecting the check boxes below the Handout Layout pop-up menu.** You can include presenter notes, slide numbers, or the filename and date.

7. **In the Options area, select the following check boxes for the options you want to use:**

   - **Print slide backgrounds.** Select this check box to include the slide backgrounds. If you're printing on a monochrome printer, you may want to leave out the slide backgrounds to make the text and other objects easier to see.

- **Print each stage of builds.** Select this check box if you want to print a separate slide for each stage of a build. This can be helpful when you're creating a handout for the presenter to use when preparing the presentation, but the audience doesn't usually need to see the builds.

- **Include skipped slides.** Select this check box to include any slides in the presentation (or in the selection) that are marked for skipping. This setting is useful when you need to provide the audience with more information than the presenter can deliver in the allotted time.

8. **Choose the number of copies in the Copies box.**

9. **Click Print to print the handout.**

Sharing a Presentation in Other Ways

Delivering a presentation from Keynote is great because you have total control over what your audience sees and hears. However, Keynote on OS X also makes it easy to share your presentation in other ways — everything from creating a PowerPoint slide show to making image files or web pages of your slides.

Table 13.2 summarizes when to use these different sharing options.

Table 13.2 Ways of Sharing Your Presentations

Sharing Type	Share Your Presentation This Way When
Share Link via iCloud	You want to make the presentation available for other iWork users to view or edit.
Send a Copy	You want to enable others to view or edit the presentation in Keynote on their Macs or iOS devices.
Create a PDF file	You need to share a presentation as a printable document. You can choose between including just the slides or the slides along with their notes.
Create a QuickTime file	You need to create a playable movie of the presentation.
Create a PowerPoint presentation	You need to work with people who use Microsoft PowerPoint (either on Windows or on the Mac).
Create images	You want to create images of individual slides that you can share as needed (without involving iPhoto).
Create an HTML document	You want to create a presentation that consists of a series of linked web pages with images.
Keynote '09	You want to create a version of the presentation document that people can view and edit in Keynote '09 for OS X.

Chapter 2 explains how to share links via iCloud and send copies of documents via Mail and other means of communication. The following sections explain how to use the other options to share a presentation.

Saving a presentation as a PowerPoint slide show

When you need to share a Keynote presentation with someone who uses Microsoft PowerPoint, you can export or save the presentation as a PowerPoint file with just a few clicks. Follow these steps:

1. **Open the presentation.**

2. **Choose File ⇨ Export To ⇨ PowerPoint to display the Export Your Presentation dialog with the PowerPoint pane at the front (see Figure 13.16).**

13.16 Use the PowerPoint pane of the Export Your Presentation dialog to create a PowerPoint file from a Keynote presentation.

Genius At this writing, PowerPoint has no conversion filter for importing Keynote presentations. So if you need to move a presentation from Keynote to PowerPoint, use Keynote's export feature, and then adjust any slides that don't convert perfectly.

3. **If you want to protect the exported presentation with a password, select the Require password to open check box.** The Export Your Presentation dialog then expands to reveal the controls for specifying the password and a password hint (see Figure 13.17). Otherwise, go to step 6.

13.17 Type the password and password hint for the exported presentation, and then click Next.

4. **Type the password in both the Password box and the Verify box.**

5. **If you want to use a password hint, type it in the Password Hint box.**

6. **Click Next to display the Save As dialog.**

7. **Type the name for the PowerPoint file in the Save As box.**

8. **Choose the folder in which to store the exported presentation.**

9. **Click Export.** Keynote exports the presentation, displaying a progress dialog as it does so, and then displays your Keynote document again without further comment.

Genius

If you have a PC available but not Microsoft PowerPoint, download the free PowerPoint Viewer from the Microsoft website (www.microsoft.com/downloads) to check the Keynote presentations you export to PowerPoint format. The Viewer lets you open and view PowerPoint presentations. You cannot edit a presentation, but you can check that it has exported satisfactorily.

Exporting a presentation to a QuickTime movie

If you want to turn your presentation into a movie file that will play on both Windows and on Macs, create a QuickTime movie like this:

1. **Choose File ⇨ Export To ⇨ QuickTime to display the Export Your Presentation dialog with the QuickTime pane at the front (see Figure 13.18).**

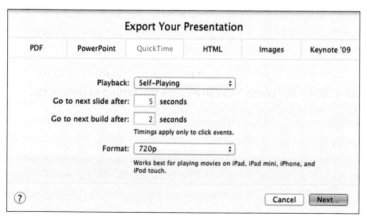

13.18 Use the controls in the QuickTime pane of the Export Your Presentation dialog to specify the type and format of QuickTime file to create.

2. **Click the Playback pop-up menu, and then click the type of playback you want:**

   - **Self-Playing.** The movie advances on-click slides after the time you set in the Slide Duration box and on-click builds after the time you set in the Build Duration box. Slides and builds with automatic timing use that timing.

   - **Slideshow Recording.** The movie uses the timing you've recorded into it. This option is available only if you've recorded the slide show.

3. **Click the Format pop-up menu, and then click one of the following formats for the QuickTime movie:**

   - **1024 × 768.** This resolution is very widely supported, so it is a good choice for movies that will need to play on many types of computers. This resolution has a 4:3 aspect ratio, so it does not work well for widescreen presentations.

   - **720p.** This widescreen format uses 1280 × 720-pixel resolution and is the next step up from 1024 × 768 resolution.

Genius

The *p* in 720p and 1080p stands for *progressive scan* — 720p has 720 horizontal lines using progressive scan, and 1080p has 1080 lines with progressive scan. Progressive scan draws the lines in sequence, giving a smoother image than interlacing, which draws the odd lines and the even lines alternately. The corresponding interlaced formats to 720p and 1080p are 720i and 1080i.

   - **1080p.** This high-definition widescreen format uses 1920 × 1080p and gives a high-quality image at a widely used resolution.

   - **Custom.** If you need to use a movie resolution other than 1024 × 768, 720p, or 1080p, click the Custom option, and then type the horizontal resolution and vertical resolution in the boxes that appear (see Figure 13.19). For example, you might need to use a lower resolution, such as 800 × 600 pixels. You can also use this setting to choose the compression type. Select the H.264 option button or the Apple ProRes 422 option button as needed.

Genius

Use the H.264 compression type unless you know you need to use the Apple ProRes 422 compression type.

4. **Click Next to display the Save As dialog.**

5. **Type the name for the QuickTime movie file in the Save As box.**

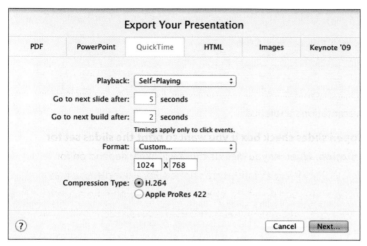

13.19 To create a custom resolution, select the Custom format, and then type the horizontal and vertical resolutions.

6. **Choose the folder in which to store the movie file.**

7. **Click Export.** Keynote exports the presentation, displaying the Creating movie progress dialog as it does so, and then displays your Keynote document again.

Creating a PDF file of a presentation

A PDF file lets you create an online document that contains the presentation in a format that can be viewed on almost any computer or operating system. Here's how to create a PDF from a presentation:

1. **Choose File ⇨ Export To ⇨ PDF to display the Export Your Presentation dialog with the PDF pane at the front (see Figure 13.20).**

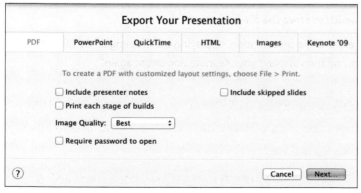

13.20 Exporting your presentation to a PDF is a great way of sharing it in a widely viewable format.

2. **Select the Include presenter notes check box if you want to include the presenter notes in the PDF.**

3. **Select the Print each stage of builds check box if you want to print each build stage as a separate image.** Printing the builds can be helpful when you are creating the PDF for a colleague to review, but you probably won't want to include the builds for PDFs you distribute to the presentation's audience.

4. **Select the Include skipped slides check box if you want to print the slides set for skipping in the presentation.** Whether you include these will likely depend on for whom you're creating the PDF and why the slides are skipped. For example, you may want to include slides skipped to keep down the presentation's running time but not slides skipped because they contain extra information the presenter summons up only In response to specific questions.

5. **Click the Image Quality pop-up menu, and then click the image quality you want: Good, Better, or Best.** Here are a few things to keep in mind:

   - Best is normally what you want because it produces a full-quality PDF. Keynote keeps each image at its full resolution.

   - If you find that Best produces files that are too large for the way you're using to distribute them, experiment with the Better setting or the Good setting to produce a smaller file. Better reduces the image quality to 150 dots per inch (dpi); Good uses 72 dpi.

6. **If you want to secure the PDF file, select the Require password to open check box.** Type the password in the Password box and the Verify box, and then type a password hint in the Password Hint box if you want to include one.

7. **Click Next to display the Save As dialog.**

8. **Type the name for the PDF file in the Save As box.**

9. **Choose the folder in which to store the file.**

10. **Click Export.** Keynote exports the presentation, displaying the Creating a PDF file progress dialog as it does so, and then displays your Keynote document again.

Creating image files from slides

You may sometimes find it useful to create image files from your slides. Keynote makes this easy to do. Follow these steps:

1. **Choose File ⇨ Export To ⇨ Images to display the Export Your Presentation dialog with the Images pane at the front (see Figure 13.21).**

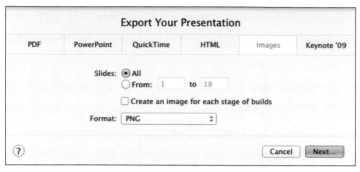

13.21 When creating image files from a presentation, choose which slides to include, whether to include builds, and the format for the images.

2. **In the Slides area, choose which slides to export.** Select the All option button if you want them all. Otherwise, select the From option button, and then type the starting and ending numbers in the boxes — for example, from 6 to 11.

3. **Select the Create an image for each stage of builds check box if you want a separate image for each build.** This is handy if you will use the slides to show the presentation as the audience would normally see it.

4. **In the Format pop-up menu, choose JPEG (High Quality), JPEG (Smaller File Size), PNG, or TIFF, as appropriate.** As you'd imagine, JPEG (Smaller File Size) gives lower quality than JPEG (High Quality).

Genius

Use JPEG files when you want to produce widely readable files with a smaller file size and you're prepared to lose some quality. See whether JPEG (Smaller File Size) gives good enough results for your needs; otherwise, use JPEG (High Quality) instead. Use PNG files when you need high-quality files for computer use. Use TIFF files when you need high-quality files for print publishing.

5. **Click Next to display the Save As dialog.**

6. **Type the name in the Save As box.** Keynote uses this name both for the folder and as the base name for the files, adding 001, 002, and so on to the base name to create the filenames.

7. **Choose the folder in which to store the folder of image files.**

8. **Click Export.** Keynote exports the presentation, displaying the Creating image files progress dialog as it does so, and then displays your Keynote document again.

Exporting a presentation to web pages

Sometimes, you might want to turn a presentation into web pages so that you can post them to a website. Here's how to do that:

1. **Choose File ⇨ Export To ⇨ HTML to display the Export Your Presentation dialog with the HTML pane at the front (see Figure 13.22).**

Export Your Presentation

| PDF | PowerPoint | QuickTime | HTML | Images | Keynote '09 |

Create an HTML document that can be viewed with Safari or another web browser.

Cancel   Next...

13.22 Keynote offers no options for exporting to HTML, so simply click Next in the HTML pane of the Export Your Presentation dialog.

2. **Click Next to display the Save As dialog.**

3. **Type the name in the Save As box.** Keynote uses this name both for the folder and as the base name for the HTML files, adding 001, 002, and so on to the base name to create the filenames.

4. **Choose the folder in which to store the folder of HTML files.**

5. **Click Export.** Keynote exports the presentation, displaying the Creating HTML document progress dialog as it does so, and then displays your Keynote document again.

Exporting a presentation to Keynote '09 format

Here's how to export a presentation to Keynote '09 format:

1. **Choose File ⇨ Export To ⇨ Keynote '09 to display the Export Your Presentation dialog with the Keynote '09 pane at the front (see Figure 13.23).**

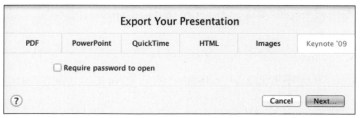

Export Your Presentation

| PDF | PowerPoint | QuickTime | HTML | Images | Keynote '09 |

☐ Require password to open

Cancel   Next...

13.23 Use the Keynote '09 pane in the Export Your Presentation dialog to create a presentation file that is compatible with Keynote '09.

2. **If you want to secure the exported file, select the Require password to open check box.** Type the password in the Password box and the Verify box, and then type a password hint in the Password Hint box if you want to include a hint.

3. **Click Next to display the Save As dialog.**

4. **Type the name for the Keynote '09 file in the Save As box.** Use a different name or a different folder unless you want to overwrite the existing presentation.

5. **Choose the folder in which to store the file.**

6. **Click Export.** Keynote exports the presentation, displaying the Creating a Keynote '09 file progress dialog as it does so, and then displays your Keynote document again.

Reducing the Size of a Presentation

If your presentation consists of only text, it'll be compact — but as soon as you add high-resolution pictures, audio files, or movie files, the presentation file can quickly grow to a large size.

If you create a presentation to give from your Mac, you may not need to worry about the presentation's size. However, if you need to transfer the presentation to another computer or distribute it via the Internet, you will probably want to reduce its file size as much as possible. To do so, choose File ➪ Reduce File Size.

The main way Keynote reduces the file size is by cutting out unused material. For example, if the presentation includes a two-minute movie but plays only 10 seconds of it, the remaining 1 minute 50 seconds is a waste of space. Similarly, if you've added any large images but cropped off or masked significant parts of them, those parts represent dead weight.

Finish creating your presentation before you reduce its size like this. Otherwise, you may find Keynote has clipped off the extra part of the movie that you now realize you need to show. If you need to enlarge an image you've made smaller, you can do so, but you lose some image quality.

Index

The Genius is in.

The new
iPad
PORTABLE GENIUS

978-1-118-17303-9

iPhone 5
PORTABLE GENIUS

978-1-118-35278-6

iPod & iTunes
PORTABLE GENIUS
Third Edition

978-1-118-16628-4

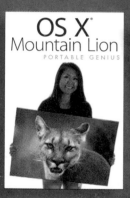

OS X
Mountain Lion
PORTABLE GENIUS

978-1-118-40142-2

MacBook Pro
PORTABLE GENIUS
Fourth Edition

978-1-118-36361-4

iPod touch
PORTABLE GENIUS

978-1-118-06352-1

iMac
PORTABLE GENI
Fou Edi

978-1-118-42063-8

iOS App Development
PORTABLE GENIUS

978-1-118-32989-4

MacBook Air
PORTABLE GENIUS
Fourth Edition

978-1-118-37020-9

Aperture 3
PORTABLE GENIUS
Second Edition

978-1-118-27429-3

Microsoft
Office
for Mac 2011
PORTABLE GENI

978-0-470-61019-0

Designed for easy access to tools and shortcuts, the Portable Genius series has all the
information you need to maximize your Apple digital lifestyle. With a full-color interior
and easy-to-navigate content, the Portable Genius series offers innovative tips and tricks
as well as savvy advice that will save you time and increase your productivity.

e **Available in print and e-book formats.**

WILEY

Wiley is a registered trademark of John Wiley & Sons, Inc.